THE
ANXIOUS
YEARS

*Politics in the Age
of Mulroney and Chrétien*

JEFFREY SIMPSON

Canadian Cataloguing in Publication Data

Simpson, Jeffrey, 1949–
    The anxious years : politics in the age of Mulroney and Chrétien

ISBN 1-895555-98-1

1. Canada – Politics and government – 1984–1993.
2. Canada – Politics and government – 1993–
I. Title.

FC635.S56   1996   971.064'7   C96-930989-9
F1034.2.S56   1996

The publisher gratefully acknowledges the assistance of the Canada Council
and the Ontario Arts Council.

Lester Publishing Limited
70 The Esplanade
Toronto, Ontario
Canada M5E 1R2

Design: Leah Gryfe
Electronic formatting: Heidi Palfrey

Printed and bound in Canada

96 97 98 99 6 5 4 3 2 1

Contents

Acknowledgements

The privilege of writing a national affairs column for *The Globe and Mail* was first given to me by editor-in-chief Norman Webster, and my efforts have subsequently been encouraged in every possible way by his successor, William Thorsell. To both of them, friends and fine journalists, I owe much, as I do to so many colleagues at *The Globe and Mail* over the years, especially those who have put up with me in the paper's Ottawa bureau.

Lawrence Martin, an author and another friend, first suggested the idea of pulling together columns in book form to publisher Malcolm Lester who, in a fit of hope over experience, decided the idea might have some merit. That this volume appeared is largely due to Lawrence's inspiration and Malcolm's work, and I am grateful to both.

My greatest debt goes to my family, who put up with the vagaries of a writer's life: my splendid children, Tait, Danielle and Brook, whom I love deeply, and my wife, Wendy, who remains *sine qua non*.

Introduction

George Bain, a journalistic craftsman and the first modern-day Ottawa columnist for *The Globe and Mail*, offered characteristically sensible advice before I wrote my first column in the space he had pioneered in 1954. If you should ever become dispirited, he counselled, or if you might wonder some day whether there might be more respectable ways of earning a living, just remember that you've been given two front-row seats to the best show in town.

Bain's counsel, gratefully accepted and frequently recalled in subsequent years, has remained my guide. To write a column in *The Globe and Mail* is a privilege of the highest order, given my paper's exceptionally intelligent readers, its national and international focus, the standards demanded of its writers and the freedom it offers those paid for their opinions. I have always remained grateful to colleagues past and present who helped me learn the craft of journalism, and to the editors who offered me a column on the editorial page and encouraged me to carry on even when, as not infrequently occurred, my opinions did not jibe with theirs. Since January, 1984, I have written about 1.2 million words in some two thousand columns, a fraction of which are reproduced in these pages.

A columnist is like a baseball pitcher, if you will forgive a metaphor from my preferred sport. Column-writing has its own rhythm because one performance inexorably leads to another but no two performances are the same. The columnist who endures must mix his offerings, like a successful pitcher who must vary his pitches, because the enemy of interest is the failure to surprise. Just as the same pitch repeatedly delivered to the same place will eventually alert batters, so a column written on the same subject with the same slant will eventually suggest to readers that they have considered all this before and need not bother again. A columnist therefore must change subjects, and even approaches, always remembering that there are bread-and-butter matters to which he must return, like a pitcher who in a pinch delivers what he throws best.

When I first began writing columns, I resolved (and was supported in this resolve by my editors) not to become a captive of the Ottawa fish bowl. The first brush with knowledge about Canada lies in appreciating its diversity, and in understanding that the national capital can be as removed from that diversity and its attendant complexity as anywhere in Canada. Ottawa's conceit consists in believing that it knows best and that only it fully appreciates the entire country. Such is the hubris of capitals everywhere, but that hubris is especially acute in countries such as Canada, whose capitals are essentially political creations unleavened by daily exposure to the perspectives and struggles of people outside government.

So I began travelling early on, all across the country and frequently abroad, trying to turn an Ottawa column into what could more properly be called a national affairs one. This was undoubtedly hubris on my part, since no itinerant, however determined, can appreciate the regions of Canada as fully as those who live there. But punditry gains coin only if alloyed with the basic tenets of reporting; and reporting means wearing out shoe leather in order to travel, read, listen and distill what people are thinking, saying and feeling outside the sometimes closed circles of the capital. My only frustration with this volume is that the demands of space eliminated much of the writing I have tried to do from Canada's regions and from abroad.

A newspaper column is a curious creature: part news, part commentary, a journalistic zoom camera that can zero in on the minutiae of issues, then pull back for the broad sweep. The enduring merit of the best columns, I think, consists in placing today's events in a wider context. Some columnists use their space to hammer home a certain ideological perspective; others delight in cutting up those they write about. Whatever choice columnists make about how they will use their space—and there is room for all kinds of approaches—the choice eventually reveals something of themselves. My strong preference has always been to let opinions arise from the columns rather than shoving myself forward through the first-person pronoun. Columnists are above all journalists, not personalities; observers not actors. Journalists are chroniclers who should never inflate their own importance beyond the events and people they cover. Nor should they assume that those on the stage of public affairs are somehow less gifted than themselves. Such an assumption, extremely widespread in contemporary journalism, usually leads to misplaced cynicism and overbearing arrogance. Nothing is easier, or more fatal to sound journalism, than for a columnist to adopt the pose of moral or intellectual superiority, since among the hazards of this pose is the dead-ringer certainty that some readers know more about the issue at hand than the writer. I certainly have preferences, often forcefully expressed, but I prefer not to have too many certainties.

My experience as reporter, foreign correspondent, author and columnist suggests that issues are often more complicated than we journalists believe. A columnist kids himself and breaks faith with readers when pretending to be an expert on every subject that catches his attention. Inevitably, however, a columnist trying to capture the quicksilver of events must leap to judgment, and there are days when such leaps painfully expose hasty judgments, suspect conclusions or errors of fact. As I scoured through almost two thousand columns to select a fraction for publication again, I cringed at some facile assumptions and downright errors. But other columns I am immodest enough to think wore rather well. Readers, the supreme arbiters as always, will decide.

A columnist can play many roles, and from time to time I have played them all: scold, satirist, reporter, commentator, analyst. There is another role that brings risks but fulfils an important journalistic function—that of preparing readers for tomorrow. In politics, as in life, certainty about the future is what many seek and none finds, but there are balances of probabilities which correctly assessed at the time of crucial decisions can make the difference between success and failure. For these attempts to warn, cajole and predict, no apologies are offered, since figuring out where decisions might lead is one of a columnist's bread-and-butter pitches.

It is also a recipe for unpopularity, I discovered, since I have consistently been arguing across a range of issues that hard decisions postponed today make for even harder ones tomorrow. To govern is to choose, after all, and choices bring results. The honourable work of political leaders is to explain tomorrow to today, a task from which too many flee for fear of electoral retribution. A columnist must face readers regularly but electors never, and therefore can make predictions, offer assumptions and present analyses from which politicians shy. A columnist's world is free; a politician's boxed in. A columnist can look courageous; but the politician really needs the courage. A columnist flies solo; a politician in formation.

Happily for me, although not necessarily for the country, my column began and has continued through anxious years of tumultuous, difficult choices for Canada. Shortly after I began writing in January, 1984, the political universe shifted with the departure from office of Prime Minister Pierre Trudeau and his replacement by another Quebecker, Brian Mulroney. The Mulroney years were so filled with drama that a scriptwriter could not have imagined richer material. Not only did a party long removed from a sustained period in office arrive in Ottawa, but its years in power were marked by continuing upheavals, the effects of which still mark Canada of the 1990s. Think of the battles during those Conservative years over free trade, the deficits and debt, the Goods and Services Tax, the first decade of the Charter of Rights and Freedoms, the failed attempts to change the Canadian constitution with the Meech Lake and Charlottetown accords. Who would have believed when the Conservatives, with a massive parliamentary majority, replaced the Liberals in 1984 that nine years later they would be not only defeated but obliterated as a political force in

Canada? The struggles of the Mulroney years not only ripped up the country, they destroyed the Conservative Party.

The Conservatives in turn were replaced by their old rivals, the Liberals under Prime Minister Jean Chrétien, a leader of the old style who preferred the avoidance of risk to the expenditure of political capital. Yet the pace of change scarcely abated under the Chrétien Liberals, who spent much of their time in office eating many of their words in opposition. Out of office, the Liberals screamed and shouted, heaved and sighed, opposed almost everything suggested by the Conservatives, blinded themselves to realities that were evident to those with eyes to see, capitulated before their own shop-worn ideas, and then, in a burst of electoralitis, assembled their nostrums for the 1993 campaign in something called the "Red Book," whose piety masked its unreality, and whose central tenets were ditched as soon as decently possible after the Liberals' 1993 victory. Safely elected, the Liberals conducted themselves like Conservatives in a hurry. Having assailed the Conservatives' attempts to tackle the deficit/debt problem, the Liberals introduced budgets that went further, faster than the Conservatives in lowering government spending, privatizing Crown corporations and otherwise scaling back the operations of government. Having campaigned vigorously against the Canada–U.S. free-trade agreement, then having criticized the North American free-trade negotiations to include Mexico, the Liberals signed on to NAFTA and became enthusiastic boosters of new free-trade agreements. Having bemoaned the Conservatives' attempts to change social policy, the Liberals introduced major changes to unemployment insurance and radical ones to pensions. Having criticized the Conservatives'constitutional reform attempts, the Liberals found themselves after the Oct. 30, 1995, Quebec referendum proposing constitutional changes themselves.

Canada during these anxious years has been in ceaseless transition. What George Bain had rightly described as the best show in town never failed to surprise. So many consequential events occurred during these years that I cannot do justice to them in this collection—leadership conventions, elections, constitutional conferences, referenda, international crises. These were the staged events that necessarily commanded attention, but of greater lasting importance were the underlying social and economic forces that produced anxiety, and someone in my position had no choice but to pay them heed.

Quebec's place in Canada has roiled the country for three decades. As an undergraduate student in the late 1960s and early 1970s, I became interested in Canadian federalism and Quebec's place within it, without ever dreaming that a healthy chunk of my working life would be spent writing about those very problems. Nor did I ever imagine when *The Globe and Mail* hired me after the summer of 1973 that I would be plunged immediately into Quebec politics. A mere two weeks after I received my first paycheque, the then city editor approached my desk in the corner of the newsroom late one Friday afternoon and inquired, "You speak French, don't you?" I had indeed made an effort to learn the language but I was hardly fluent, so I lied a trifle by answering "Yes." "Good," he replied, "then go down to Quebec Monday morning and help cover the campaign."

I was placed, quite properly, at the bottom of our correspondents' totem pole, but what an opportunity I had been afforded. For six weeks, I moved around Quebec—my territory being the eastern part of the province—from Quebec City through the Gaspé up to Saguenay–Lac Saint-Jean, down to the Beauce and as far along the St. Lawrence River as Sept-Iles. The sovereignty movement had turned by then into a political party, the Parti Québécois, led of course by René Lévesque. What a thrill for a kid barely out of graduate school with improving but far from perfect French to be covering him and the other PQ pioneers—Jacques Parizeau, Bernard Landry, Camille Laurin, Robert Burns, Jacques-Yvan Morin, Claude Morin—of whom it was said after the PQ took office in 1976 that they constituted the best English-speaking Cabinet in Canada.

I was not "present at the creation" of the Parti Québécois nor the modern-day Quebec nationalist movement, but I did hop aboard early in the movement-cum-party's development and have seldom been too far removed from it. Shortly after arriving in Ottawa after covering the Quebec election of 1976, I was assigned the so-called national unity beat in *The Globe and Mail*'s Ottawa bureau, which meant reporting on the struggle between the Péquistes and the federal government under Trudeau. That struggle culminated, in a temporary manner of speaking, in the referendum of 1980.

After almost five years of reporting on the file—I subsequently became bureau chief and squeezed in a book about Joe Clark's short-lived government (*Discipline of Power*)—I longed for a break from Canada's national unity debates. Even while I was far removed from Canada, however, the Quebec file followed me. Assigned to London in 1981 as *The Globe and Mail*'s European correspondent, I was soon followed across the Atlantic by Trudeau's proposal to amend the Constitution, including, among other alterations, patriating it from Britain. The battles back home were played out in the salons of London as federal and provincial governments wined, dined and otherwise lobbied British MPs and policy makers. I was in the press galleries scribbling away when the House of Commons and House of Lords finally approved what had been negotiated in Canada. After filing my last dispatch, and after the constitutional changes became a *fait accompli*, I assumed, utterly wrongly, that I had seen the last of constitutional reform stories for my journalistic career.

Trudeau announced that his constitutional changes would last for a thousand years and that "separatism was dead." Subsequent developments mocked both predictions. How they were mocked framed the national debate from soon after I began this column until the present day. The Meech Lake accord, which I supported, ripped the country apart and laid bare conflicting visions of Canada. The Charlottetown accord, which I considered a mish-mash of proposals best buried, represented yet another unsuccessful attempt to satisfy Quebec and other regions of Canada. If I have not been far away from the "national unity" file as a columnist, it is because the file has seldom been removed from the spotlight of national attention. There are, I assure you, vastly more interesting but regrettably few more important national issues than whether the nation will survive its constitutional agonies. Given the results of the Oct. 30, 1995, referendum in Quebec, the file bids fair to remain absolutely central.

If the national unity file frustrated and divided Canadians, so did the wrenching changes to the nature of government. When I arrived in Ottawa in 1976, Canada had just entered the era of persistent federal deficits. The Auditor-General in that year, reporting on a deficit of $3.8-billion, warned that Parliament was close to losing control of the public purse. Subsequent higher deficits piled up throughout the 1980s and 1990s, so that an ever-larger share of taxpayers' money went to pay interest on the staggering federal debt. Provinces, too, felt the burden of higher debts, partly as a consequence of reduced federal transfers to them. Weighed down by debt payments, governments struggled to reduce spending, slash programs and eliminate others. They also raised taxes—the ratio of taxation to gross national product rose faster in Canada in the 1980s than in any advanced industrial country, a state of affairs that not surprisingly produced the widespread tax fatigue of the 1990s. While governments trimmed their activities, free-trade agreements and the vagaries of foreign lenders to whom Canada became increasingly indebted further circumscribed governments' margin for creative activity. For many years after the string of deficits began, Canadians stubbornly resisted acknowledging the deepening severity of the problem. Only in the early 1990s, at first in some provinces, then belatedly in Ottawa, did governments find the necessary public support to begin attending to their weakened fiscal positions.

Anyone who raised the problem of the deficit in the 1980s risked being labelled a neo-conservative or Cassandra. This dismissal gradually receded to the margin of public discourse as more people belatedly understood the remorseless arithmetic of deficits and debt. The tragedy of the last two decades, however, lies in the failure of politicians and the Canadian public to face up sooner to this problem of indebtedness, so that when remedial action was eventually taken, the decisions were exceptionally painful. Much of the anxiety of our time can be traced to the uncertainties and unheavals caused by that remorseless arithmetic of debt-repayment and persistent deficits. For neo-conservatives, of which I am not one, the reduction in state activity represents a joyous end in itself, since they believe that the less government the better; whereas I lamented the deficit/debt trap, and tried repeatedly to alert people to its consequences, because once the state was ensnared in the trap, the opportunity for it to take creative action declined because debt repayments gobbled up so much money.

I believe in selective, creative use of the state for collective purposes such as the fostering of national identity, furthering social justice and the enlargement of what the German sociologist Ralf Dahrendorf called "life chances" for the largest number of citizens. The free market is the best mechanism ever devised for the delivery of goods and services and for sending signals to consumers and taxpayers to guide their behaviour. But the market cares little for social justice, and a cohesive society must search endlessly for a balance between justice and efficiency, rights and responsibilities, so that the agency of government is needed to lean against the injustices and disequilibriums caused by the free market. But this balancing was less possible with governments burdened down by unsupportable deficits and debt.

My deepest frustration as a Canadian observer was that for so long our political culture remained blind to what we were doing to ourselves. When finally we awoke, it was to the cheerleaders of the radical right whose political gains were exceeded only by their ascendancy to the commanding heights of the nation's media. Complexity's foes, the brassy ideologues were always going on about "the people" without revealing in their writing that they had actually met very many. Their prescriptions read sometimes like formulae for building temples to humanity, having first banished all the humans.

The story line of these anxious years has also been one of declining faith in politicians, although this phenomenon, much remarked upon, has been somewhat exaggerated for having been conflated with the visceral and almost universal loathing for former prime minister Brian Mulroney. That loathing poisoned each of his government's wells, with the exception of free trade, which he managed to pull off despite fierce domestic opposition. Some day, but not any time soon, a more balanced view of the Mulroney years will emerge, since the Chrétien Liberals pursued many Conservative policies, demonstrating again that imitation can be the sincerest form of flattery.

Mention of Brian Mulroney brings me back to George Bain's comment about the two best seats in town. Ideas matter in public affairs, but so do politicians. No columnist trying to convey the texture of events and the thrust of ideas can leave out the personalities who defined them. I have known personally most of my subjects, some better than others, of course, but none of them well. There is a fine and not easily explained line between actor and critic, politician and journalist, which I have defined, at least to my satisfaction, as knowledge without friendship. I cannot fathom how journalists think they can write intelligently and accurately about public figures while scorning their acquaintance; nor do I know how journalists can walk the other side of the street by befriending them, thereby making it exceptionally difficult to render a critical picture, when necessary, of their activities. The fascination of politics is the clash of ideas and personalities, and a rendering of one without the other deforms both. I hope in some of the columns to have caught something of the essence of those who have been up there on that stage.

As will become apparent to those who read on, I have sometimes been sharply critical of and disappointed in political leaders, but I have also tried to give each his or her due. It is quite old-fashioned to believe public service can be a noble calling, and there are some people who make it hard to sustain that belief. I persevere in that belief, and therefore have tried to be fair to those I wrote about and to recognize, even when I disagreed profoundly with them, that they were displaying a bravery beyond mine by subjecting themselves to the vicissitudes of public life. I cannot shake the thought, strange I suppose for a columnist, that if I were up there on the public stage I might not do any better. In selecting these columns, it is painfully obvious that I made errors in judgement, but readers are entitled to their own opinion about how many. I do have my pet peeves: craven compromises of those with power; the knee-jerk reaction of opposition for its own sake; the prefabricated positions of the interest groups who equate their interest with that of the general public; popinjay premiers without a sense of the national whole.

Columns are pen sketches of time and place, their observations quickly forgotten, their phrases seldom memorable, their context usually lost. They are like the proverbial moving finger that, having writ, moves on. Collected together later, they may recall, however, those times and places, and remind us of what we have lived through, and perhaps what lessons we have thereby learned. They are, if you like, the first draft of history, with a twist.

PART 1 *The Deficit*

As the Social Fabric Frays, the Troubled Future Becomes Visible (September 14, 1995)

Statistics Canada placed its finger this week on a key factor explaining some of our political stresses.

The federal agency reported that, in 1993, median family income declined after inflation by 2.9 per cent from 1992. Husband-and-wife families with two or more children saw their incomes rise marginally; all other family types saw incomes decline. The sharpest decline was recorded for single-parent families—a dispiriting fall of 6.9 per cent.

Those single-parent families are overwhelmingly led by women. They are most dependent on transfers from government. Statistics Canada estimated that single-parent families received $53.84 in transfer payments for every $100 of employment income.

Those transfer payments, as we know, are under pressure from fiscally strapped governments that are reducing welfare and unemployment-insurance benefits, curbing legal aid and cutting funds for such programs as shelters and emergency hot lines.

Meanwhile, governments continue to be structured, bureaucratically and financially, to pay heed to regional and particularistic lobbies rather than society as a whole with its widening income divisions. In the age of the Charter, courts are emboldened by particularistic lobbies, in the name of equality, to spread scarce resources to designated or newly designated groups.

Here are the seeds of future trouble, as the social fabric frays and the dysfunctional behaviour that can accompany endemic poverty and too many single-parent families (the two often going together) produces more crime, undereducated young people and blighted areas.

Statistics Canada's latest numbers, piled atop numerous other studies, also point to the costs associated with split families and the huge handicaps that accompany teenage pregnancy. The defence of the nuclear family can easily be portrayed as a return to the days of Ozzie and Harriet, but the signs are unmistakable that broken families are more likely to lead to a series of problems for children than nuclear ones.

The state obviously cannot dictate sexual mores or family composition, and it would be fruitless to try. But every government, given the evidence of the costs associated with family breakups, needs to reassess whatever policies it can that favour nuclear families, or a fairer distribution of assets for broken ones.

Declining real incomes also help explain the anger with politics and particular governments. When incomes decline, people look for scapegoats. They also check their bank-books, where they found that until recently taxes were rising faster than incomes, leaving people with less disposable income. Sadly for all of us, the mountain of debt incurred by governments (that is, by us) in the last generation means many years of either tax increases or spending cuts, or both. A problem that took two decades to create will take many years to put right.

Sharp political analysts check the growth or decline of real incomes to measure the public mood. Unemployment may weigh heavily on the minds of those unemployed, underemployed or scared of losing their jobs. Declining real incomes hit a majority of the population, and therefore pack a political punch beyond unemployment.

These trends—widening income disparities, a strained social safety net and real income declines—are occurring simultaneously with another: some people, especially at the very top of the income pile, are doing handsomely. The old monied families and the nouveau riche, the technological sophisticates and the jugglers of fancy concepts are generally thriving.

While what has been called the "glass-tower elite" of traditional plutocrats and talented *arrivistes* thrive in their enclaves of affluence and reinforce each other's complaints about the world—complaints echoed both by a braying business press and by Poujadiste tabloids—their world is increasingly divorced from the one lived in by their fellow citizens and portrayed through the prism of Statistics Canada numbers.

Crush of the Deficit   *(January 21, 1984)*

Three years ago, the federal government's deficit was around $10-billion, and both Liberals and Conservatives pledged to bring it down. Now the deficit exceeds $31-billion; yet apart from a few platitudes, a pall of indifference has apparently spread over the issue.

In other countries, with less onerous deficits than our own, a week seldom passes without the budgetary deficit sparking furious political and economic debate.

Last weekend, for example, the two leading contenders for the Democratic nomination in the United States clashed bitterly. What were Senators Walter Mondale and John Glenn arguing about? How to reduce the United States's deficit, which, in proportional terms, is about two-thirds the size of the Canadian federal government's?

The American debate is bipartisan. Six former secretaries of the treasury—Republican and Democratic—recently published an open letter urging a smaller deficit.

In Western Europe, budgetary deficits preoccupy governments everywhere. No one needs reminding of British Prime Minister Margaret Thatcher's views. But in France, Socialist President François Mitterrand has decreed the budgetary deficit should not exceed 3 per cent of French gross national product. Spending cuts and tax increases are now the order of the day in Socialist France.

In the Netherlands, Belgium and Denmark, conservative coalitions are trying a variety of devices to control spiralling deficits. And the Christian Democrats in West Germany, like the Social Democrats before them, are trying to run a tight fiscal ship.

Yet in Ottawa, few people are screaming about a federal deficit amounting to more than 6 per cent of gross national product (GNP). Maybe the steam left the debate in 1982 when the deficit soared. Maybe the Tories, adding new financial commitments (health, defence), are afraid to say anything before an election. Maybe people believe the Finance Department's projections that the deficit will shrink later in the decade. Or maybe Canadians prefer to hope the problem will go away.

If provincial deficits and surpluses are included, the national picture improves slightly. In 1982, the combined federal and provincial deficits amounted to 5.3 per cent of GNP. That was still higher than in any of the major seven industrial countries except Italy.

The Liberals thought in their 1983 budget papers that the deficit problem would ease in a couple of years. Great pains were taken to explain that the deficit was more "cyclical" than "structural." With recovery, predicted the Finance Department, will come a sharp contraction of the deficit, from 6 per cent of GNP in 1982 to 2 per cent in 1987.

The trouble is that what was considered "cyclical" (namely, high unemployment) looks unfortunately like becoming "structural" (i.e., permanent). Few economists are now willing to predict significantly lower unemployment during the 1980s. And servicing the government's debt, which took up 7.1 per cent of the government's budget in 1976-77, now eats up 13.6 per cent.

Continuing deficits of staggering size increase pressures on interest rates, on inflation, on Ottawa's room to introduce new programs, on transfer payments to the provinces, on Canada's international economic credibility. Whichever party wins the next election will smash against the hard realities of the deficit. Yet the pall of indifference spreads, and the prospects for its lifting in an election year are not promising.

The Market's Role *(March 19, 1987)*

Whether we recognize it or not, Canadians are being asked this year to give their verdict on the operation of the free market.

Attitudes toward the market, either emotional or rational, subliminal or overt, will shape the reaction of many Canadians toward the two great coming issues of national politics—free trade with the United States and tax reform.

Both of these initiatives by the government will essentially let the market play a greater role in allocative decisions. That is, they will prevent or make more difficult some of the things governments have done to curb the flow of market forces.

The debates on free trade and tax reform will be especially intriguing because Canadians have often manifested a deep ambivalence about market forces. Some critics have pointed to the large degree of foreign ownership as an example of what the free market can bring. Others have argued that the market, given a free rein, will favour central Canada at the expense of peripheral regions. Still others have insisted that the market allows the rich to grow richer while the poor grow poorer.

In almost every case, governments have been pressured, not necessarily to make the market work better, but to curb its excesses, or even its natural tendencies. The free-trade initiative, if an agreement is reached, will prevent federal and provincial governments from engaging in certain activities they have favoured to redirect market forces. There may be a greater good in all of this—improved access to the U.S. market and a free flow of goods and services within Canada. But the price will be the elimination of such policies as preferential purchasing, certain forms of subsidies, provincial liquor policies and impediments to investment, to name but a few of the tools governments have used to stymie market forces.

These tools have large constituencies dependent on them, and the members of those constituencies will fight to preserve what now protects them from a freer flow of market forces. Those groups include employers and employees in the textile industries, owners of border broadcasting stations, farm groups, brewers and their employees, autoworkers and many others.

The same point applies to tax reform, the purpose of which will be to produce a more neutral tax system with fewer deductions, exemptions and tax dodges. Those items have been included in the existing tax system usually for defensible reasons, because the government wanted to encourage certain kinds of economic activity—that is, to steer the market in directions in which the government believed the market would not otherwise move.

By circumscribing these deductions and exemptions, the government will be reducing its intervention in the market. Again, this may be for the greater good of a more rational allocation of the nation's resources. But all kinds of groups depend on the provisions of the existing system, including holders of flow-through shares in the mining industry, capital gains–tax claimants, those socking money away in retirement savings programs and recipients of aid from various social programs.

Much of what has defined Canada has been wrapped up, for better or worse, in government initiatives to block, redirect, discourage and otherwise shape the forces of the free market, whether those forces occurred in Canada or emanated from beyond our borders, usually in the United States. That's why the debates about free trade and tax reform cannot be limited to debates about economics and statistics.

How Canadians feel about the market is largely a debate about the history of the country, about how they see themselves and what kind of country they want.

Pain Postponed (February 11, 1988)

An experienced foreign diplomat, ending his Ottawa stint not long ago, wrote in a long, final dispatch to his government that the federal deficit represented Canada's most serious long-term problem.

Whether it's the most serious problem or just one among several, the deficit and accumulating national debt will be around to plague whichever party forms the next government.

The deficit has fallen from $38-billion when the Conservatives arrived in office to $29.3-billion in 1987-88. It is expected to decline only marginally for the next two years, ending up at $28.6-billion in 1989-90.

That's progress of a sort. It means that the growth in the national debt— and in the key indicator of debt as a percentage of GNP—has slowed. But the growth continues.

The legacy of fiscal improvidence bequeathed to the country by the previous Liberal governments still haunts us. In the past four years, the fastest growing budgetary expenditure has been interest charges on the debt. In the next two years, the government expects to add $57.5-billion to the national debt, driving up that key indicator of debt as a percentage of GNP to a staggering 56.1 per cent.

It is almost a maxim in federal budgets that the Finance Department predicts substantially lower deficits—three, four or five years down the line. Various budgets presented by Liberal finance ministers used to provide marvellous examples of this pie-in-the-sky forecasting.

Now the Conservatives are up to the same tricks. The Finance Department predicts that by the early 1990s there will be sharp declines in the deficit, and growth in the national debt at the same rate as general economic growth.

Those predictions are based on a rosy view of the economic future—real growth of 3.2 per cent from 1990 to 1993. Praise be if we can manage that. If an economic downturn ensues, let alone a recession, you can throw those predictions out the window.

Unless Canada gets five more years of strong economic growth, following on the past five years, the next government will face severe upward pressure on the deficit. Ten consecutive years of strong economic growth is therefore what the government is counting on, presumably with crossed fingers, since that would defy the laws of economic probability.

It was unthinkable, of course, that in an election year the government would give deficit reduction any sort of priority. On the contrary, it got a revenue windfall this year from better-than-expected economic growth, and quickly set about allocating most of the money for new spending.

That's the major reason why yesterday's budget was a crashing bore. The government had already put in place big spending programs, and all we needed to know were the details of the revenue and expenditure predictions.

The Mulroney government is now nicely positioned to paper the country with money from programs already announced—the regional development agencies for the Atlantic, the West and northern Ontario, the cash payments to grain farmers, the research "centres of excellence" for universities and, of course, the income tax reductions on July 1. It has also provided for a large contingency fund should some additional worthy program strike its political fancy.

It's the next government that will be burdened with these costs and additional ones for day care, defence purchases and agricultural subsidies. A betting man would give short odds on a fiscal squeeze followed by another round of spending cuts early in the mandate of the new government.

Unless Canada gets awfully lucky in the next five years, the Minister of Finance circa 1990 or 1991 will be one beleaguered person.

The Muffled Alarms   *(March 16, 1989)*

A bit of history should be recalled in the weeks ahead when the Conservative government tries to persuade an indifferent or skeptical public to worry about the federal deficit.

For nearly two decades, governments have intermittently sounded the deficit-reduction tocsin, only to have the sound fade. In the circumstances, it was hardly surprising that Canadians didn't take the matter seriously. Not only would deficit reduction have demanded unwelcome sacrifices from them—indeed, a sea change in the Canadian political culture—but the public kept hearing confusing and even contradictory sounds from Ottawa.

When Pierre Trudeau came to office in 1968, and for some years thereafter, he mused publicly about lowering Canadians' expectations. His rhetoric usually conflicted with his government's fiscal performance, however, especially after the 1973 oil crisis led Ottawa to prime the fiscal pump.

Eleven years ago, in the early summer of 1978, Mr. Trudeau announced without warning that there would be $2-billion in spending cuts. He had not even bothered to inform his finance minister, Jean Chrétien, who stumbled through an encounter with the press trying to explain his boss's decision.

The cuts seemed terribly important at the time. Bureaucrats fussed. Politicians speechified. Journalists reported and opined. And within a few months, the whole deficit-reduction crunch passed as in a dream.

Mr. Trudeau, stung by criticism from his friend West German Chancellor Helmut Schmidt, had suddenly got interested in doing "something" about the deficit. That "something" turned out to be as crude as it was fruitless.

A year later, Prime Minister Joe Clark took office. Building on some bureaucratic work begun under Mr. Trudeau, he restructured the Cabinet system and introduced the much-vaunted "envelope" system for government spending. That system, recently dropped by the Mulroney government because it failed, was designed to force ministers to restrain expenditures. The Clark government's first budget gave Canadians a chance to vote for "short-term pain for long-term gain," including an 18-cents-per-gallon excise tax on gasoline. Canadians voted, and the Conservatives returned to opposition.

Re-elected in 1980, the Liberals attempted again to curtail government spending, but abandoned the effort when the recession hit in 1981. For the next three years, government spending grew by leaps and bounds and government revenues slumped. By the time Brian Mulroney's Conservatives arrived in office, the deficit had reached $30-billion and was heading toward $36-billion.

Five years later, on the eve of another Conservative budget, the deficit stands at about $29-billion and the national debt is rising toward $350-billion. Fifteen years ago, in 1973-74, the federal government was running a balanced budget.

In short, four different governments have tried a variety of institutional and policy responses to curtail the federal deficit, yet the situation in 1989 is appreciably worse than fifteen years ago.

Fundamentally, governments have played at the margin of the problem, while taking a series of decisions that made the core of the problem tougher to resolve. In fact, because they have already raised taxes sharply and trimmed the costs of government operations, the Conservatives now have no choice but to attack the core of the problem, something they resolutely refused to try from 1984 to 1988.

Far from solving the problem in their first mandate, the Conservatives became part of it by accepting, rather than challenging, the political culture of Canada. They won re-election last November all right—in part by not breathing a word to Canadians about what they intended all along to do.

The Fallout from Political Timidity

(February 21, 1990)

> "The growing public debt has become a severe handicap to economic progress and the most serious obstacle to economic growth."
> —*Agenda for Economic Renewal*, Nov. 8, 1984.

> "The debt is still growing faster than the economy—faster than our ability to pay."
> —Finance Minister Michael Wilson's budget, Feb. 20, 1990.

Five-and-a-half years after coming to office, the Tory dog is still chasing its tail.

Bequeathed staggering deficits and debts by the Trudeau Liberals, the Tories are still struggling with that legacy, and will continue to do so for some years to come. The struggle, of which yesterday's budget was a small part, was made worse by the Tories' own timidity.

Since they came to power in 1984, the political and economic cycles have been mostly out of sync. From 1986 to 1988, with the economy booming, the Tories should have driven down the deficit. Had they done so then, yesterday's budget would have been much easier. But their eyes were fixed firmly on re-election in those years.

Once the Tories were safely re-elected, the political winds were favourable for attacking the deficit/debt problem, but the economic climate worsened. So, at a time when the Tories are clamping down modestly on government spending, the economy is slowing down. This is bad economics made necessary by political timidity.

Deep in the budget lay one apparently obscure phrase that explained everything else: "It [the expenditure control plan] does not entail any permanent structural changes in major programs."

With those words, the government closed off most of the realistic options for long-term reductions in public spending. By leaving major programs untouched, it could only put a series of variable restraints on the increases for about two-fifths of ongoing programs.

These restraints, along with the ending of three programs (the Polar 8 icebreaker, the pre-election oil sands boondoggle called OSLO, and the flow-through share incentives for mining), are the pith and substance of the budget. If these changes amount to a "tough" (Prime Minister Brian Mulroney's word) budget, throw out your dictionaries.

These reductions will still leave Ottawa $500-million short of its $28-billion deficit target for next year. By next year, of course, the election will be looming on the horizon.

The 1989 budget, properly maligned for raising taxes, at least had the virtue of attacking "structural changes to major programs" such as Via Rail, unemployment insurance and defence. This budget shies away from such a politically risky but economically necessary approach. It thus postpones difficult trade-offs imposed by the levels of deficit and debt. The budget even grants defence, of all departments, a 5 per cent increase.

Money market analysts convinced themselves before the budget that Messrs. Wilson and Mulroney needed only to keep next year's deficit close to $28-billion to reassure foreign investors who are increasingly financing Canada's debt.

They should not be misled. A third of the "spending cuts" come from unspecified contributions from Crown corporations, "enhanced collection of accounts receivable" and earlier remittances from the Bank of Canada to the central treasury. Another third of the cuts come from freezing a few programs for two years. Freezes, as we know, inevitably melt before elections.

These changes have nothing to do with "structural changes in major programs," the most important approach to long-term deficit reduction and debt write-down.

Markets beware.

Mr. Wilson Chips Away at the Debt Left Over from the Nightmare Years *(February 27, 1991)*

Finance Minister Michael Wilson's seventh budget confirms yet again the overwhelming fiscal weakness of the federal government.

Ottawa became a fiscal cripple in the years 1975 to 1984, when the federal government accumulated nearly $200-billion of debt. Compounded interest on that accumulated debt cost another $120-billion by 1989-90. So the total bill for these ten nightmare years of economic mismanagement, 1975 to 1984, is in the vicinity of $320-billion.

It was obvious by the time the Tories took power in 1984 that, having spent a decade getting into an utterly untenable fiscal situation, Canada would need more than a decade to extricate itself from trouble. That difficult and painful process of escape is still going on, and will be for some years yet.

Only in 1995-96 can the federal government foresee a balanced budget, and that forecast should be taken with a mountain of salt, given Ottawa's lamentable record of medium-term predictions. The balanced-budget prediction can be easily overturned by international events, economic growth projections, political expediency in the run-up to an election, or a constitutional crisis.

The weakness brought on by this legacy of indebtedness is everywhere apparent: in continuing reductions in transfers to the provinces, in public-sector wage restraint, in privatizations, in spending cutbacks and in relentless tax increases.

All these policies, which have been hallmarks of Mr. Wilson's previous budgets, were repeated again yesterday in an especially austere budget. Perhaps only a government whose popularity is just above the interest-rate level, reckoning it could not fall any lower, would have offered this austerity. About the only kind of cod-liver oil Mr. Wilson did not suggest yesterday was another round of tax increases, but he still managed to increase the burden on individuals by upping unemployment insurance premiums.

This budget will create a predictable furore, since it offers no relief to any group afflicted by the recession. Ottawa is withdrawing from the economy, and all those groups that depended upon government involvement will be profoundly unhappy.

The nightmare years, coupled with the Tories' inability or unwillingness to tackle the legacy with the necessary persistence in their first term in office, left the country terribly vulnerable to recession, higher interest rates or both.

This double whammy destroyed the projections for deficit reduction in the previous two budgets, and forced the government into yet more spending cuts yesterday. Still, spending on programs will increase by a whopping 6.9 per cent, largely because of higher unemployment insurance payments.

High interest rates, of course, have made the fight against the deficit/debt problems more difficult to wage. Indeed, the entire budget might be described as a treadmill: higher interest rates make deficit reduction more difficult, large debts make deficit reduction more difficult, recession makes deficit reduction more difficult. Hence, more of the same.

But the fundamental problem remains the size of the debt, close to $400-

billion. If the debt were modest in size, say $150-billion, Ottawa's interest payments would be about $16-billion instead of about $42-billion, even at these high rates of interest. The cost of paying the interest on this mountain of debt—let alone writing down the principal—would be the grim task of any federal government.

In one important respect, Mr. Wilson offered something new. He proposed legislation to keep overall program-spending increases to 3 per cent for the next few years. Governments usually open the spending taps as an election approaches, as the Tories did in 1987 and 1988. By foreclosing that option, Mr. Wilson is trying something decidedly brave.

There is every likelihood that this is his last budget. Seven budgets later, he has chipped away at the debt left over from the nightmare years. His successors, Conservative or Liberal or New Democrat, will be plagued by the same problem throughout the 1990s.

Long After His Death, John Maynard Keynes Is Dying Yet Again in Ontario

(May 4, 1991)

Who killed John Maynard Keynes? The Keynsians done it.

They killed their hero, the British economist whose theories were once so influential on how to manage an economy, by not listening to all their master's teachings. Instead, they picked up only what they wanted to hear, and, like the Ontario New Democratic Party government, put half the master's teachings into practice. The rest they conveniently forgot.

Keynes, to put matters very crudely, saw government as an important agent in levelling economic cycles. In economic slowdowns, he considered government spending and stimulus entirely appropriate. But when economic activity picked up, government spending had to ease off and the debts incurred in the bad times had to be paid down. Otherwise, economies would be vulnerable the next time the bad times arrived, and inflation would certainly be at hand.

So Keynes's message, boiled down, was simple: spend in the lean times, retrench in the fat ones.

This now seems like elementary common sense. When first propounded, however, the theory was heresy to many who believed in small, lean, parsimonious government all the time.

Keynes's theory got into trouble when the practitioners forgot the second half of it. They spent, often lavishly, in the lean times, as the NDP proposes to do in Ontario. But they clamoured for even more spending, as the NDP did in opposition, during the fat times.

Remember the last Ontario election campaign? Everywhere he went, NDP Leader Bob Rae poured scorn on the Liberals for not having spent enough. The Liberals had thrown Keynes out the window, spending like sailors during boom times and driving up spending by double digits each year. Yet Bob Rae accused them of ignoring real social needs, of not spending enough. He made common cause with all manner of interest groups, and thereby left himself open as Premier to disappointing some of them.

Interest groups, too, were lambasting the Liberals for spending too little in the boom times. They could see the revenues rolling in, and, disregarding Keynes's teaching, said: spend it. Don't withdraw during the fat times to prepare for the bad times. Spend. On us, of course.

Keynes could not envision entitlements and interest groups. His was a much more elitist society. He could not imagine that discretionary government decisions to spend, or favour one group of taxpayers with a one-time decision, might immediately become entitlements of citizenship for those favoured.

Nor could he see how politicians, caught by regional pressures and interest groups (and by the need to get re-elected), would find compressing expectations excruciatingly difficult. Good intentions, and Keynes, fell victim to politics.

Consider three examples:

- A problem with pensions? Create registered retirement savings plans, and blow a huge hole in federal revenues. This is now an inviolable middle-class tax break. Woe unto any government that touches it.
- Regional development, under Jean Marchand and Tom Kent, was designed to assist tightly targeted areas of high unemployment. But Montreal ministers in the Trudeau years said their city had to be designated, and this was done, because they had clout. Subsequently, all of Canada became eligible except Southern Ontario and the lower mainland of British Columbia.
- Create an unemployment *insurance* scheme. Unemployment rises. Make it far more generous. Then add regional variations. Wind up building government programs around finding ten weeks of work for people so they can claim UI for the rest of the year.

The examples are endless, and costly. It's easy to expand spending, and economically defensible, in bad times. But retrenching has become difficult and politically painful when the bad times are over.

Ontario illustrates perfectly why Keynes died. If he were alive, the Liberals should have put the brakes on spending instead of overheating the economy. The New Democrats, if they believed in Keynes and understood him, should have damned the Liberals not for spending too little but for spending too freely.

Now the NDP is treating Ontario, and through it the rest of Canada, to the ghost of Keynes. Ghosts, after all, offer only the appearance of reality, which is how the NDP interprets Keynes.

Keynes's theories themselves died some time ago, killed by erstwhile believers.

Troubled Tories Taking Another Tilt at the Windmill *(February 26, 1992)*

Eight budgets later, the Mulroney government still tilts at the windmill of the federal deficit. As always, the budget papers show a sharp decline in the deficit—a few years from now.

Unfortunately, for this year and next, the government will miss the deficit targets set in the last Michael Wilson budget a year ago. This year, the overshoot will be about $1-billion; next year, about $3.5-billion.

By 1995-96, if all goes well, the government's borrowing requirements will be zero. By 1995-96, the chances are excellent that the Tories will no longer be in office, lots of unanticipated factors will have intervened, and the minister of finance will be producing budgetary figures showing zero borrowing requirements by . . . pick your year.

It took Canada about a decade, from 1975 to 1984, to get into serious fiscal trouble, and it will take at least that long, and probably much longer, for Ottawa to return to the fiscally prudent decades between the end of the Second World War and the 1970s.

By spending cuts and tax increases, the Tories have struggled against the debt legacy they inherited. And they made their own burdens worse in 1987 and 1988 when they eased up on restraint. Safely re-elected in 1988, they resumed the struggle, only to be hit by recession and their own inability to stay away from pet projects.

Now, Finance Minister Don Mazankowski is back with a budget that predicts 2 per cent inflation but 3 per cent increases in federal spending. In short, the government will grow less rapidly than the overall growth in the economy but faster than the inflation rate.

The savings announced yesterday are largely in defence and social housing. Defence will lose $2.2-billion over the next five years; Canada Mortgage and Housing (which Ottawa proposes to transfer to the provinces anyway), $647-million.

In addition, the government proposes cosmetic savings from such devices as eliminating first-class air travel for its employees and duplication in its services.

It also seeks chicken-feed savings by winding up or consolidating forty-six agencies, boards, commissions and advisory councils. These will save the grand total of $22-million per year, and several of the cuts are extremely unwise.

In particular, the closing of the Economic Council of Canada robs the country of a credible, independent source of economic information. This decision is partly pure spite by the Finance Department, which has feuded with the Council. The opposition would do us all a favour to fight hard against this silly move.

Amid this restraint, the government continues to spend hugely for farmers (annual subsidies up 9.5 per cent since 1984), the elderly (spending up 7.1 per cent a year), the unemployed (up 7.1 per cent a year), Natives (up 10.8 per cent a year) and, of course, debt repayment (up 9.1 per cent). Add to those increases the 5.4 per cent average hikes to provinces and 4.8 per cent for defence in the period since 1984, and it's no wonder the deficit battle seems like windmill-tilting.

After the administration of selective pain through eight budgets, and with only one more budget to come before an election, it was time to give people a small break.

Taxpayers will now be able to raid their retirement savings programs for new-home purchases, and the personal income-tax surtax will be slightly reduced over two years. There will also be a useful overhaul of child benefits to put slightly more money in the hands of low- and moderate-income Canadians.

If growth resumes as the government anticipates, and if selective spending restraint continues, there will be room for further tax cuts in the final budget before the next election. At their convention last summer in Toronto, some senior Tories were speculating (drooling?) over tax cuts in 1993. Yesterday's budget leaves the door open for that politically motivated response next year.

A tax cut and the high-profile but essentially cosmetic expenditure reductions have as their target angry Conservatives, some of whom have drifted over to the Reform Party.

Tories have not been pushed down to between 11 and 16 per cent in the polls by the Liberals, but by losses to the Reform Party and the Bloc Québécois. Getting those voters back somehow is the Tories' only path to survival.

A Quarter-Century of Folly, and Another Decade to Go (May 1, 1992)

For a quarter-century, from 1965-66 to 1990-91, taxes in Canada increased more rapidly than growth in the economy. However, they grew less rapidly than overall government spending.

The pecking order of increases for an entire generation has been: (1) spending; (2) taxation; (3) economic growth. Here are the numbers, for a quarter-century: government spending grew on average by 12.3 per cent; revenues by 11.8 per cent; the economy by 10.3 per cent.

Those numbers have produced a crisis in public-sector finance. No matter what the political stripe, governments are whipsawed by the bitter edge of this twenty-five-year trend. The trend brought, most obviously, huge and apparently intractable public-sector borrowing, debt repayments and deficits. Governments, in good times and bad, spent more than the country's economic growth could bear. They were therefore forced to borrow to pay the excess. Then they raised taxes to pay the debt, and thereby contributed to dampening growth.

The trends have also led to "tax fatigue," abetted by yesterday's Ontario budget, which grabbed another $1-billion. When taxes grow faster than incomes, people get unhappy. When taxes grow faster than incomes, and government services decline because spending must be capped, taxpayers are doubly angry. Taxpayers who feel they are paying more but receiving less are generally correct, and their anger and mystification contributes to souring attitudes toward all politicians.

In 1991, for example, recession drove down real incomes, but prices rose by 5.6 per cent, largely because of government tax increases, including the Goods and Services Tax. Government-regulated prices rose by 9.6 per cent, compared with 4.5 per cent for non-regulated prices. In other words, the market responded to the recession much better than governments did.

No party was blameless in the blind advance toward the crisis over a quarter-century, although partisan attacks now lead them to blame others, as the Ontario NDP did yesterday.

Conservatives ruined Saskatchewan's finances. Conservatives are driving up Alberta's deficit. Socreds bequeathed a deficit to B.C.'s NDP. Liberals shamelessly squandered Ontario's golden years of growth in the 1980s. The Trudeau Liberals ran the federal deficit from zero to $36-billion in a decade.

Now, all governments must grapple with a quarter-century of folly.

In Ontario, an NDP administration raised taxes yesterday, modestly capped spending, yet still saw its own, already large, deficit-projection numbers exceeded. The recipe for the future: more of the same, because the accumulating deficits of the NDP years must be paid down by still higher taxes later.

In Quebec, the government faces a $4-billion deficit. It's talking about casinos to raise revenues, and cuts to medical services. In Saskatchewan shortly, the new NDP government will trim spending, raise taxes and still produce an eye-popping deficit that will cost the province a couple of bond-rating points. British Columbia, weathering the recession better than any other province, still has a $1.6-billion deficit despite a so-called tough NDP budget, almost half as large per capita as that in recession-battered Ontario.

In Ottawa, deficits of $30-billion a year have become a fixture of contemporary budgets. A national debt of $420-billion offers little prospect of short-term relief.

In the early 1980s, burgeoning federal deficits were partly offset by provincial surpluses. Now, a large federal deficit is compounded by large provincial deficits. On a cumulative basis, therefore, the debt problem has spread like a stain from Ottawa to the provinces, and now to the municipalities, school boards, hospitals and transit systems. Ottawa has transferred some of its problem to the provinces; provinces are "offloading" their problems onto school, university and hospital boards and municipalities. In recession, tax increases from governments starved for money, and spending driven by entitlements, run far ahead of economic growth. The deadly combination of tax hikes plus spending rising faster than economic growth pushes up deficits which, in turn, sows the seeds for future tax increases.

After the recession ends, it will take about a decade of reversing the quarter-century order of taxes, spending and economic growth to restore some degree of equilibrium to the nation's finances. There are only some flickering signs that political leaders and electorates understand the challenge ahead.

It Wasn't a Socialist Shopping Binge That Gave the Country a Hangover

(February 9, 1993)

"There's no doubt that the debt is a very real problem, and one which deserves our attention, if not for ourselves but [*sic*] for our children who will inherit the burden."

Now, who do you suppose said that? A bank president? Prime Minister Brian Mulroney? No, surprise of surprises, the words came from NDP Leader Audrey McLaughlin in a recent column she penned for *The Whitehorse Star*.

Some years ago, when the nation's debt problem began to get serious, neither the federal NDP nor its provincial cousins would even acknowledge it. Most New Democrats considered the problem either irrelevant or far less consequential than a host of other concerns.

Now, however, the relentlessness of the deficit/debt spiral has borne down on NDP governments in Ontario, Saskatchewan and British Columbia. The NDP premiers of Ontario and B.C. told *The Toronto Star* recently that the spiral was so serious that a full-scale federal-provincial conference should be devoted to it.

In the incremental world of Canadian politics, we are making progress. At least there is agreement across the political landscape that the country's deficit/debt situation is unsustainable. What to do about it remains the subject of intense political debate.

On the political right, fingers are always pointed at the Left for reckless tax-and-spend policies. Those on the right preach restraint and portray themselves as the only safe custodians of public finances. Elect the socialists, they cry, and the country will find itself under a mountain of debt.

Until recently, the Left in Canada has been out of office. Here, and in the United States, the Right remained politically triumphant. Yet while the self-described custodians of fiscal virtue governed, deficits and debt skyrocketed.

The United States, for example, has just emerged from twelve years of Republican presidential rule, during which the country became the largest debtor nation in world history. It now falls to a Democratic president to expend his political capital to clean up the Republicans' mess.

In Canada, the Conservatives have governed since 1984. They inherited a debt of $200-billion and a deficit of $36-billion. Eight years later, the debt is $460-billion and the deficit $33-billion.

True, the Trudeau Liberals left the country in a fiscal bind. Much of the debt amassed by the Tories has represented interest payments on the debt inherited from the Liberals. And the Tory deficit of 1992-93 is much lower as a portion of the country's gross national product than when the Liberals left office.

Still, the Tory years have included crushing deficits and ever-accumulating debt. It will take another decade of fiscal austerity in Ottawa, regardless of which party finds itself in office, to bring the nation's finances into some semblance of order.

Provincially, the New Democratic Party has not brought high deficits. In Saskatchewan, NDP premier Allan Blakeney's government left the books in reasonable shape when his party lost to the Conservatives in 1982. It was the Tories who then ran the province's finances into the ground.

In Alberta, Premier Ralph Klein now preaches fiscal restraint and balanced budgets. But who presided over the deterioration in Alberta's finances? The Conservative Party.

In B.C., the Social Credit Party claimed to have balanced budgets, but it accomplished this more through creative bookkeeping than anything else. Now it's the NDP in that province, as in Saskatchewan, that must cut back.

In Ontario, Liberal premier David Peterson presided over the boom years. Those years were wasted in excessive wage settlements and large spending, and the NDP was handed a much weaker fiscal position than a prudent Liberal government would have bequeathed.

Not long ago, a leading Conservative politician privately warned a group of businessmen against letting the NDP get its hands on fiscal matters. He said it would be like giving a compulsive shopper free rein with a credit card.

But the country's conservative forces held that credit card for much of the 1980s. They were the ones that racked up the huge bills that left accounts overdrawn. It's worth remembering this the next time a preacher from the political right comes calling.

At Last, There's a Political Consensus that the Debt Problem Is Serious *(March 11, 1993)*

The massive changes at Ontario Hydro—4,500 fewer jobs, spending cuts, contracts cancelled, plants to be mothballed—are the latest blows to the Ontario economy, once the golden goose of Canadian federalism.

Ontario government revenues fell two years running, courtesy of the recession. Unemployment soared, taxes rose and the deficit skyrocketed. Some jobs left because of free trade; others because the province's manufacturing productivity had lagged for years. Its education system, the plaything of educational theorists and bureaucrats, proved grossly inadequate for the competitive demands of the 1990s.

Now, what used to be the province's crown jewel and a motor for its economic development has fallen on disastrous times. Combining the province's burgeoning debt with that of Ontario Hydro has caused moneylenders to wonder about whether they should make further loans at the most favourable rates. Add that worry to the continuing large deficits of the NDP provincial government and Ontario looks less like a golden goose than a plucked chicken.

The results for Canadian federalism are impossible to predict accurately, but several possibilities commend themselves.

The first is that Ontario governments, whatever their political stripe, are likely to greet with less than unbridled enthusiasm any federal-provincial fiscal arrangements designed to distribute Ontario's wealth to other parts of Canada.

For some months, NDP Premier Bob Rae has been snarling at the federal Tories' reduced increases in their payments to the province. He even asked for a special payment to take account of the recession's severity, a demand that Ottawa predictably dismissed.

Some of Mr. Rae's thunder is undoubtedly *la bonne guerre* between a provincial government and Ottawa; but some of it speaks to the deeper issue of the province's assertive Ontario-first attitude.

That attitude was manifested once before in recent memory: during the spat over oil prices in the late 1970s and early 1980s that eventually led to the National Energy Program, when Ontario defended its interests as an oil-consuming province.

Sensing its vital interests threatened, Ontario mobilized public opinion to defend them and succeeded in pressuring the Joe Clark and Pierre Trudeau governments to restrain Alberta's ambitions as an oil-producing province.

Apart from this Ontario-first attitude, Ontario's diminished fiscal standing has also brought home the reality of deficits and debt to the NDP. The same sobriety has overtaken the NDP governments in Saskatchewan and British Columbia, although they had fewer illusions about the reality of the problem.

The Ontario NDP has learned that there is a left-wing way of looking at the world and a right-wing way, and then there is arithmetic. Alas, the arithmetic of deficits and debt is so immutable, and so crippling, that the NDP premiers, including Mr. Rae, are now ringing the tocsin about the problem.

At last, therefore, a political consensus exists in Canada that the problem is serious. After years of denial, the responsible political left acknowledges the gravity of the country's fiscal situation and can debate solutions without insinuating that the problem is part of a right-wing conspiracy.

From this maturity flows the idea, first raised by the NDP premiers, of a serious First Ministers' conference—or series of conferences—after the next federal election on the crisis of fiscal federalism.

The idea is an excellent one. It would focus public attention on a problem that many citizens still feel does not exist. It would cement the idea that the governments are in the same boat and cannot afford to row in different directions. It would—or at least might—induce the two levels of government to hold each other accountable for jointly negotiated targets for spending and taxing.

Finally, it would let governments use the political protection of federal-provincial agreements to make the difficult decisions that lie ahead.

Of course, the whole exercise could degenerate into name-calling, finger-pointing and federal-provincial squabbling. My guess, however, is that the crisis has become so severe, and the recognition of its severity is so widespread, that something constructive and urgent might come from this NDP idea.

And Now, the Main Political Event: Governments Versus Their Employees

(May 14, 1993)

The critical dividing line in Canadian politics these days is less the traditional one of partisanship than that between governments and their own employees.

From Newfoundland to Vancouver, and regardless of political stripe, governments are grappling with restraining the growth in their expenditures. This necessarily turns attention to the size and cost of their public sectors.

Every government wants to root out that old curmudgeon, "waste and inefficiency." But as any serious analyst of government can attest, rooting it out won't save huge sums. If governments want to address their costs, they must look at their own bill for wages, salaries and benefits.

Cast an eye across Canada and see the dividing line of governments against their own employees.

In Newfoundland, Premier Clyde Wells was thumpingly re-elected in the teeth of a vigorous attempt by the Newfoundland Teachers Association to defeat him because Mr. Wells had proposed attacking their pension fund.

In New Brunswick and Nova Scotia, provincial governments froze public-sector wages. In Quebec, the Liberal government negotiated a previous freeze and proposed this week to freeze the salaries of its employees for two years beginning July 1. For their part, the unions are already threatening the end of labour peace.

In Ontario, of course, the government is attempting to claw $2-billion back from its nearly one hundred thousand employees as part of what Premier Bob Rae calls a "social contract."

In Manitoba, the government proposes additional days off for employees this summer, without pay. In Saskatchewan, NDP Premier Roy Romanow has no good cheer for the government's employees, as the province wrestles with a staggering deficit bequeathed by one of the worst provincial governments in recent Canadian history, the Conservatives under former premier Grant Devine.

In Alberta, Premier Ralph Klein is breathing fire about public-sector restraint. In British Columbia, the government has negotiated a restraint package with health-sector employees. In Vancouver, the teachers are on strike again, an event about as regular as the Canucks' *el foldo* routine in the Stanley Cup playoffs.

Ottawa, of course, has frozen public-sector wages, although the Public Service Commission reported this week an astounding bit of news: the number of public-sector employees grew by 2.6 per cent last year. So much for restraint. (And the blessed Ottawa Board of Education, one of the nation's leading bloated bureaucracies, just slapped a tax increase of 5 per cent on citizens in a city where many people's incomes are frozen.)

What underlies this universal trend is the sad fact that not a single government in Canada can produce sufficient revenues to balance its expenditures. Without this kind of restraint, their fiscal situations would deteriorate even more markedly.

Governments could, of course, raise money through higher taxes, as Ontario is planning. But taxes rose faster in Canada during the 1980s than in any other G7 country, according to comparative figures from the Organization for Economic Co-operation and Development. No wonder there is tax fatigue across the country.

Even higher taxes on the "wealthy," the leitmotif of the unions, would produce only a fraction of the money required to dent the deficits.

To wit, Osgoode Hall Professor Neil Brooks' most recent article on tax reform suggests that Ottawa could raise another $5-billion in additional taxes on the wealthy. Even if he were correct—his analysis is partly right and partly wrong—where would that leave a government with a $35-billion deficit? Still staggering.

The lag between economic activity and the public sector's response is also driving governments to distraction. Governments cannot restructure themselves as quickly as private corporations. So much of their spending is locked into programs whose beneficiaries consider the programs to be entitlements of citizenship.

So, it matters little which party governs, since the fiscal crisis of Canadian federalism compels all governments to examine the money they spend on their own employees. This is the new dividing line of Canadian politics, and it is a much deeper one than traditional, tired partisan cockfighting.

Ghosts of Finance Ministers Past Sing a Tired and Familiar Chorus *(October 19, 1994)*

"In building up a debt we are bankrupting our children," Finance Minister John Donald Jean John Allan Marc Michael Donald Martin, sometimes known as Paul Jr., told the Commons finance committee Monday.

Memories:

John Turner, budget day, Jun. 23, 1975: "I come now to specific measures. None is more important than the control of public expenditures."

Donald Macdonald, budget day, May 25, 1976: "Now that the recovery is well established and private spending is rising, it is equally appropriate that these record deficits should recede."

Donald Macdonald, budget day, Mar. 31, 1977: "For some time, our policy has entailed a sizable deficit. As the slack in the economy is taken up, the deficit will decline."

Jean Chrétien, budget day, Nov. 16, 1978: "Significant reductions in the deficit can be expected."

John Crosbie, budget day, Dec. 11, 1979: "The fundamental objective of our fiscal plan is to bring about a steady reduction in our deficits."

Allan MacEachen, budget day, Oct. 28, 1980: "I am convinced we must slow down the growth of public debt charges, and this is one of the reasons I am determined to reduce the deficit."

Allan MacEachen, budget day, Nov. 12, 1981: "I believe we must reduce our deficit and our borrowing requirements substantially."

Allan MacEachen, budget day, Jun. 28, 1982: "The government cannot responsibly add to the deficit."

Marc Lalonde, budget day, Apr. 19, 1983: "We must manage the deficit now to ensure that it will come down as quickly as possible."

Marc Lalonde, budget day, Feb. 15, 1984: "In the medium term, the deficit will fall."

Michael Wilson, budget day, May 23, 1985: "I am implementing a clear and realistic medium-term plan to control our debt."

Michael Wilson, budget day, Feb. 26, 1986: "When the government came to office, we encountered a debt problem of massive proportions. . . . The buck was passed to us. Well, the buck stops here."

Michael Wilson, budget day, Feb. 18, 1987: "While great progress has been made on the nation's deficit problem, there can be no holiday from fiscal responsibility."

Michael Wilson, budget day, Apr. 27, 1989: "We . . . have a serious problem: our large and growing public debt. . . . The sad reality of debt is that it feeds on itself. It places a nation on a treadmill."

Michael Wilson, budget day, Feb. 20, 1990: "We will reduce the deficit to $28.5-billion next year. We will cut it in half to $14-billion in three more years. We will reduce it further to $10-billion in the year after that."

Michael Wilson, budget day, Feb. 26, 1991: "We will put government finances on the course to a balanced budget."

Don Mazankowski, budget day, Feb. 25, 1992: "We will substantially reduce the deficit."

Don Mazankowski, budget day, Apr. 26, 1993: "I am presenting a budget that will deliver . . . a strong, positive initiative for a co-operative national attack on all government debt."

Paul Martin, budget day, Feb. 27, 1994: "For years, governments have been promising more than they can deliver, and delivering more than they can afford. That has to end. We are ending it."

Memories:

Budgetary deficits: 1974-75, $2-billion; 1976-77, $6.2-billion; 1978-79, $12-billion; 1980-81, $13.5-billion; 1982-83, $27.8-billion; 1984-85, $38-billion; 1986-87, $30-billion; 1988-89, $29-billion; 1990-91, $32-billion; 1992-93, $41-billion; 1993-94, $45-billion; 1994-95 (projected) $39.5-billion.

Memories:

Net public debt: Pierre Trudeau takes office, 1968-69, $17-billion; Pierre Trudeau leaves office, 1984-85, $199-billion; Brian Mulroney leaves office, 1993-94, $508-billion, about half of which is compound interest on the Trudeau government's debt. Net debt forecast for this year: approximately $550-billion.

Memories from Monday:

Mr. Martin states: "We are in hock up to our eyeballs."

Memories:

Yogi Berra (undated): "It's *déjà vu* all over again."

The Shrinking of the State Is the Underlying Story of Our Time *(January 23, 1996)*

Unionized workers demonstrate on the lawns of Queen's Park in Toronto. Seasonal workers in New Brunswick protest changes to unemployment insurance. Health-care workers complain loudly in Alberta.

Here and there across Canada, organized groups are decrying reductions in government spending, especially in social programs. Some groups—such as teachers, nurses and doctors—complain because the money they are paid might shrink, others—such as seasonal workers—complain because their benefits might drop.

By no means is social peace threatened as it was recently in France. Apart from the one-day partial shutdown in London, Ont., by some unions, government services continue to be delivered. Public-sector unions make noise, predictably enough, but the more important political calculation for governments is the level of tolerance for these reductions by citizens who use government services rather than work for the government.

The shrinking of the state, which has been going on for some years and will continue for some years yet, is the underlying story of our time, a story made necessary by too many years of expansion of government activities with borrowed money. By the end of this fiscal year, the combined federal and provincial debts will be $871-billion, very close to the country's total gross domestic product.

Belatedly, the three fiscal fatties of Canada—Ottawa, Ontario and Quebec—

are beginning to confront their problems, albeit with quite different timetables and objectives.

Ottawa under the Chrétien Liberals is slowly reducing the federal deficit—from 3 per cent of GNP in 1996-97 to 2 per cent in 1997-98. Meanwhile, the federal debt piles up, albeit at a slightly slower pace.

The Quebec government, under Premier-in-waiting Lucien Bouchard, is already working on a round of cuts. Mr. Bouchard has called off a 1 per cent increase in the provincial sales tax scheduled for July 1, which would have raised about $500-million, and told his future ministerial colleagues to find savings of about the same amount. Quebec is already the most heavily indebted province on a per capita basis. When federal, provincial, municipal and other tax-supported debts are added together, each Quebecker shoulders a public debt of about $33,500.

The Mike Harris Conservatives in Ontario, with their sharp ideological bent, are slashing $6-billion in government spending and promising a tax cut. The results of these actions, which have scarcely been felt, will be reduced government services and a proliferation of higher fees for certain government services. University tuitions will rise by about 20 per cent, municipalities will be imposing fees for certain services previously financed out of general revenues, hospitals will close.

The angst that people feel about these structural shifts in state spending is unlikely to diminish, in part because the full impact of cuts already announced has not been felt. Ottawa's reductions to the provinces for post-secondary education, health and welfare have not yet worked their way through public finance. Ottawa's changes to unemployment insurance (UI), designed to take $1.2-billion out of the system, are still before Parliament and have not hit UI payouts. Some of the additional user fees that Ottawa planned are only now taking effect for such services as national parks, fishing licences and passports.

Some economists, including Ernie Stokes in the latest issue of *Canadian Business Economics*, predict that, depending upon interest rates, at this rate of improvement in government finances it might be possible for governments to offer tax relief in the first decade of the next century. Tax relief and/or lower real interest rates might be possible by then, but only if public finances continue to improve.

Politically, the question remains how long people will accept the changes required by the debt build-up of the past two decades. Apart from public-sector unions, whose unhappiness is understandable, the general population seems for now to accept changes to the scope of government imposed by parties from the centre-left to the neo-conservative right.

There will come a time, however, when a broad public fatigue with these changes will set in. A race is therefore on between the arrival of that fatigue and the stabilization of public finances.

PART 2 *Free Trade*

So Glad You Called *(October 23, 1984)*

"Hello, Mr. President. Brian Mulroney here."

"Brian who?"

"Brian Mulroney, Prime Minister of Canada."

"Oh yes. How are you?"

"Fine, sir. You were terrific in the debate the other night. We were rooting for you."

"Ah, thanks. That's awfully nice of you."

"Sir, I know you're busy, but I just thought we could talk a bit about the things Joe Clark and George Shultz discussed last week."

"George who?"

"George Shultz, sir. Your Secretary of State."

"Oh yes. Well, fire away, as we say down here."

"Right. Well, first there's acid rain. Joe sort of gave George a hard time on that one. George wouldn't budge. So I'm wondering, sir, if in light of our special relationship you might do something about the problem."

"Problem? As I've said before, Bill, acid rain comes from trees. And dammit, I can't stop the trees from growing."

"I see. But you could stop the arms race. At least talk to the Soviets about an anti-satellite weapons treaty or something. We're kinda worried about that up here, being as we are between you and the Russians."

"Dammit, Bill, you sound like that guy you replaced who was always trying to tell me how to run the world."

"I meant no disrespect, sir. I realize your awesome responsibilities, and you can count on us to do our bit. It's just that people are a bit nervous up here, and I've got to make the right sounds."

"You don't know what the Ruskies are like. I had old Gromski or Grominko or whatever his name is in here for a chat. I laid on the charm. Big smiles. Nice wine. Asked about his kids. He just spouted the old propaganda about evil empires, military buildups and his country standing tall again. I couldn't get anywhere."

"Well, perhaps we could agree, in light of our new relationship, on stopping the Garrison diversion project."

"The what?"

"The dams in the Dakotas that might flood parts of Manitoba."

"How many electoral college votes are there in Manitoba?"

"Well, perhaps we can talk about Garrison another time. But what about sectoral free trade? Can we agree to give those talks a push?"

"I'm all for free trade. What sectors did you have in mind?"

"Well, the ones we've been talking about for the last year."

"Which ones are those?"

"Agricultural implements, rapid transit equipment, steel and infometrics."

"Infowhat?"

"Infometrics. Computers. High-technology transfer of information. That sort of thing."

"You interested in one of my Teleprompters? Maggie Thatcher bought one. Greatest little invention since talking pictures. Makes you look like you've memorized the speech."

"No, thanks. I give the same speech every time so I don't think I need one."

"Too bad."

"Sir, could we resume negotiations on the West Coast salmon treaty now that the International Court has settled the other case?"

"The hell it has. If the Commies in Nicaragua or any other pipsqueaks think we're going to pay attention to some doddering old judges they're in for a shock. We had to mine those harbours, Bill. The Soviets were pouring in the arms."

"Yes, well. . . . You'll be pleased to know, sir, we've decided not to send observers to the Nicaraguan elections. This is what you asked us to do. But if I might suggest it, a somewhat more positive response to the Contadora Group's peace plan would go down well here."

"What peace plan? We want the Contras to fight. We've got to stop those Commies before they spread subversion everywhere down there. Ever heard of the Monroe Doctrine?"

"Yes, I have. Perhaps we can talk more about it at our next meeting in Ottawa."

"Where?"

Talking Free Trade (June 4, 1985)

Since the Shamrock Summit, there has been a marked surge of intellectual momentum for free trade with the United States, but no one yet knows whether the Mulroney government is impressed.

The government, having focused its attention on the budget, has kept trade relations with the United States in the shadows since Quebec City.

Not only did the Americans inconveniently change trade negotiators just when things were getting interesting, but the Mulroney government needed more time to feel its way. Since Quebec, International Trade Minister James Kelleher has been moving quietly across the country and around the Cabinet, testing the waters.

Probably nothing will happen until the Macdonald Royal Commission brings down its report. Donald Macdonald, the chairman of the Commission into Everything, has already suggested that Canada should take the "leap of faith" into the free-trade embrace. (Critics of free trade might recall that Tirpitz used the same phrase in urging unrestricted submarine warfare by Germany in the First World War.)

Presumably, therefore, this bipartisan commission will soon add its loud and costly voice to the many now urging the Mulroney government to seize the moment. If the Mulroney government does intend to head for free trade, it makes sense to wait for Macdonald and Company's prior endorsement.

In recent days, one of Canada's most eminent economists put his shoulder to the free-trade wheel. Richard Lipsey, whose economics textbook taught some of us everything we have since forgotten, argued in a compelling C.D. Howe Institute monograph that Canada's continued economic well-being lies in free trade.

Free trade and political/cultural sovereignty are not irreconcilable, Mr. Lipsey argues. On the contrary, a declining standard of living might weaken the national will to resist the pull of continental political integration.

The key to prosperity, argued Mr. Lipsey, lies in improving productivity through greater economies of scale and more value-added production. Free trade would bring/force both. Humane adjustment policies and a phasing in of free trade could ease the pains.

Please note that we are talking here of free trade. As George Bain wrote yesterday, there is an abundance of what we might call terminological inexactitude floating around on this issue. So we are talking about free trade. Not freer trade. Not trade enhancement. Not an umbrella agreement. But free trade. No tariffs. No restrictions on trade or services except for those negotiated and placed in a mutually acceptable treaty.

Last month, the premiers of the four Western provinces favoured free trade, although Manitoba's NDP Premier Howard Pawley muted his enthusiasm. Alberta Premier Peter Lougheed promises a Canada-wide speaking tour to promote the idea. At the Regina First Ministers' conference, the Atlantic premiers seemed committed to free trade.

The Business Council on National Issues, the big-business bullhorn, is ready to consider free trade. So, surprisingly, is the Canadian Manufacturers' Association, some of whose members might presumably feel the pinch of lower tariffs.

Still, opposition resides in the provincial governments of Ontario and Quebec, in the trade unions, in university sociology departments and among the entrepreneurs of ideas (such as editorial boards of Toronto newspapers).

A discernible shift, however, has been toward the proponents of free trade, whose preference creates the fewest problems in Washington and in international trading circles. Free trade does not create the fewest political problems for the government in Ottawa. Hence the hesitation.

Into the Trade Talks *(September 19, 1985)*

There will be no snow in Saskatoon this winter and the tides will cease in the Bay of Fundy if Prime Minister Brian Mulroney does not soon announce the opening of trade talks with the United States.

Whatever he chooses to call the goal of the talks—trade enhancement, trade liberalization, freer trade, secure access, reciprocal trading advantages—we will be into negotiations with the United States this winter.

The glacial movement toward these negotiations began long before Mr. Mulroney became Prime Minister. Previous Liberal governments tried trade diversification—the so-called Third Option—then sectoral free trade with the United States. These initiatives failed, leaving Canada without improved access to the markets of either Western Europe or the United States.

As protectionism grew in Western Europe and protectionist sentiments mounted in the U.S., Canada's trading options were narrowed to the one Mr. Mulroney will announce this week. But so uncertain are the psychological reactions of Canadians to this new policy that the Mulroney government has been moving with great caution.

Now all the preparatory work has been done. The refusal to participate in Star Wars and the strong statement on Arctic sovereignty allow the Tories to fend off attacks that Canada's margin for manoeuvre in foreign policy will be curtailed by trade integration. Very soon, Communications Minister Marcel Masse will issue a major statement on cultural sovereignty to reassure those who think trade integration means a loss of national identity.

The search is on for a negotiator to lead the team. A private-sector committee, led by Walter Light, formerly of Northern Telecom, is in place to advise the government negotiators. And a fall meeting has been set with the provincial premiers to get their input before the talks formally begin.

Once the negotiations begin, the government risks being placed on the public-relations defensive. All those groups favouring the talks, including the Macdonald Royal Commission, have already had their say. The opening of negotiations will be the starting gun for all those opposed to closer trade links to mobilize their forces.

In Parliament, the Liberals and NDP will pound the government with questions about the nature and objectives of the talks. Their goal will be to raise all sorts of hypothetical and scary scenarios, forcing the government to commit itself in advance.

Until the talks end in success or failure some time in 1986 or 1987, the battle will be largely a phony war, with the opposition and government both debating speculative outcomes.

Thus far, the government has sold its case for trade talks without adequately preparing Canadians for what we might be asked to give up. This is especially so for provincial premiers who clamour for free trade without ever admitting that their non-tariff barriers are among those the Americans find the most unacceptable. Since it is axiomatic that the less we are willing to yield, the less we will get in return, the talks may eventually be narrowed to something far more restrictive than the Macdonald Inquiry's call for a free-trade agreement monitored by a bilateral commission.

The wider the scope of any trade package, the better the chance of acceptance by the U.S. Congress. A narrow package could be picked apart by lobbyists without the Administration being able to use "reasons of state" arguments. Either way—wide or narrow—the package will make its way with difficulty through the Congress, especially in the eighteen months preceding the next presidential election.

A Song at Twilight *(January 24, 1987)*

"Hello, George. How are you?"

"Fine, Mr. President. Just back from Ottawa, where I got an earful from Brian."

"Brian who?"

"Brian Mulroney. The Prime Minister."

"Oh yes. He's the fellow who sings so well."

"Well, Mr. President, they're not happy with our action on acid rain."

"Acid what?"

"They say we're not living up to the Quebec Declaration."

"The Quebec what?"

"The document you and the Prime Minister signed to use your best efforts to stop protectionism."

"Oh yes. I think I remember that. Was that before or after the singing?"

"Before, I think. But anyway, they say we're harassing their exports. They specifically mentioned shakes and shingles."

"Shakes and Shingles? Do they sing? Is that a rock group? Any musicians are free to play in the United States. What are they talking about?"

"They don't think we're doing enough to push along the free-trade initiative. They're really annoyed at Peter Murphy's statements."

"Peter who?"

"Our free-trade negotiator. They think he should shut up about the Auto Pact."

"The autowhat?"

"The treaty that allowed duty-free passage of cars made in Canada and the United States. Murphy hinted that maybe we should re-examine the safeguards."

"Whose safeguards? I've never been in favour of the pill, and anybody in my administration who promotes promiscuity is going to get the chop. I campaigned on the right to life. Tell Murphy to shut up or he'll be fired."

"Speaking of firing, Mr. President, I should tell you that the Prime Minister is in hotter soup than we are. Just before I arrived he had fired a Cabinet minister for some fishy land deal."

"Gave him the old Poindexter treatment, did he?"

"Yes, and called in the Mounties."

"Must be serious. Every movie I ever saw had the Mounties getting their men."

"Mr. President, the Prime Minister's in trouble partly because he's seen as a little too close to you."

"What's the matter? Didn't he like my singing? I thought I did pretty well, considering he all but dragged Nancy and me on stage. He didn't give me any time to rehearse."

"That's true, Mr. President. And you did swell. But he's made a big deal about being friendly with you, and now he feels you're not delivering."

"We delivered those gosh-darned arms, got the hostages out, and now we're being criticized. I call that ingratitude."

"Well, maybe. But he thinks we've got to give them something he can sell back home."

"Look, I know the arms weren't all that modern, but given what I hear about the state of their armed forces, he should be bloody well grateful."

"He'd especially like us to recognize their sovereignty in the Arctic. There's a body of water somewhere up there called the Northwest Passage. We apparently sent a ship through there, and they didn't like it."

"I didn't hear anything about this. Maybe Ollie North authorized the mission. He's a great patriot, you know."

"I got the clear impression the Prime Minister will be looking for quite a performance from us during your Ottawa visit in April."

"Well, I'm happy to co-operate, but only on one condition."

"What's that, Mr. President?"

"He's got to give me more time to rehearse."

Invisible, Inc. *(April 2, 1987)*

WASHINGTON—"It's like chicken soup. Of course they're in favour of it."

That's the graphic way Robert Strauss, one of the wise old birds in the Democratic Party, described American legislators' reaction to the prospect of a trade deal with Canada.

"People aren't negative about it," he said. "They simply haven't given it a thought." Mr. Strauss should know. He's a former U.S. trade negotiator, a prosperous Washington lawyer and a wheelhorse in the Democratic Party.

Indeed, as you move through Congress and the lobby organizations in Washington, you find a small network of people interested in the negotiations and following them rather closely. But this network is alive in an overwhelming atmosphere of indifference.

After spending three days in the U.S. midwest last week—in Nebraska, Missouri and Minnesota—I can fairly observe that free trade with Canada stirs as much interest in the American heartland as the trade-weighted value of the Spanish peseta.

Mind you, there's absolutely no reason why Americans should be informed, or any way that they could be. The negotiations are still continuing, so there's little concrete to debate. Their media are almost wholly indifferent to the issue, and U.S. politicians aren't talking about it.

Trade in general, on the other hand, stirs politicians in both parties. In the early stages of the presidential race, the buzz within the Democratic Party is all about improving American productivity, getting tough with Japan and other "unfair" traders, protecting American jobs and revamping American education.

That's the climate awaiting the Canadian trade initiative. Broadly speaking, there are two ways that climate could influence U.S. attitudes toward a Canadian deal.

If protectionist sentiment just keeps growing, if Americans feel they cannot afford any more liberalized trade for a while, the Canadian deal will obviously get a rough reception. There will be no exceptions for "our good neighbours to the north."

If, however, the deal incarnates certain principles and specifics that Americans can use for their broader trading purposes, the deal may get a surprisingly warm reception. And, although it sounds corny to report, there is a broad feeling of goodwill toward Canada throughout the United States.

The United States is understandably preoccupied with its $170-billion trade deficit. With overall world trade stagnant, there is simply no way the country can boost its exports enough or reduce its imports sufficiently to eliminate the deficit in the next few years.

What the United States needs is expanded world trade on terms more favourable to itself. That means more liberalized treatment of services (which Americans define to include what Canadians call cultural industries), intellectual property, agriculture and investment opportunities for multinational companies which direct trade and dividends back home. (The United States is also running a $60-billion trade deficit in automobiles, $6-billion of which comes from trade with Canada. That explains why Americans simply cannot ignore the Auto Pact and such decisions as the Canadian subsidy to keep General Motors' plant afloat in Ste-Thérèse, Que.)

A U.S.–Canada trade deal, which in Canada will be judged largely on its intrinsic merits, will be judged by Americans partly or mainly in the much wider framework of their international trading dilemmas.

For now, Americans are focusing on trade, but not on the trade deal with Canada. This fall, the two issues will dovetail, and Canada's interests, as is so often the case, will be considered as only one small part of a superpower's broader strategic needs.

Choosing the Lesser of Two Evils: Free Trade Isn't Risk-Free But Neither Is Battling U.S. Protectionism (October 9, 1987)

Jeffrey Simpson was the Skelton-Clark Fellow at Queen's University at the time of writing this piece.

KINGSTON—The U.S. Constitution speaks of "life, liberty and the pursuit of happiness"; the Canadian of "peace, order and good government." Those two phrases, contained in the basic laws of profoundly democratic societies, illustrate different assumptions about how best to achieve the same objective—the maximization of human liberty.

Those different assumptions, which have so coloured the entire histories of the United States and Canada, lie at the heart of the free-trade debate. But because the economic arguments for free trade grate more against the Canadian assumptions than the American, the free-trade debate in Canada will likely be as searing as any since those at the creation of Confederation itself.

When you strip away the details, the debate is really about the operation of the free market and the appropriate role for government. And here is where the different assumptions of Canadians and Americans collide.

In the United States, the free market is surrounded by liturgy. And why not? The free market has been the driving force behind making the United

States an enormously wealthy country, a military superpower, a magnet for tens of millions of immigrants who sought to share in its bounty.

The great protest movements of U.S. history have usually been populist; that is, disaffected groups trying, not to fetter the market, but to make it more receptive to their interests. Many of the wonderful U.S. social critics—Upton Sinclair, Sinclair Lewis (of Babbitt fame), Thorstein Veblen—pilloried or parodied the excesses of the free market, not the market mechanism itself.

Henry David Thoreau perhaps best typified the ultimate U.S. reaction against the consequences of the market—commercialization, urbanization, impersonalization. He retreated, to Walden Pond, just as the protesters of the 1960s turned, not to fundamental economic reform, but to their own Walden Ponds of hippyism, drugs, dropping-out, back-to-the-land.

And even today, what we would call the members of the opposition party, the Democrats, are alive with ideas, not of blunting the free market, but of trying to make it work better—everything from education vouchers expanding freedom of choice to work incentives for those on welfare.

The United States has had its presidents ready to interfere robustly with the free market: Andrew Jackson, in his way; Teddy Roosevelt; Franklin Roosevelt, after much hesitation; and Lyndon Johnson. But it has had more leaders, such as James Polk, Grover Cleveland, Warren Harding, Calvin Coolidge, Dwight Eisenhower and Ronald Reagan, who remained decidedly skeptical, or downright hostile, to the expansion of government in areas properly left to free-market forces.

Of course, you can draw this picture far too sharply. The tensions between the Jeffersonians and Hamiltonians have run through U.S. history, and they remain evident today. Ask the horde of lobbyists who swirl around Washington what they are doing. The truthful answer would be that they are trying, in many cases, to blunt the operation of the free market, to protect their interests from competition, or to turn the market to their advantage through government decisions. And there has always been an enormous gap between the liturgy surrounding the free market in the United States and its practice.

But the assertion remains valid: that in no other country in the Western world, including Canada, is the free market so revered, so trusted, so credited with having delivered so much as in the United States. The whole notion of "life, liberty and the pursuit of happiness" requires only a minimum of government, notably the protection of personal safety and property. "Peace, order and good government," by definition, requires something more from government. It presumes, as the U.S. Constitution does not, that the maximization of human liberties depends, at least in part, on the exercise of government power.

Government in Canada is not the foe of liberty, as many Americans believe government to be, but its friend, or at least its protector. From the beginning of Canada, for reasons of a forbidding geography and scattered population, the Canadian state (and the provincial governments) has been asked to do things that in the United States were left to the free market.

In addition, those who fought the American Revolution and built the U.S. government worried profoundly about concentrations of political power, and so scattered authority through three branches of government, whereas Canadians fighting for responsible government never dreamed of breaking up executive and legislative authority. What they wanted—and got—was the takeover of that government, with all its powers intact, by politicians who could use it for their own ends and those of the people.

So the temptation to use government has always been prevalent in Canada, whichever political party ruled. The business community historically favoured government intervention for its ends; social reformers wanted it for their own purposes; regions wanted it to assist their economic development; and, not to put too fine a point on things, the Canadian people wanted it to achieve national objectives that would otherwise not have been accomplished, or would have been done by the British or Americans.

This has meant a substantially greater direct involvement in the operations of the free market in Canada than in the United States. And what free trade essentially asks is that Canadians turn over to the free market more of the decisions about allocating resources, distributing benefits and meting out punishments. Why? Because in a number of areas, the proposed agreement—and the subsidy code that is supposed to be ready in five or seven years—will constrain Canadian governments from doing some of what they have traditionally or occasionally done.

The list of these constraints is impressive. We will no longer be able to screen most investment, adjust energy prices to protect domestic consumers, direct government purchases to Canadian suppliers, use tariffs to protect domestic producers (tariffs being an implicit subsidy), shield some agricultural producers through low import quotas, assist cultural industries if such assistance runs afoul of U.S. notions of intellectual property, provide comfortable rules for banks and financial institutions, and, in all probability, continue to offer a full panoply of assistance programs to depressed industries and economically disadvantaged regions.

In addition, Canada is forgoing existing protection for generic-drug manufacturers and, if the well-founded rumours are correct, will stop substituting Canadian commercials for those broadcast by U.S. TV stations near the border. Canada should give up some of these practices, because they are either flagrantly discriminatory or economically counter-productive. But

they do illustrate the kind of measures Canadian governments have historically taken. And, if the two sides agree on a subsidy code, the government's
capacity to distort the market will be further fettered. This fettering may
lead, as many studies maintain, to enhanced economic growth through a
more competitive economy, but it grinds against what has been a large part
of the Canadian political culture.

Talking about turning over more decisions to the blind hand of the free
market is deceptive, because in the North American context, free-market
forces will inevitably be U.S.-driven. It cannot be any other way, given the
sizes of the two countries. And this raises an absolutely critical question that
will pour fuel on the forthcoming debate: do further economic links lead
inexorably toward cultural, social and even political integration?

If the past thirty years or so count for anything, the answer is probably no.
The Canadian economy, by all sorts of measures (trade and investment
flows being two), has never been more tightly bound to the U.S. economy as
during this period. Yet, during that same period, Canada launched massive
social programs quite different from their U.S. counterparts—national pensions, publicly financed health care, substantially enriched unemployment-
insurance benefits and workers' compensation programs, job-creation
schemes (social-insurance programs in disguise) and perhaps quite soon a
form of publicly financed day care.

In addition, the outpouring of Canadian cultural products, low- and high-
brow, has never been so great, although not as great as perhaps a mature country should enjoy. And although some observers note the "Americanization" of
our political system, it remains in many essential ways distinct from the
American. But is the recent past a necessary guide to the future under a free-
trade agreement? If, in the restructuring of the Canadian economy, Canadian
firms find that they cannot compete with their U.S. counterparts, is it possible
they will demand reductions in their costs of production, some of which
would be contributions to government social programs or taxes used to pay
for these social and cultural programs?

They may be forced to consider this, because they will be impeded under
the free-trade agreement from running to government for bailouts, subsidies, quotas, tariff protection and every other kind of protectionist scheme.

By turning more over to the free market, Canadians will be de-politicizing
many economic decisions. Every subsidy decision, every government intervention, is basically a political act. That's why so many of them have been
of dubious economic validity. But the political forces behind propping up
the textile industry, clothing manufacturers, shoe producers, farmers of all
kinds, Sydney Steel, Sidbec, Domtar's plant at Windsor, Que., Cominco's
smelter at Trail, B.C., the Faro mine in the Yukon, General Motors' Ste.-

Thérèse, Que., plant, the wine industry of Ontario, British Columbia and Nova Scotia, pulp and paper plant modernizations, Maislin—the list runs on and on—have all impelled government to intervene.

Once again, de-politicizing decisions may be an economic blessing, but it does represent possibly the triumph and certainly the assertion of the U.S. assumption about the proper role for government over the previously held Canadian one.

The proposed agreement provides important specific benefits for Canada. The elimination of tariffs will mean lower prices and less inflation. Enhanced energy access means continued uranium exports (now under protectionist assault) and further sales of hydro-electricity from Quebec, Manitoba and perhaps other provinces. It could also mean a better market for Nova Scotia and Alberta natural gas. Canadian financial institutions will be exempted from the amendments to the Glass–Steagall Act.

Producers of meat, horticultural items and sugar will have better access. The harmonization of standards, easing of visa requirements, simplification of customs procedures are all laudable achievements. Canada also must be notified if new anti-dumping or countervailing duty laws are enacted, and if those laws apply to Canada such changes must be specifically written into the law.

The United States, on balance, gets more. In addition to preventing future Canadian governments from doing many things the United States finds disagreeable, Canada will end transportation subsidies for agricultural products shipped south of the border; increase global import quotas for poultry and eggs; drop protection against U.S. grain imports; eliminate mark-ups against U.S. wine; open up the energy field, with some restrictions on ownership; end the duty-remission scheme for third-party automotive parts; phase out tariffs in the auto sector; liberalize access for U.S. banks; weaken substantially review powers over investment; and end preferential postal rates for Canadian magazines.

Tariff reductions, which should help both countries, disproportionately benefit the United States because average Canadian tariffs are higher. Similarly, opening up government purchasing will assist both countries, but unless the Canadians can crack open more defence contracts, the balance of advantage goes to the United States. Its market is roughly ten times larger, but the amount of government purchasing made available under the proposed agreement is only six times greater.

All of which leads to the now-famous bilateral dispute-resolving mechanism. This is the device upon which the Canadian government hung so much of its case. It's the principal tool the government believes will "secure market access." Will it?

The mechanism won't achieve what had been the overriding, albeit naive, Canadian demand: special exemption from U.S. trade-remedy laws and an end to harassment of Canadian exports. Both sides keep their own existing laws and agencies for interpreting those laws.

What the binational tribunal will do is replace court review. And that means ensuring that due process has been followed by each side in applying its laws.

The grounds for an appeal on procedural or legal points is therefore wide, but on substantive questions probably limited. The problem for Canada is that many rulings go against exporters not on procedural or legal grounds, but on substantive, even political, ones. The tribunal also would play a role in disputes under new trade regulations either side has found discriminatory. In such cases, an appeal to the tribunal would require compulsory consultation. If that failed, the aggrieved party could (1) terminate the whole free-trade agreement, or (2) retaliate. Termination is probably a hollow threat, especially for the smaller partner, since so many interests will have become dependent on the new trading arrangement.

It's hard to imagine Canada throwing over the whole arrangement because it's sore about U.S. treatment of, say, blueberries, or even steel. Retaliation makes no sense in the product categories under dispute, since chances are, the other country's producers are sufficiently hard-pressed that they aren't exporting. Retaliation in other areas is like buckshot: it can hurt a lot of innocent people. What the bilateral mechanism will do is give Canada additional moral leverage, a few avenues of procedural appeal, the chance to avoid being sideswiped by U.S. protectionism directed against others that might hit us, and a few not terribly impressive weapons. It will not give us "secure market access." Perhaps, under the prevailing political circumstances in the United States, this is all Canada could reasonably have achieved. Perhaps with a new bilateral subsidy code in a few years, each side will lay aside for the other its own trade-remedy laws.

But these are what we might call "leaps of faith." If, over time, this mechanism grows teeth, then a free-trade agreement that, on balance, seems to provide benefits to both, but more to the United States than Canada, will resemble a fairly balanced deal.

And nobody should forget—although many politicians already have—that having no trade deal may be much worse than having this one, because protectionism in the United States is not a transitory phenomenon. Its root causes run deep into the accumulated trade deficits, monstrous budgetary deficits, and a challenge to U.S. superiority on all fronts.

We can try to "fight 'em in the trenches," as some bombastic politicians will suggest, without the slightest guarantee that we will not be hammered. Or we can try this agreement, with all the risks it poses, with all the interests it will gore, with all the challenges to the Canadian political culture, with all the profound questions it raises about what we think of the free market, of the government's role in society and of what we shall become as a nation.

The Soul in the Suds *(October 24, 1987)*

Prime Minister Brian Mulroney delivered on his promise to protect Canada's cultural sovereignty in the free-trade negotiations. He protected Canadian beer.

How the Canadian brewers succeeded in exempting themselves from free trade must remain a mystery, until we remember their indispensable role in defining Canadian culture.

I mean, could we really consider ourselves a country if the Montreal Canadiens were owned by Miller? Or the Quebec Nordiques by Coors? Mind you, the Toronto Maple Leafs would be better off being owned by either company than by Harold Ballard, the George Steinbrenner of Canadian sports.

Even in baseball, Canadian beer represents the thin red line of national self-respect. We've taken to their game like red-blooded Americans, rooting for American players who are directed by American managers and traded by American front-office personnel, but watched by fans drinking Canadian beer. Their beer is so much weaker than ours that it would have taken months rather than weeks of solid drinking to ease the pain of the Blue Jays' monumental collapse.

Speaking of the Blue Jays, one of their owners, Labatts, used to pretty much run the Ontario Conservative Party, or perhaps it was the other way around. In any event, Ontario just wouldn't have been the same if Auggie Busch had had the direct line to the premier's office.

American brewers would never stand for selling their products in government-run stores. What more defines the average Canadian's weekend than running the empties back to some dismal place in a suburban shopping centre? The tolerance which defines the Canadian culture has far less to do with the weather than with accepting the endless frustration of trying to find a government-run beer store open when you really need one.

That great Canadian nationalist, Premier David Peterson of Ontario, knew how important those stores were to the national psyche. He got elected by promising to abolish them, made a half-hearted attempt to allow sales by corner stores, then beat a retreat. Canada lives.

For generations, work in those stores represented one of any provincial government's little treasure troves of patronage. And what, pray tell, has ever been more unfailingly Canadian than political patronage? Scrap the way we market beer and you might just as well abolish the Canadian Senate.

What would a summer weekend on the dock in Haliburton, the Okanagan or the Townships be if we had to drink Pabst? It's one thing to drive American cars, watch American television programs, read American magazines, root for the Pittsburgh Steelers or Chicago Bears, but we'd have nothing left if they took away our Carlsberg or O'Keefe, which, come to think of it, are now owned by the Aussies. Oh well, at least the Aussies know how to brew beer that tastes like beer.

The structure of the brewing industry is so typically Canadian—too many plants with short lines of production—that changing the structure would deal a body blow to our political culture. The brewers represent the triumph of politics over economics, and what could be more Canadian than that?

They survived the threat of free trade by lobbying the provinces, which, in turn, put pressure on the federal government. That, too, is typically Canadian.

We may be selling our economy, even our souls, in this trade deal. But we are keeping our beer, and so our culture, just as the Prime Minister promised. Mel Hurtig can sleep easily tonight.

Is Culture Protected? *(January 12, 1988)*

Various artists and cultural administrators have insisted that the Canada–U.S. trade deal threatens Canadian culture.

A parade of eloquent ladies and gentlemen so argued before the Commons committee on the free-trade deal. Rather than focus on the details of the deal, the majority of objectors based their case on vigorous flag-waving, a flood-tide of rhetoric and broad assertions that they did not wish to become Americans.

They didn't make a terribly persuasive case, perhaps because they missed the point. The trade agreement, after all, states quite baldly: "Cultural industries are exempt from the provisions of this agreement. . . ." If words mean anything, Canada's existing gambit of so-called cultural policies should be safe.

But what of the future? Another clause, the kind that lawyers love, reads: ". . . a party may take measures of equivalent commercial effect in response to actions that would have been inconsistent with this agreement but for paragraph 1," the one about exempting cultural industries.

One interpretation of this clause, concurred in by an official of the Canadian negotiating team, is that the United States will have the right of compensation—"equivalent commercial effect"—for any future move the Canadian government makes in the cultural field which the Americans feel injures their economic interests. They can legally do that now under U.S. law, but the trade agreement may widen the ground for U.S. action.

Future policies to promote Canadian culture therefore could bring a price—one that any Canadian government would have to weigh in deciding whether to proceed. Of course, we pay a price now, a heavy price, to support Canadian cultural industries, but we pay that price to ourselves after debate in our own country, not to another country which disagrees with our policies.

The potential for misunderstandings is great, but not because of the trade deal. Many Americans simply don't understand Canadian cultural concerns, because south of the border culture is viewed as another service industry. That's the natural reaction of a cultural superpower whose products flood the world marketplace. After all, you can't blame somebody from Kansas City for not understanding what it's like to live in a Canadian city where most of the movies, books, television programs and magazines are foreign.

Under the trade deal, an American firm that feels aggrieved by a new Canadian cultural policy can ask its government to invoke the mandatory consultation and dispute-resolving provisions of the agreement. Indeed, it's a reasonable guess that over time Americans may make more use of these provisions than Canadians will.

That isn't the conventional wisdom about these provisions. So far, almost all Canadian public debate has focused on whether these provisions adequately protect Canadians from U.S. protectionism.

That's a perfectly valid concern, given the number of past or looming threats to Canadian exports in the United States. But Canadian governments have historically intervened more frequently in the marketplace than American governments, so it may be that U.S. interests will use these provisions frequently to object to this or that emerging Canadian policy. Certainly under the U.S. system, with all its pressure points, the chances that some group or other will object to Canadian policy are great.

Nobody can predict how the consultation and dispute-resolving provisions will work until they are tried, but it seems axiomatic that Americans may be tempted to use them. Future Canadian cultural policies—maybe the emerging film distribution policy?—may provide an instructive case in how the Americans can use the trade agreement.

Why Canada Must Be Involved in the U.S.–Mexico Free-Trade Deal *(September 6, 1990)*

With considerable political trepidation, the Mulroney government will shortly announce Canada's entry into another set of free-trade talks—this time with Mexico.

The government needs these talks like the proverbial hole in the head, but feels Canada has no choice. The Mexican and the American administrations have agreed in principle to negotiate a free-trade agreement between their two countries. That raises the prickly question of whether Canada can afford to remain aloof.

The government thinks that Canada's interests can be protected only by participating in the negotiations; in effect, turning them into trilateral talks aimed at a North American free-trade agreement. But the Cabinet remembers—who could forget?—the rancorous debate over Canada–U.S. free trade, and the prospect of re-visiting that debate through the back door of North American free-trade negotiations is one ministers would rather not have faced.

The world, unfortunately for them, waits for no one. The Mexicans, who have been liberalizing their economy at break-neck speed for five years, now see free trade with the United States as the logical and urgent next step. If, as expected, U.S. President George Bush asks for and receives congressional approval to launch these negotiations, they'll begin early in 1991.

Without the imminent prospect of Mexican–U.S. negotiations, the Cabinet would never dream of a bilateral trade deal with Mexico. Mexico ranks seventeenth among Canada's trading partners. Bilateral trade was only about $2.2-billion in 1988, with a $1-billion surplus in Mexico's favour. Mexican products represented only 1.3 per cent of total Canadian imports; Mexico took 0.5 per cent of Canada's exports. Canada's biggest bilateral worry with Mexico is the $5-billion Mexicans owe Canadian banks.

There are undoubtedly ways of intensifying economic relations—Spar Aerospace and Northern Telecom both won recent contracts in Mexico—but bilateral trade remains small beer, certainly not enough to justify a free-trade deal. After all, as Michael Hart wrote in a recent monograph for the Institute for Research on Public Policy, the bulk of Mexican exports to Canada face extremely low tariffs.

No, the case for Canada turning the bilateral negotiations into trilateral ones is to preserve the gains from the Canada–U.S. trade deal, which might become the model for a trilateral agreement. Both Mr. Hart and Professor Richard Lipsey, an ardent free-trader who wrote a recent monograph for the C.D. Howe Institute, warn that a successful U.S.–Mexican deal would leave the Americans with the best of both worlds.

The U.S., they argue, would then have negotiated two bilateral deals, whereas Canada and Mexico would have only one. This would give the United States a "hub-and-spoke" trade advantage, whereby any company wishing to service the entire North American market and benefit from free trade would be encouraged to do so from the United States.

They argue—this argument is a clincher for the government—that if the United States and Mexico are serious about a bilateral trade deal, Canada's interests are better protected at the negotiating table than looking in from the outside. Nor do they think low Mexican wages are a severe problem, since investment decisions and corporate success have more to do with factors other than low wages. Low tariffs don't keep Mexican products away now; eliminating such tariffs won't make much difference.

Naturally, some of those who opposed the Canada–U.S. free-trade deal will dislike the prospect of a North American free-trade area. The Pro Canada network has already sounded the alarm. The Canadian Labour Congress is dead set against free trade with a country where wages are low and working conditions often poor. Lloyd Axworthy, the Liberal MP from Winnipeg, gave an insight into his party's likely position when he attacked the trilateral prospect in a recent speech.

This fall, the Commons external affairs committee has scheduled hearings into trade negotiations with Mexico. By then, the Mulroney government should have signalled its intentions. And Canada will be asked to think again, if only indirectly, about free trade, an issue that divided the country so sharply—and still divides it.

PART 3 *Quebec*

The World Outside *(April 11, 1985)*

It remains an enduring irony of Canada that despite the legions of French Canadians in national and international affairs, the French-language press in Quebec remains at best marginally interested in, and at worst oblivious to, what is going on outside Quebec.

These words, with their implicit criticism, lay the writer open to attacks for harbouring hostile sentiments toward Quebec. To which one can only reply that many Quebec journalists quietly deplore and lament this incessant preoccupation with self. Indeed, Gilles Paquin, a fine journalist in *La Presse*'s Ottawa bureau, is moving on his own initiative to Costa Rica to send freelance articles back to his paper from Central America.

Naturally enough, the French-language media are preoccupied with Quebec. Their readers and advertisers are there, and Quebec is a distinct society. A publisher or editor would have to be a fool not to provide thorough coverage of the political, economic, cultural and sports life of Quebec.

But the depressing facts are these: there is not a single full-time French-language reporter writing from outside the province, except in Ottawa. No one in Toronto, Vancouver, Washington, Paris or anywhere else.

Indeed, the situation is worse than it was five years ago. *La Presse* has closed its bureaus in Toronto and Washington, the only ones it had outside Quebec and Ottawa. *Le Devoir* no longer carries regular reports from freelancers in Toronto and Vancouver. Neither *Le Journal de Montréal* nor *Le Soleil* ever systematically interested itself in the rest of Canada or the world.

The Quebec print media have closed in on Quebec in a fierce struggle for circulation and survival. *La Presse*, worried about competition from the tabloid *Journal de Montréal*, has expanded its sports coverage. International news, Monday to Saturday, has been cut back. And news from the rest of Canada remains as meagre as ever.

Occasionally, something will happen in the rest of Canada—a linguistic crisis, an Ontario election—to bestir editors to send their own people briefly outside Quebec. But most of the time Vancouver might just as well be Lima, and Nova Scotia a province of Nigeria.

La Presse and *Le Devoir* have beefed up their business sections. Yet neither has a correspondent in Toronto, which, one writes without arrogance or satisfaction, has become the business capital of the country.

This curious and depressing state of affairs cannot be explained by a lack of quality French-language journalists. They exist in abundance, and many of them share these concerns.

One searches for explanations to what one hears. Money is allocated by La Presse Canadienne (the French arm of Canadian Press) for a Paris bureau. The editors turn it down.

Vacancies are posted for Ottawa bureaus. Few, if any, journalists apply. Trips to other parts of Canada are proposed. They too are nixed—"The readers aren't interested."

How can this be, when surveys have shown Quebec readers want more world news? And why shouldn't they? Quebec's economy is tied to international and Canadian trends. Its political life, by the decision of Quebeckers themselves, remains wedded to Canada's. And French Canadians are littered throughout Canadian and international affairs.

Can language be the problem? If so, why have English-speaking papers had people lining up for posts in Quebec City, Tokyo, Beijing, Paris, Mexico City? Can money be the problem? Yes, for *Le Devoir*. No, for *Le Journal*. Or for *La Presse*, an arm of Power Corporation.

Quebeckers are among the most politically sophisticated Canadians. Their papers are letting them down.

The Myth-Mongers *(February 15, 1989)*

"The distinguishing part of a myth is that truth and error, fact and
fable, report and fantasy, are all on the same plane of credibility."
—U.S. journalist Walter Lippmann, *Public Opinion*, 1922.

Had Mr. Lippmann lived to see *Disparaître*, the pseudo-documentary aired Sunday night on Radio-Canada, he could have written an entire chapter on its contribution to the myth of French-speaking Quebec.

A myth, as he properly defined it in his classic study, is simply a set of assumptions that are widely accepted as correct. A myth is believed, and as such remains impervious to rational argument, because it draws on wellsprings of emotions, usually apprehension and fear.

Disparaître, by its very title and ominous story line, spoke directly to the French Canadians' collective insecurity about their position in North America. Not surprisingly, the film's thesis is now all the fashionable rage in French-speaking Quebec, provoking newspaper series, commentaries and other assorted public manifestations of disquiet.

That thesis, simply put, suggests that French-Canadian society is teetering on the edge of demographic collapse. Why? Because Quebec has one of the world's lowest birth rates, and because immigrants pose a grave and perhaps mortal threat to French-Canadian society. Multiculturalism, profoundly misunderstood by the film's producers, offers a poisoned chalice to French-speaking Quebec.

The film suggests, despite its own evidence to the contrary, that too many immigrants to Quebec orient themselves toward English. Their strange ways threaten French Quebec's cultural harmony and emotional security. Caught between the difficulties of assimilating immigrants into a French melting pot and French Canadians' declining birth rate, French Quebec faces a future of demographic decline leading to extinction. Hence, *disparaître*.

This crude and dangerous thesis, being swallowed whole by gullible sensationalists but being destroyed intellectually by such cool heads as Lysiane Gagnon in *La Presse*, is buttressed by references to Britain, France and West Germany. The film purports to demonstrate how, in those countries, racial tensions are eating away at the fabric of stable societies, undermining British, French and German culture.

Anyone who has lived or travelled extensively in those countries knows this to be a gross, even mendacious exaggeration. Immigration has certainly produced some social dislocation and, in France and West Germany, an extreme right-wing backlash in selected areas. But to suggest that immigration threatens these countries' essential character is nonsense.

The rational evidence that contradicts *Disparaître*'s main thesis is probably helpless against the grip of myth. Still, it is worth remembering that the French-speaking component of Quebec society is higher than it was ten years ago; that the younger the children in school, the higher the percentage of French-speakers; that a majority of immigrants who remain in Quebec do learn French.

Certainly the birth rate of French-speakers in Quebec has fallen dramatically since the days of the "revenge of the cradle." The government can try to increase that birth rate, but family structure, income imperatives and social mores make the return of large families improbable.

To jump from this demographic fact to a conclusion that suggests that French-Canadian society faces extinction is preposterous. It is the stuff of myth-makers and of singers who should stick to songs.

But there was Gilles Vigneault, the celebrated bard of Quebec, rattling on in mid-film about a doomsday scenario for his people. As he spoke, Mr. Lippmann's words rolled around the mind: "What a myth never contains is the critical power to separate its truth from its errors."

The Crusade of Mr. Parizeau (*September 30, 1989*)

GATINEAU—Jacques Parizeau, forty minutes into his speech, produces another rhetorical thunderclap.

"For us, Quebec is *notre patrie, notre pays,* for which we alone are responsible. Sovereignty is first and above all else to be responsible for ourselves."

The Parti Québécois, its leader growls, makes choices, unlike the dithering, equivocal Liberals. "We make choices because we have a country to build. We want a Quebec that is solid, advancing, doing things, offering equality of opportunity. We have a vision for Quebec." That vision, friends, is independence: pure, simple and undiluted.

How will we get to the Promised Land? Mr. Parizeau asks. He smiles, as if letting his audience in on a dirty secret. First, we will demand complete control over four essential powers now shared with Ottawa: family policy, language and culture, social policy and regional development. In each case, we will hold a referendum demanding that Ottawa fork over control and money.

Then we'll set about drafting a constitution for a new Quebec. When that's completed, we'll hold a referendum on the constitution. "Not a referendum for hope or for contemplating from afar, but a referendum to make sovereignty for Quebec." And when will that climax come? "We're going to hold it when we think we have the best chance of winning."

A few more puffs of rhetoric and Mr. Parizeau vanishes for the drive back to Montreal. He persuaded no one in the hall, because they had all been persuaded before. These were the true believers, living in the shadow of Ottawa, remembering the PQ's salad days, feasting on their own identity as French-speaking Québécois.

They had waited patiently for Mr. Parizeau, who arrived half an hour late in the best PQ tradition. He did not disappoint them. Other leaders now understand that television needs only a few sound bites, and that anything more is wasted effort. But Mr. Parizeau rumbled on for fifty minutes in that growl of his, sweating through his shirt, making fun of the Liberals, skating artfully around Quebec's labour turmoil (blame the Liberals without condoning illegal strikes) and holding aloft that vision of an independent Quebec for which he returned to politics to remake the Parti Québécois in his own image.

For indeed, this is very much Mr. Parizeau's party. Brag as he might about the high quality of PQ candidates, the PQ team is a pale reflection of the *équipe de tonnerre* that swept into office on Nov. 15, 1976. The PQ of 1989 is Mr. Parizeau, the former finance minister, and a collection of recycled MLAs and not terribly inspiring newcomers. If the PQ wins next Monday's election, Quebec will have the nearest thing imaginable to a one-man government.

Whatever Quebeckers might think of that prospect, it would hardly shake Mr. Parizeau. Self-confidence oozes from every pore. When he acknowledges the crowd's applause, he raises both hands aloft, a bit the way de Gaulle communicated with his followers and the deities inspiring him. When Mr. Parizeau plays with statistics, he lets everyone know that the master is keeping things real simple for the common folk but that he'd be right at home with bankers and financial gnomes.

Mr. Parizeau is an easy man to respect but a hard one to love, perhaps because he loves himself so much. He has a roguish charm, all right, but nothing of the common touch. He could have made a fortune in business or been finance minister in a federal government. He might even have been Prime Minister of Canada with his intelligence and impeccable English.

But he chose Quebec independence, and now he pursues that goal his way.

French Canada's Blank Pages *(November 8, 1989)*

By happy coincidence for him, Quebec journalist Michel Vastel's book on Pierre Trudeau is being officially launched today just after the former prime minister returned to the news by slamming the Meech Lake constitutional accord.

Mr. Vastel's book, which I have not yet read, is a curiosity by virtue of having been written in French by a French-Canadian journalist about a major French-Canadian political figure.

The motto on Quebeckers' licence plates reads *Je me souviens*—I remember. And yet, if French Canadians had to depend on their own literary efforts to recapture their political past, they would have blank minds and stone hearts.

The curious fact of Quebec writing remains that almost all the major books about important Quebec political figures, both federal and provincial, have been produced by English-language writers.

Peter Desbarats wrote the early biography of René Lévesque. Graham Fraser bettered Mr. Desbarats' effort with the definitive account of the Parti Québécois and Mr. Lévesque's years in office. L. Ian MacDonald penned biographies of Claude Ryan and Robert Bourassa. Conrad Black's immense, sympathetic tome on Premier Maurice Duplessis, written in Mr. Black's customary rococo style, is the longest treatment of that important Quebec political figure.

Joseph Schull's biography of Sir Wilfrid Laurier far eclipses the one available in French. Alastair Sweeney's biography of George-Étienne Cartier is without equal in French. Professor Dale Thomson has written the best biographies of Prime Minister Louis St. Laurent and Premier Jean Lesage. George

Radwanski wrote Pierre Trudeau's biography, and Richard Gwyn's *Northern Magus* offered the best portrait of Mr. Trudeau's years in office. All the books thus far written about Prime Minister Brian Mulroney have been written by anglophones or, in the case of Michel Gratton, by a francophone in English.

This phenomenon is the more surprising because of the relentless preoccupation with Quebec—one might uncharitably say navel-gazing—by so many of the province's academics and journalists. Quebec in all its dimensions fascinates them, as any glance at provincial academic journals or newspapers documents. Yet they have left it to the anglophones to write the definitive biographies and major historical studies of the most important French-speaking political figures. (Historian Robert Rumilly is a notable exception, but his multi-volume history is heavily shaded by his Union Nationale sympathies.)

The rest of Canada remains a huge expanse of nothingness in the Quebec media and among the vast majority of Quebec academics. When Lysiane Gagnon, *La Presse*'s extraordinarily good columnist, recently wrote a typically perceptive and fair series on Manitoba, it was an exception that proved the rule.

The English-language media have their share of sins to account for, but failure to cover Quebec is not one of them. Whether readers choose to digest what they are offered is another matter, but they can hardly complain that over the years the major English-language media of Canada have ignored Quebec.

It remains an indefensible fact, lamented privately by many French-speaking journalists, that no French-language media operation (save Radio-Canada) has even one correspondent based anywhere in Canada outside Quebec and Ottawa.

All manner of ingenious excuses have been offered in Quebec for this state of affairs. Choosing where to deploy money and personnel is a matter of priorities. The inescapable conclusion to be drawn from the Quebec media's singular and abiding lack of interest in the rest of the country is that Canada figures extremely low in editorial priorities.

The Strong Tugs of Nationalism and Liberalism in Quebec   *(September 9, 1994)*

MONTREAL—The central paradox of contemporary Quebec is that the province has never been more similar to the rest of North America, yet it may soon consider once again the prospect of asserting politically its differences by seceding from Canada.

Perhaps the paradox is explained, as some have suggested, by Sigmund Freud's famous "narcissism of small differences," or at least a narcissism of diminishing differences.

This kind of analysis, however, is not fruitful because it can lead to the kind of creepy conclusions of Camille Laurin, a former Parti Québécois Cabinet minister and candidate in Monday's election. He viewed societies as patients on a couch requiring collective psychological treatment administered by an all-wise state run by people such as himself, of course.

So perhaps the paradox is better explored by following historian Benedict Anderson's provocative analysis of nationalism as a matter of an "imagined political community."

Even in a society such as Quebec's, people know only a tiny fraction of their fellow citizens. They do, however, develop what Mr. Anderson calls a "deep horizontal comradeship," largely through a shared language that enables them to imagine what they partake with others.

French is, of course, the language in Quebec that creates this "imagined community" for the 83 per cent of the population who speak it. And when French is threatened, in fact or perception, the "imagined community" considers it an assault upon itself. And an assault, real or imagined, provokes a response.

The many associations people experience in their lives—membership in civic institutions or international ones, work-related contacts, etc.—are seldom as viscerally felt as those of national membership. Even Marxism in Russia, China and Vietnam failed to rally people without an appeal to nationalism. Liberalism faces the same challenge.

There are richer philosophical frameworks for exploring the human condition than nationalism, but they seldom pack the same emotional wallop. Jefferson, Madison and the other great thinkers of the American Revolution, for example, are venerated in their country as patriots, to be sure, but their enduring contribution came as explorers of liberal philosophy.

This dichotomy between the tugs of nationalism and of liberalism is why the debate in Quebec so often features emotion on the nationalist side, but reason or at least pragmatism on the federalist one. It explains why most of the songs and symbols of Quebec are nationalist, and why so many of those who work with the French language—historians, writers, journalists—are drawn to nationalism.

The media, following Mr. Anderson, are critical vehicles for the creation of an "imagined community." People who read the same newspapers or watch the same television programs feel that thousands, or even millions, of fellow citizens are absorbing the same information simultaneously, information conveyed differently or not at all by media in some other place.

In an age of global economics and shared political sovereignty among states, it may seem bizarre that the "imagined community" of nationalism in Quebec and elsewhere should remain so strong.

But one set of factors may feed into the other. The very impersonal forces of global economics and shared sovereignty leave people feeling vulnerable. They cling with greater fervour to that which they find familiar and comfortable. In Quebec this is the language of the majority, the memories it conveys, the sense of shared travails and joys it offers, the "imagined community" of interests it defines.

There is something too about an "imagined community" as transmitted by language that defines and constricts membership, which is why the curious expression persists of *pure laine*, meaning all-wool but figuratively denoting French-speaking citizens of Quebec who can trace their ancestors back many generations.

In a more polyglot place such as English-speaking Canada or the United States, such a notion would seem archaic, if not offensive. Its currency in Quebec discourse, although increasingly unacceptable in intellectual circles, illustrates the sense of definition of membership that accompanies an "imagined community."

In a federal country with shared sovereignty and in an increasingly interdependent world, it is the central paradox of our time, in Canada and elsewhere, that the tenacity of the "imagined community" shows few signs of weakening.

Just What Does Quebec Mean When It Says It Wants to Be "Normal"? *(September 14, 1994)*

MONTREAL—"Normal" was former Péquiste premier René Lévesque's favourite political word. Only by becoming an independent country, Mr. Lévesque argued incessantly, could Quebeckers form "un pays normal."

Monday night, in the first flush of victory, Péquiste Premier-elect Jacques Parizeau and Bloc Québécois Leader Lucien Bouchard picked up the Lévesque refrain.

Mr. Bouchard proclaimed that the referendum would allow Quebec to become "un pays normal." Mr. Parizeau chose a slightly different phrase— "un peuple normal." It has been an article of faith for a generation of secessionists that only independence would make Quebeckers "normal." Federalism, by their definition and political logic, was abnormal and therefore contributed to whatever ailed Quebec.

Just who "le peuple Québécois" comprises is, of course, something seces-sionists resist defining, except in territorial terms. The "people" are presumed to include all those who inhabit the existing territory of Quebec. But of course nations, or "peoples," are not always defined by territory. All around the world, "peoples," defined for example by a shared language or religion or ethnicity, do not find themselves grouped within political territories.

Indeed, within Quebec there are various "peoples," according to the defin-ing characteristics used by the secessionists. These include the English-speaking community, the so-called allophones whose mother tongue is neither English nor French, and the aboriginal "peoples" whose histories run back beyond the arrival of Europeans.

Secessionists are really talking, despite occasional embarrassments on the subject, about French-speaking Quebeckers, who, they argue, can never be "normal" without independence. The other "peoples" in Quebec know the game, since they overwhelmingly oppose the Parti Québécois's seces-sionist plans.

There are many countries that fit the PQ's description of what it takes for people to be normal. The Japanese are largely a homogeneous people on their islands, save for a small Korean minority. The Danes, Swedes, Greeks, Dutch and French are the sort of peoples who share a language and a long history within a territory.

But look elsewhere around the world. The Swiss have a federation and by any standard Switzerland is a "normal country." The Germans were unified in the nineteenth century, but only became a "normal" country by being turned into a federation after making war on the European continent three times in seventy years. India is a federation and a "normal" country. The United States, with its racial mix, is a federation and a "normal" country. Australia, which faced a secessionist movement from Western Australia early in this century, is a federation and a "normal" country. Spain, with its Basques and Catalans, is a "normal" country and a federation. South Africa, for long an international outlaw because of apartheid, is now a "normal" country and recently gave itself a federal constitution. Mexico is a "normal" country and a federation, albeit one with weak states.

Conversely, Yugoslavia was an "abnormal" country created after the First World War and riven thereafter with internal divisions. Its former con-stituent parts opted for becoming "normal" with decidedly messy results. The Slovaks decided to become "normal" by seceding from the Czechoslovak federation, and now have a large, restless Hungarian-speaking minority within Slovakia. The former "republics" of the Soviet Union opted for a "normal" life as peoples and now find themselves beset on all sides by internal ethnic rivalries.

Quebec secessionists have dominated the debate over what constitutes a "normal" country for a people sharing a language and a history. It will be among their strongest arguments in the forthcoming debate.

Unless and until federalists explain that the world has at least as many, if not more, examples of "peoples" living in federations of varying kinds, they will have ceded the high ground of debate to the secessionists.

A "normal" state of affairs for a people is not necessarily what the secessionists claim. Unless federalists explain that Canada is really part of a wider, larger community of federations, and that this membership represents not just the wave of the future but a proven track record from the past, then the defence of federalism becomes utilitarian, pragmatic and ultimately weak.

Conflicting Visions Within Quebec's Secessionist Movement *(May 4, 1995)*

MONTREAL—The divisions that recently surfaced publicly among Quebec secessionists have existed in one form or another since the movement's early stirrings.

To explain them as a conflict between "hard-line" and "soft-line" secessionists is correct, but only to a certain point. Both camps seek an independent Quebec. They have differed, and still do, about the desirability and necessity of links with the rest of Canada.

Jacques Parizeau, for almost a quarter of a century, has favoured Quebec independence unconditionally. If, after independence, something can be negotiated with the rest of Canada, fine. But those links are not crucial and should not inhibit Quebec becoming independent.

What might be called the "associationists" included former premier René Lévesque, the political mentor and friend of Bloc Québécois Leader Lucien Bouchard. The associationists want Quebec independence all right, but its realization should in some way be tied to the likelihood or realization of formal, institutionalized links with the rest of Canada.

The two camps have differed in their reading of the rest of Canada. People such as Mr. Parizeau doubt that the rest of Canada will want any formal association. If Canadians do, fine. Maybe something can be worked out, provided it suits an independent Quebec.

The Lévesque–Bouchard school thinks some form of association is certainly desirable, and probably necessary. It will be achieved only if Quebeckers gather up their strength in a supreme national expression of solidarity to confront the rest of Canada.

Again last week, Mr. Bouchard called for a "regroupement des forces," a coming together of all elements of Quebec society. That coming together, expressed by a referendum Yes vote, would allow Quebeckers to feel proud, speak forcefully, express unity and, finally, to negotiate some new deal on equal terms with the rest of Canada. Not a new federalism. But confederalism, or association, or something institutional.

Mr. Bouchard has been at various times a federal Liberal, a Péquiste, a federal Conservative, and leader of the Bloc Québécois. His critics mock this inconsistency, and something about his political meanderings does suggest a mixture of emotional hills and valleys and an eye for the political chance. He is, despite his political beatification in Quebec, an opportunist. But to dismiss Mr. Bouchard as an opportunist misunderstands his ambitions. At least one constant has guided his political wanderings—a deeply felt (if often vaguely articulated) sense that Quebec must gather up its strength to secure a better deal from the rest of Canada.

Mr. Bouchard once thought that perhaps Pierre Trudeau would let Quebec stand tall. Disillusioned by Mr. Trudeau, Mr. Bouchard embraced Mr. Lévesque's sovereignty-association gambit: vote for sovereignty, then negotiate a new arrangement. When Mr. Lévesque's referendum lost, Mr. Bouchard followed his friend Brian Mulroney, believing that the Meech Lake accord would give Quebec a better deal. After Meech Lake collapsed, Mr. Bouchard opted again for the old Lévesque approach of voting for sovereignty, both as a desirable end product and as a means of putting pressure on the rest of Canada for new arrangements with Quebec.

It would never have occurred to Mr. Parizeau—indeed, it would have screamed against everything he believed—to involve himself in federal politics. But Mr. Bouchard has done so three times: as a Liberal, Conservative and Bloc Québécois, his participation symbolizing this old idea of getting a new deal with the rest of Canada.

Mr. Bouchard, whatever the smiling gloss now placed upon their disagreements, has pushed Mr. Parizeau grudgingly into adopting an associationist position. Mr. Bouchard's was a political master stroke, accomplished with the private encouragement and public support of some of Mr. Parizeau's own ministers.

The political theatre represented not just the clash of two ambitions, embedded in two proud men possessed of a deep sense of political destiny, but the conflict between two visions within the secessionist movement.

SIGN LAW

Mr. Bourassa's Options   *(December 16, 1988)*

Quebec Premier Robert Bourassa faces only two realistic options following yesterday's Supreme Court ruling against his province's language law.

The first, and least desirable, would be to override by legislation Quebec's own Charter of Human Rights, which, the Supreme Court ruled, renders unconstitutional provisions requiring French-only commercial signs.

The second, but perhaps more risky politically, would be to take the court's broad hint and allow signs in two languages, with French predominating.

Either choice would upset a segment of Quebec society. Nationalist groups, the Parti Québécois opposition, some editorial writers and citizens who like Bill 101, the language law, as is will want the override option. English-speaking Quebeckers and moderate francophones will want, or at least accept, the two-language approach, with French predominating.

Putting matters this way probably oversimplifies the cross-currents in Quebec, where many citizens like Bill 101 but at the same time won't object to bilingual signs. But if the debate polarizes, as it may in part because Mr. Bourassa has dithered for so long, the interests of the English-speaking minority may well be sacrificed.

Mr. Bourassa, it should be remembered, is haunted by the spectre of "social peace" unravelling in Quebec. He also faces a strongly nationalist opposition which, apart from the language question, is going nowhere in Quebec. The Parti Québécois knows, and Mr. Bourassa fears, that language turmoil may be the PQ's only lifeline to political competitiveness.

Mr. Bourassa is nothing if not a political animal. Faced with a choice between squelching a nationalist revival and satisfying English-speaking Quebeckers, he may be tempted to opt for political safety regardless of the human-rights issues involved.

He must know, however, that spurning the Supreme Court's ruling would cost him several, if not all, of his English-speaking ministers. They campaigned on signs in two languages—the party's platform. They took abuse from their constituents for agreeing with a silly National Assembly resolution deploring certain observations by the federal Commissioner of Official Languages, D'Iberville Fortier; but they told their electors to hold their fire for the larger battle over signs.

Their resignations—if it came to that—would send a signal to the rest of Canada far more direct than any interpretation of a sometimes arcane Supreme Court ruling. The signal would be that, in matters where the perceived collective rights of French-speakers (remember the "distinct society" clause in Meech Lake) clash with fundamental human rights as defined by the Canadian and Quebec charters, collective rights will prevail.

As for Prime Minister Brian Mulroney, he too finds himself in a difficult position.

He gave what was arguably his most effective speech since entering politics when, as leader of the Opposition, he spoke in defence of French-language rights in Manitoba. He has championed the rights of linguistic minorities, and he himself is a member of one of those minority-language groups.

But he has also made common political cause with Premier Bourassa on a range of issues, including free trade and Meech Lake. Provincial Liberals, including the Premier, materially assisted the Conservatives' political cause from 1984 to today. The Prime Minister's Quebec caucus is chock-a-block with mild nationalists and even a few former active supporters of the PQ.

The Prime Minister could opt for expediency in supporting restrictive action by Mr. Bourassa. Or he could be Prime Minister of the whole country, standing up for constitutionally sanctioned rights wherever they are threatened.

Effects of the Blow *(December 20, 1988)*

"There can be no question as to where the obligation of a national political party lies. It lies today, as it shall tomorrow, in ensuring that our minorities in Canada are treated at all times with dignity and justice."
—Brian Mulroney, Leader of the Opposition, Feb. 24, 1984.

Those were brave, important words Brian Mulroney spoke shortly after entering the House of Commons. He uttered them while the House wrestled with French-language rights in Manitoba. What he said then for French-speaking Manitobans, and what he repeated for French-speaking minorities elsewhere, applies equally today to Quebec's English-speaking minority.

Premier Robert Bourassa's decision on language rights—a repudiation of his own party's election platform, and of court rulings in Quebec and Ottawa—will unleash a series of unfortunate consequences, the prospect of which fills an observer with almost unrelieved gloom.

For starters, English-speaking ministers in Mr. Bourassa's Cabinet have no alternative but to resign. They cannot in conscience be a party to a decision that repudiates all their efforts. Their resignations will send a powerful signal, not only to their own communities in Quebec but elsewhere in Canada, that when the "collective rights" of the majority conflict with individual rights of the minority, even if those rights are upheld by the courts of the province and of the country, the majority will win a complete or largely complete victory.

The political defeat of the English-speaking ministers must cause them and their community to reflect on how, or whether, they can participate in the collective future of Quebec. They have played the political game within the Liberal Party, played the judicial game through the Quebec courts, counselled patience and a generosity of spirit toward the legitimate concerns of the French-speaking majority, and lost the issue they had identified as important to their community.

The failure of their efforts will make the plight of French-speaking minorities elsewhere in Canada that much more precarious, an elementary observation that has somehow escaped the spokesmen for the Federation of Francophones outside Quebec. The federation, in applauding Mr. Bourassa's decision, has failed utterly to understand that the Liberals and the Parti Québécois have written them off. Their fate is therefore dependent on action by English-speaking provincial governments whose electorates' generosity will be strained by recent developments in Quebec.

Meech Lake, too, has been compromised by Mr. Bourassa's decision, since it confirms a fear of some critics of that accord—that it would not protect minority-language groups. Manitoba Premier Gary Filmon yesterday withdrew the Meech Lake resolution from the legislature, justifying his action by citing Quebec's decision.

Nationalists in Quebec are aflame, feeling that Mr. Bourassa's modest concession—allowing other languages than French to appear in a secondary position within commercial establishments—represents a dangerous blow to the French language and culture. Scattered unpleasant incidents have already been reported. A confrontation between inflamed nationalists and a sullen, hurting English-speaking minority is not a recipe for constructive dialogue, let alone harmony.

Men and women of goodwill toward Quebec can only feel saddened by what has happened. The dream articulated by Mr. Mulroney (which he hinted at again yesterday in the Commons) of a tolerant, generous, outward-looking, confident Canada—a dream to which we English-speaking Canadians have most assuredly done our own fair share of harm—has taken a knock.

Christmas cannot come too soon.

A Collision of Minorities *(December 23, 1988)*

To paraphrase Rainer Maria Rilke, it is not so much the collision between two solitudes that explains what has happened in Quebec, but the collision between two minorities, each fearful for its future and incapable of forgetting the other's past.

French-speaking Quebeckers are a strong majority in their province, but a minority within Canada and North America. That minority status produces reflexes and complexes, reinforced by their sense of French Canadians' historical struggle to survive, which make them especially sensitive to a notion foreign to English-speakers—collective rights.

This notion, so bizarre to Anglo-Saxons, is invoked to defend the exercise of political discretion by the French-speaking majority to defend its own interests, especially in the fields of language and culture.

Collective rights, therefore, represent the political weight of the French-speaking majority acting with the reflexes of a minority. Thus it became logically consistent to use the "notwithstanding" clause in the Charter of Rights and Freedoms, because the use of that clause was a political act of a parliamentary body dominated by French-speakers.

Quebec's English-speaking minority, without sufficient political clout in Quebec, pinned its defence on individual rights, the classic defence of a minority. It won where it expected to win—in the courts of Quebec and Canada—but lost in the political arena, despite having sent to that arena admirable representatives whose departure was lamented by all but the fierce nationalists.

Bedevilling the clash between the two minorities is that each sees the other as a majority. The French-speakers see the anglophones as part of the North American whole, and therefore as the obstinate camel's nose under the French-speaking tent. The anglophones see the francophones as a majority in Quebec and cannot understand why they are not more generous.

Only a few French-Canadian commentators have derived any pleasure from the events of the past week. The majority in the serious press and in the National Assembly have been clearly torn up by this conflict. Le Devoir, the defender of French Canadians since its creation, was willing in an editorial to accept bilingual signs with French predominating. Even those who agreed with Robert Bourassa's decision have recognized the individual-rights arguments on the other side.

This may seem cold comfort, but it represents progress of a sort. The anglophone ministers who resigned and Alliance Quebec, the organization representing English-speaking Quebec, have also understood, while not accepting, the arguments about collective rights.

But it will not be easy to make progress on linguistic matters for a while. The sign issue, whatever its importance, was more symbolic than anything else. It sent a signal to people about their place in Quebec society, and how they were viewed by the other minority.

The anglophones are legitimately asking what role they can play in Quebec as long as the cultural insecurity of French Canadians remains. They sent excellent representatives into Quebec politics, and those representatives were defeated. They went to the courts, basing their case on individual rights, and lost in the political arena of collective rights.

There are francophones who would agree with the estimable journalist Michel Roy, who wrote, "When the indications of a strengthening [of the French language] become clear, Quebec will have to give to its English-speaking community full freedom of commercial expression." When, indeed? The answer can be given only by the French-speaking community itself. And the only ray of light in an otherwise dark week came from those, such as Mr. Roy, who were willing to ask that question.

REFERENDUM '95

The Czech and Slovak Republics
Present a Sobering Example for Quebec

(January 5, 1995)

Two New Year's Eves ago, the Czech and Slovak Federal Republic ceased to exist. Slovakia seceded from the federation, ultimately pushed out by fed-up Czechs. Are there lessons in this split for Canada, itself facing dismemberment in 1995?

Every circumstance of the Czech and Slovak split was different from those of contemporary Canada, except for an essential similarity: clashing national identities. The Slovaks, fired as minorities usually are by a sense of having been history's victims, dreamed of becoming independent while maintaining an economic association with the Czechs. Theirs was an ambition worthy of the Parti Québécois: to be politically free and economically bound.

Everything the Slovaks had assumed would occur after the split turned out to be wrong, except that they would be independent.

Robert Young of the University of Western Ontario reminds us of these miscalculations in a monograph called *The Breakup of Czechoslovakia,* which makes for sobering reading for anyone who considers secession a walk in the park.

Before the split, Slovaks assumed they had negotiated a monetary union, uninterrupted trade patterns and a customs-free border with the Czechs. The common-currency agreement fell apart thirty-nine days after Slovak independence because of speculative pressure and runs on Slovak banks.

Slovakia had to devalue its own currency, raise its value-added tax and watch bilateral trade drop 50 per cent. Soon after the split, the Czechs began to enforce controls at border posts.

For almost two years before the formal split, Slovak nationalists pushed for the disintegration of Czechoslovakia. They made demands, set timetables, denounced compromises, thundered at injustices; until the Czechs, angered by this ceaseless hectoring and dismissive of Slovak desires for what Mr. Young calls "vague confederalism," realized the Slovak nationalists could not be satisfied, turned exclusively to examine their own self-interest, resolved to yield no further and indeed to make many demands of their own, and so negotiated a hard bargain with the numerically smaller, economically weaker Slovaks.

The Czechs and the Slovaks differed in their understanding of certain matters during the negotiations, but the Czechs usually won out because, as Mr. Young writes, "as ever in international relations, where these readings were in conflict, matters would be settled by the relative power of the sovereign states."

Since the split, the Czechs have enjoyed political stability and economic growth, and Slovaks have suffered political instability and economic stagnation, until a very recent modest burst of growth. Slovaks, incidentally, are citizens of only their own new country. They had proposed a "union regime" under which people of the two countries would have one citizenship. When the Czechs obviously rejected this absurdity, the Slovaks suggested "dual citizenship." This, too, the Czechs rejected.

The Czechs rejected these Slovak suggestions on citizenship and in many other areas because, to the Slovak nationalists' apparent surprise, the Czechs were no longer interested in seeking compromises. The Czechs came to define their own self-interest less through the prism of maintaining the federal union than in preparing for the Czech Republic's own independence; that is, life without the Slovaks.

Compromisers were therefore shouldered aside by the hard men of Czech politics. Even President Vaclav Havel, long a voice for tolerance and compromise, ultimately recognized that he could neither persuade the Slovak nationalists to remain within the country nor dissuade the Czech political elite from kicking them out.

Public-opinion surveys showed that a majority of neither Czechs nor Slovaks wanted separation. However, the dynamics of secession, once unleashed, could not be stopped; indeed, they were encouraged by political actors on both sides.

Czechoslovakia, created in the 1920s, dismembered by fascism in the 1930s, oppressed by the Soviets until the Velvet Revolution of 1989, has now fallen apart. It will not be put back together.

Quebec's Politicians Catch a Disease
Shared by Poets and Intellectuals

(September 7, 1995)

Thomas Jefferson, author of the U.S. Declaration of Independence, can rest easily in his grave. His pre-eminent reputation for economy and eloquence of language remains untouched by the crafters of a similar document for a sovereign Quebec.

Yesterday, the six-person committee charged with producing a ringing preamble for the bill on Quebec secession unveiled its efforts. Minutes into the reading of their interminable text, it became abundantly evident that the six had become enamoured along the way of their own verbosity, an occupational hazard of poets and intellectuals.

None had evidently read—or if they had, they had forgotten—Abraham Lincoln's Gettysburg Address, which conveyed in 258 words infinitely more than that day's main speaker, Edward Everett, offered in more than two hours. The Quebec six therefore neglected the golden rule of great speeches: that economy of language carries more punch than endless repetition.

Their effort indeed read like the work of a committee, with bits of ersatz poetry jumbled with dry history and lists of good intentions to make something that offered reassurances for everyone. It may be that some Quebeckers will wade through the verbal swamp, but the majority will get lost early on and skip to the important part—the last line—wherein the authors declare: "Quebec is a sovereign country."

This preamble was delivered at Le Grand Théâtre in Quebec City before a secessionist rent-a-crowd of the kind political parties regularly assemble for staged events. In theory the crowd was assembled to hear a preamble that distilled what the fifteen regional commissions into Quebec's future had heard earlier this year while circulating around the province.

In fact, the preamble was fabricated by six committed secessionists who included the famous Quebec singer Gilles Vigneault, four other long-time secessionist preachers from literature, sociology and law, and Premier Jacques Parizeau's own special adviser, Jean-François Lisée. As such, it read like a piece of political propaganda, which is indeed what it was always intended to be. It will now be affixed to the referendum question to be revealed today.

The whole spectacle at Le Grand Théâtre, replete with a video of scenic Quebec and the provincial flag, smacked of a theatrical show, and as such represented an aspect of Quebec politics somewhat foreign to the politics of the rest of Canada.

Quebec politics, especially of the secessionist variety, has always featured certain theatrical flourishes. The whole layered language of Quebec politics is replete with the vocabulary of "people" and "nation" and "historic rights" and other such weighty phrases that speakers employ to impart a kind of solemnity to their pitches.

Secessionists, in particular, like to wrap their events in the trappings of sovereignty: flags and titles and formality underpinned with language which purports to identify their cause with that of the true interests of Quebec. The event at Le Grand Théâtre was therefore partly an attempt to capture attention to give momentum to the secessionist campaign, and partly a reflection of this theatrical quality of Quebec politics in general.

The rent-a-crowd, of course, enjoyed itself hugely, bathing in the videos and the interminable preamble, all determined to believe, or at least to act, as if they were part of something historic. They may actually have thought that the images of this spectacle would truly inspire Quebeckers and turn them toward secession, although few of them, if honest with themselves, could actually have imagined that their neighbours and friends would rush out to read such verbiage.

Missing in action, and notable for their absence, were the other secessionist leaders: Bloc Québécois Leader Lucien Bouchard and Action Démocratique Leader Mario Dumont. They had begged off, rather curiously, on claims of other business. They presumably knew in advance what would be in the preamble and therefore correctly figured that there were better ways to spend part of an afternoon than listening to it.

There Are Two Kinds of Economic Association, and They're Very Different

(September 8, 1995)

There will be economic associations between Canada and Quebec should it vote to become a separate state, but there will not be the kind of Economic Association proposed by the Parti Québécois in its secessionist bill introduced yesterday.

This distinction between economic associations and an Economic Association, or partenariat, as the PQ bill calls it, is not just a matter of semantics. The distinction lies at the heart of a misunderstanding that in turn is central to the debate in the weeks leading to the October 30 vote.

Canada, as currently constituted, has economic associations with many other sovereign countries. Canada trades with other countries, invests else-where and accepts investment from overseas, and even enters into formal trading arrangements such as the North American free-trade agreement. When asked by pollsters, Canadians have replied that yes, they wish those kinds of economic associations to continue with a separate Quebec.

In no case, however, does Canada carry out these economic associations with any of the institutional structures proposed by the Parti Québécois. These include the possibility of common citizenship and passports, the use of a common currency, or a political superstructure with some kind of joint parliamentary arrangement. The economic associations Canada carries out are those with other sovereign states and therefore are more restrictive in certain respects than those among Canadian provinces.

What the PQ wants is an Economic Association that would keep the ground rules existing among Canadian provinces, at the same time that Quebec becomes a separate state. The contradiction is obvious and profound.

Yet another contradiction appears. The PQ, ignoring the evidence from other breakups of federations, expects the negotiations toward an Economic Association to move entirely in one way; that is, toward a redefined integration between Canada and a separate Quebec.

In fact, from Canada's point of view, any negotiations with a separate Quebec would not be about reintegration, but about disintegration. A country would be breaking up if Quebec left, and quite apart from the emotional wallop that breakup would carry in Canada, it would force Canada to consider above all how to protect its self-interest in divvying up the assets from what had been 130 years of history.

It is hard to imagine, therefore, how negotiations could simultaneously be about reintegration and disengagement. It is even harder to imagine— indeed it is inconceivable—that the rest of Canada could negotiate any-thing, since something called the "rest of Canada" does not exist, in fact or in law. There are no institutions or constitutional provisions defining some-thing called the "rest of Canada" or Canada without Quebec.

The federal government does not represent the "rest of Canada." Nor do the provincial premiers, except in some loose confederative sense. It would take a long time for the "rest of Canada" to agree on how to structure itself, who should negotiate and what should be the aims of the negotiations.

At a minimum, such a process of self-definition would require extensive public consultations as options were debated and leaders selected. That process might involve constituent assemblies, a referendum and/or general elections. And most of the debate would centre on how to protect Canada's interests in a negotiation about disengagement, not reintegration.

The PQ and its secessionist allies will of course brush aside all the self-evident problems and confuse for its own purposes economic associations and an Economic Association. But the problems and the contradictions are so obvious that over time it will become clear that what Quebeckers are really being asked to pronounce themselves on is only the first part of the PQ's question, the one about the "sovereignty of Quebec."

Yes or No to that is the question. It's the only one rooted in the real world, as opposed to the fictional one that secessionists have constructed in their mind's eye to try to enlarge support for their abiding objective: Quebec independence.

The Federal Argument Is Harder to Sell Today Than It Was in 1980 *(October 19, 1995)*

QUEBEC—Prime Minister Jean Chrétien gave it the old college try in Quebec City yesterday, warning of the dangers of secession and vaunting the merits of federalism. Alas for him and for federalism, the case for Canada is less easily made in Quebec in 1995 than in the 1980 referendum.

Canada, whether federalists like to admit it or not, has done itself quite a bit of damage since the last referendum. Three attempts to change the Constitution either exploded (Meech Lake and Charlottetown) or ended in controversy (patriation). While these constitutional efforts sapped energy and created controversies, the country's fiscal situation deteriorated significantly.

In 1980, the federal government had been running deficits for only six fiscal years and the brutal recession of 1981-82 had not yet laid its hand upon the country, dramatically worsening the government's fiscal position. Now, fifteen years later, the Auditor-General reminds us that the federal debt has reached almost \$550-billion. By adding in provincial debts, the national indebtedness stands at almost 100 per cent of the country's gross domestic product.

In 1980, politicians such as Jean Chrétien could plausibly argue that secession would divorce Quebeckers from a fiscal powerhouse, evidence for which abounded in federal programs, many of high visibility in Quebec. Now, there is little defence against the correct secessionist prediction that the federal government will be cutting social programs and changing publicly financed pensions in yet unspecified ways. Any federalist politician who denies these cuts are coming would be lying, although they can properly reply that an independent Quebec would be forced into economies even more substantial than those forthcoming from Ottawa.

Then there were the constitutional defeats. Of course, it is somewhat disingenuous for the secessionists to lament these defeats, since both Meech Lake and Charlottetown were condemned by most secessionists. Still, the memory of Meech Lake still hangs around in Quebec, its demise a symbol of the difficulty of changing the federal system to allow more autonomy for Quebec and a reminder of the denial by the rest of Canada of Quebec's desire to be recognized both symbolically and in reality as a "distinct society."

The chances are excellent that very few Quebeckers can remember the five items in the Meech Lake accord. If they recalled anything it would be the emotionally loaded "distinct society" clause, the very part of Meech Lake that stuck in the throat of the rest of Canada.

The Trudeauiste view of Canada, and Quebec's place within it, resonated powerfully outside Quebec and in the heart of Jean Chrétien and francophones like him in Quebec. But that view, whatever its power in Quebec when Mr. Trudeau was Prime Minister, has diminished to a considerable extent, and Mr. Chrétien is irrevocably saddled with the political consequences of that decline. It is not just among secessionists that his part in opposing Meech Lake is recalled.

There is no point, therefore, in even talking about changes to the federal system in the referendum, except by oblique and uninspiring references to flexible federalism, such as Mr. Chrétien offered his audience of business people yesterday. If Mr. Chrétien tried anything as dramatic as Mr. Trudeau's promise to put his neck on the line for constitutional changes—whatever that startling but variously interpreted promise meant in the 1980 referendum—he would open a Pandora's box of skepticism.

These defeats—constitutional and fiscal—rob federalists of certain optimistic and forward-looking messages they might otherwise have been able to deliver. They have been driven instead into a campaign of warnings of an increasingly apocalyptic variety about the consequences of secession and the unreality of the political and economic association suggested with the rest of Canada.

Federalists are therefore playing the cards the last fifteen years have dealt. The cards are somewhat less powerful than the ones they were able to play fifteen years ago.

The Gospel of Nationalism According to Saint Lucien *(October 25, 1995)*

MONTREAL—"We have wasted the last thirty years," cried Bloc Québécois Leader Lucien Bouchard. "You, the young people, you must avoid the errors we have made."

For three decades, he told the throng of students, we knocked on all the doors, invented all kinds of formulas, elected all sorts of different politicians, always trying to convince English Canada that we were a people. And what did we get? Nothing. Worse than nothing.

We got, Saint Lucien explained, the Constitution of 1982, Pierre Trudeau's and Jean Chrétien's work that diluted the powers of the National Assembly. They cooked it up behind René Lévesque's back in the bars and hotel rooms of Ottawa. The gang of them—Trudeau and Chrétien and the English-speaking premiers—stabbed us in the back. Now, fifteen years later, it's inconceivable we would let them do it again. It's the same man, Chrétien. Do you think Quebeckers will give him a blank cheque again? Never!

We lost so much time, Saint Lucien explained, his voice dropping to almost a whisper. All those sterile discussions, those constitutional intrigues. All those blasted hopes. All those false promises. And look, before our very eyes, they are starting the same charades again.

Pierre Paradis, the provincial Liberal House Leader, says the rest of Canada should do something to help the federalists. Daniel Johnson dreams of a "distinct society." And Jean Chrétien tells them to get lost. He doesn't want to do it, and he can't do it.

Saint Lucien mentions the name of Newfoundland Premier Clyde Wells. Immediately the entire hall erupts in waves of booing. Wells, he explains, has done it again: he told Quebeckers he'll always oppose any constitutional recognition of their distinctiveness.

A No vote means putting Quebec at the mercy of Clyde Wells, Jean Chrétien and English Canada. After all the defeats, they still want us weak and pliable. They think they can trample us down again. Well, we're not going to stand for it. "Il faut jamais supplier les autres"—we must never beg the others.

As one, the crowd rises to their feet. "Lucien. Lucien," they cry. "Un pays. Un pays." But he has not finished just yet. There are more emotional chords to be plucked, more individuals to assail, more demons to invoke.

Look what's coming from English Canada. Heartless and cruel policies. In Ontario, they're cutting welfare rates. The weakest members of society are being hurt. They can do what they like in English Canada. They're a democracy. But we in Quebec, after a *Oui*, we'll protect the poor. More roars. We want social justice and economic equality in Quebec. We've got to protect Quebec from the merciless politics practised in Ontario and out there in the rest of Canada. And what happens in Ottawa after a No? Cuts to unemployment insurance. To pensions. To university funding, so your fees will rise. (Booing resumes.)

Then Saint Lucien returns to where his heart lies. We've been too weak, he complains. We never gave our premiers the support they needed to negotiate with *les autres*. They were alone, and they were defeated.

Why? Because we Quebeckers were divided. But after October 30 (we are nearing the peak of his crescendo now) we're going to have a real *rapport de forces*. Quebeckers will be united, for the first time. We're going to negotiate as a people!

We'll negotiate calmly, but from strength. And English Canada will have no choice, because they will know the people of Quebec have spoken. And this economic and political partnership, so sensible among sovereign states, will happen because the rest of Canada will have no choice. Their jobs depend upon it. It will be in their interest. You'll see.

So, finally, after all these years and so many defeats but only if we have the necessary courage next Monday, there will be a real negotiation—people to people!

"Un pays! Un pays!" chant the students.

Saint Lucien smiles.

If the Quebec Referendum Is Close, the Crisis Will Deepen Profoundly (*October 27, 1995*)

MONTREAL—Barring a major change in voting intentions, Canada will find itself Monday night in yet another deep crisis. Whether the Yes or No side wins, the margin will probably be narrow. Whatever the legal outcome, the political fact will be that a majority, perhaps even a strong majority, of francophones will have voted against Canada.

Canada has been many things, but central to its existence has always been the willingness of French speakers, largely concentrated in Quebec, to live with English-speaking people in a federal Canada. And vice versa. If they should vote with a strong majority Yes on Monday, as now seems likely, they will be saying in a negative way that they do not like Canada as it is, and in a more positive sense that they want their own country, whatever the risks.

Those are political facts, hard and perhaps irreversible. Either a narrow Yes or No would follow the last federal election in which the Bloc Québécois whipped the Liberals in Quebec, even capturing 50 per cent of the popular vote, and the last provincial election, in which the Parti Québécois won a solid majority of seats, although with less than half of the popular vote.

Three contests, then, between secessionists and federalists. Two defeats already for federalist forces, admittedly for particular reasons relating to political circumstances, and now a closely contested referendum. If federalism wins narrowly Monday, the Prime Minister, the Liberal Party and federalism generally will still have received a mighty blow.

It was not supposed to be like this. If one had listened to Prime Minister Jean Chrétien, he of the sunny ways, the "separatists" would be defeated handsomely. It now appears they may be defeated, but even in defeat they will have won a political victory.

The rest of Canada probably considered Mr. Chrétien statesmanlike when he appeared on national television the other night. People there would have liked his message. In French in Quebec, he looked like a man cornered, plaintive and raising *en passant* the very subject on which he lacks total credibility—the Constitution.

Mr. Chrétien used to be called yesterday's man, but he turned that taunt on its head by proving that being someone from yesterday—reassuring, patriotic, pragmatic—was precisely what English Canada wanted. He let the rest of Canada think that Quebec would be quiet, and that come the mighty confrontation between secession and federalism, Canada would knock 'em dead.

Who knows? Maybe the results will be 58-42 for federalism, or even 60-40 or 62-38, as many federalists confidently predicted when the campaign began. In which case, Mr. Chrétien can turn to his detractors and spit in their eye, and turn to English Canada with a smile.

But if the result is close, as seems more likely, he will have misread the campaign. More profoundly, yesterday's man will have been shown to be just that. More profoundly still, his vision and those who agreed with him will have been not just found wanting, but part of the fundamental cause of the problem.

History resonates in the "imagined community" of francophone Quebec and impresses itself upon contemporary events. Mr. Chrétien has discovered that whereas being "yesterday's man" plays well in English Canada, in Quebec it recalls not just his own previous constitutional positions, but the inability or unwillingness of the rest of Canada to come to terms with francophone nationalism, at least as nationalists define the problem. The referendum campaign suggests this problem remains. Perhaps no synthesis is possible.

Thousands of No supporters, some from far away, will march the streets of Montreal today exhorting Quebeckers to say Yes to Canada. They may even influence a few wavering voters. They should not kid themselves in their expressions of genuine patriotism that this referendum has demonstrated anything other than a deepening of the crisis of Canada.

The Life of Battered Canadian Federalism Hangs by a Thread *(October 31, 1995)*

MONTREAL—The cliché that a week is a long time in politics has just saved Canadian federalism, at least for now.

A week ago, following three or four disastrous days of campaigning, the federalist forces in the Quebec referendum were reeling. Prime Minister Jean Chrétien and the leader of the No forces in Quebec, Liberal Leader Daniel Johnson, had become ensnarled in problems over the recognition of Quebec as a distinct society. Newfoundland Premier Clyde Wells had weighed in with a spectacularly ill-timed and club-footed intervention. Finance Minister Paul Martin's credibility blew sky-high with his prediction that secession would imperil one million jobs.

Meanwhile, Bloc Québécois Leader Lucien Bouchard had ignited secessionist passions, making wavering francophones believe in the inevitability of an economic and political partnership with the rest of Canada. Saint Lucien was converting skeptics and animating the faithful. Canadian federalism, whose easy victory had seemed assured before the campaign began and during the first two weeks, was definitely teetering.

In the end, Canadian federalism survived, battered and bruised, in spite of the fact that 60 per cent of francophone Quebeckers voted last night for secession. But it survived only because federalists had put away their pocketbook arguments and pulled out the flag. The flag appeared not only in Quebec, but across the country in rallies, letters and other manifestations of love for Canada and affection for Quebec.

Canadian federalism, therefore, got the scare of its 128-year life yesterday. Quebeckers answered the questions put to them with characteristic determination not to be pushed into a corner. Although there was only one question on the referendum ballot—the one about sovereignty coupled with an offer of an economic and political association with Canada—there were, in fact, two being posed.

Secessionists were offering their question; federalists, as the Prime Minister kept saying, were offering Canada. That is, they were offering Canada as it is with very little prospect of change in the years ahead. Federalists tried therefore to push Quebeckers into a corner, betting that in a choice between "separatism" and Canada, Quebeckers would strongly reject "separatism."

But Quebeckers did not like the stark options: "separatism" or Canada as it is. They kept signalling to the secessionists that they would not buy the Parti Québécois/Bloc Québécois message, so it was changed to incorporate the offer of a partnership with Canada. They didn't like the Canada that federalists were offering either, as the Prime Minister was forced to belatedly recognize with his promise of change, even by constitutional means. By voting as they did, Quebeckers signalled a determination to keep pushing for substantial changes in Canadian federalism without discarding the secessionist option. They voted, in other words, to keep the pressure on without, for now, doing anything irrevocable.

Had they voted strongly No, they would have signalled their general satisfaction with the state of federalism. Had they voted Yes, they would have embarked on a risky journey. That a majority of francophones did vote Yes testifies to how attractive the Yes option has become. Or, to put matters another way, how reduced are the fears of secession's consequences.

That Yes majority among francophones now represents the biggest challenge to Canadian federalism. Whether hearts will harden against the non-francophone population which voted massively No, thereby frustrating the ambitions of Quebec francophones, remains to be seen. It is true in democratic theory that all citizens are equal and every vote counts the same; in politics, things are not always that neat.

Canadian federalism survived to fight another day, but the Prime Minister and the very idea of Canada as we have known it saw their legitimacy destroyed in Quebec last night. Canadian federalism, to have any chance for survival, has no choice but to be radically changed in a short period of time. The secessionists won the referendum campaign; they nearly won the vote.

They will win another vote in the future if Canadians cannot find the ingenuity to alter the federal system.

With No Clear Thinking, Canada Was Ill-Prepared for Its Dismemberment

(November 8, 1995)

TORONTO—So what if the vote had been the other way ten days ago—50.6 per cent for the Yes?

At least three repercussions would have been felt almost immediately in Quebec: the financial markets would have plunged and interest rates would have risen. Aboriginals would have stepped up their opposition to inclusion in a sovereign Quebec. And fresh legal challenges would have been launched against secession.

Outside Quebec, confusion bordering on chaos would have been the order of the day. Shock, anger, resignation, determination—these would have been among the emotional reactions. As for clear thinking about alternatives, there would have been a void.

It's scary to contemplate how ill-prepared the rest of Canada was for its dismemberment. Even in Ottawa, senior bureaucrats began to sketch out possibilities with only ten days remaining in the campaign and the Yes side ahead in the polls.

Such lack of preparation should never happen again. Having nearly won the referendum, and having captured 60 per cent of the French-speaking vote, secession remains politically alive in Quebec. Plenty of secessionists now think the departure of Quebec is just a matter of time. So do lots of people outside Quebec.

Nothing is inevitable except death and taxes. But there are balances of probabilities, and the referendum results suggest that what had been considered a long shot now must be given shorter odds. That means, as a sheer matter of prudence, people outside Quebec should spend time thinking what had been the unthinkable so that if secession should occur, the rest of Canada will have some research to rely upon.

Obviously governments are the last institutions that will encourage such thinking. They are into the Save Canada mode, as they should be. No elected official will stand up and say he or she is preparing for a world without Quebec, since such a statement could be portrayed as the wish being the father (or mother) of the thought.

Indeed, for a long time the fear of giving comfort to the secessionists impeded people outside Quebec from thinking about the unthinkable. The C.D. Howe Institute, to its credit, commissioned a series of studies about various aspects of deconfederation. There have been a few books and articles on the subject, but that's about it.

What should people think about? For starters, there's the problem of how to conduct negotiations over the terms of secession. More fundamental, what would the rest of Canada consider its self-interest to be? Do we need an economic and political partnership as proposed by the Parti Québécois? What about passports, citizenship? How do we prevent a fiscally irresponsible Quebec government from putting unacceptable pressure on a shared currency?

How does Canada fulfil its fiduciary and treaty obligations to the Native people of Quebec? What about boundaries? Should secession be declared illegal, and how would such an illegality be stopped?

What about government payments to people in Quebec when they are no longer residents of Canada? What practices of Quebec would be deemed injurious to Canada's interests within the North American free-trade area? Would there be areas where the two countries' interests might coincide?

The disappearance of Quebec from the country's radar screens, especially in Western Canada, will call up The Ontario Problem on those same screens. Alberta and British Columbia, economically strong and politically consequential, will demand quite properly that the political power of Ontario be fettered. How?

What about Maritime union, since the small Maritime provinces would be without any bargaining power whatsoever? What about Newfoundland? Will Alberta and British Columbia, to say nothing of Ontario, be willing to subsidize the Atlantic provinces?

What about the central government? Should this be a loose confederation of regions or provinces, or a country with a strong central government to resist where necessary north–south pressures and defend Canada's interests against a sovereign Quebec?

These are just a few of the questions Canadians outside Quebec, with their potentially superior bargaining power, need to think hard about so that if the unthinkable happens, Canada will be ready.

Canadians Don't Want to Go Down the Path to a Distinct Society Again *(November 15, 1995)*

"What experience and history teach is this—that people and governments never have learned anything from history, or acted on principles deduced from it."

—G. W. F. Hegel.

That night in the Verdun arena, six days from the referendum, the cheers of the federalist crowd could not obliterate the sound of a trapdoor opening.

Prime Minister Jean Chrétien had come to Verdun to rally the worried spirits of the No campaign. He promised Quebeckers changes in the Canadian federation if they voted No. Specifically, he promised them recognition of a "distinct society" and a veto for the "people of Quebec" over constitutional changes that might affect their province.

No sooner had the words escaped from his lips than the trapdoor swung open. The government of Canada and the provinces—and through them the country—are now suspended above this trapdoor. Canada has tried repeatedly to include a distinct-society clause in the Constitution and to give Quebec a veto in a revised amending formula.

Not only has Canada failed in both objectives, its failures have inflicted considerable harm.

Why, then, does the Chrétien government propose to drive the country down a path it does not wish to take? Why does it risk another failure?

Why, indeed, does it even think about constitutional changes when the last twenty-five years of Canadian history demonstrate with painful clarity that constitutional debates are inherently divisive, result in stalemate and heartbreak, and leave the country's institutions bruised? Is the Chrétien government so insensitive that it cannot read the lessons of history?

This Liberal government spent two entire years refusing even to talk about the Constitution. They banned the dreaded c-word from their vocabulary. Then, in the dying days of the campaign, the provincial Liberals panicked and blurted out the need for Quebec's recognition as a distinct society.

Mr. Chrétien hurried to patch the split, thereby committing himself to pursuing this objective in his Verdun speech. Because the Prime Minister spoke, the government is now stuck with this promise without knowing how to achieve it and apparently underestimating the risks.

No solace should be taken from recent polls—and resolutions passed in the New Brunswick, Newfoundland and Ontario legislatures—showing a willingness to recognize Quebec as a distinct society. These polling data and these resolutions merely cloud the issue. They are symbolic recognitions of the obvious without imparting a willingness to allow Quebec to be treated, or to treat itself, differently.

That is, of course, what Quebec wants, or at least what the provincial Liberals want; and it is precisely what the rest of Canada will not grant, at least not in a constitution. Outside the Constitution, yes; inside a constitutional document or in a series of parliamentary resolutions, no.

As for a Quebec veto, that too is a trapdoor. There is not only a visceral dislike of the idea outside the province, but endless meetings were spent in the 1970s and early 1980s wrestling with an amending formula that contained a veto for Quebec. All the sensible formulas were rejected, sometimes by Quebec itself, in favour of the ones we now have. A veto for Quebec will be met with a demand for a veto for British Columbia and another for Alberta, and off we will head down a dead-end street.

Open the Constitution and wait for the aboriginals to demand their time and place. Wait for the Charter Canadians to line up. Wait for the surfacing of all the resentments these debates invariably create. Wait, in short, for Canadian federalism to offer more proof positive to the secessionists that it lacks coherence.

And yet, the Quebec Liberal Party, rather than being creative—that is, non-constitutional—in its demands, repeats the old formulas that won't work; and the federal Liberals, totally surprised by the referendum turn of events, swallow all their previous declarations and place themselves and the country above the trapdoor.

Has the Government Lost Its Nerve or Just Lost Touch with Canada? *(December 20, 1995)*

Canadians live in an age of discontinuity presided over by a managerial government.

This gap between the pressures for change and the government's preference for management explains the widespread but still vague sense that Prime Minister Jean Chrétien's government has rather suddenly lost its way.

That the Chrétien government lost its nerve presumes that it had any. Nerve implies a willingness to take risks, to raise the bar; or conversely, to stay the course when all hell breaks loose. Instead, the Chrétien government has been characterized by a strong preference for incremental movement.

For a while, incrementalism seemed just what Canadians wanted and the country needed. Deficit reduction, but slowly. Unemployment insurance reform, but gradually. Constitutional change, not at all. Social policy changes, very cautiously. The country had been battered by governments proposing dramatic changes (wage and price controls, the National Energy Program, constitutional change, budget cuts, free trade, the GST) and people wanted a rest, or at least change at a more measured pace.

Presiding over this incrementalism was the ultimate pragmatist, Jean Chrétien, who turned his former critics' taunts about being "yesterday's man" into political virtue. Canada is Number One, he cried. Sure, we have a deficit problem, but let's not get our knickers in a knot over it. National unity. What, me worry? The United Nations says Canada is the "best country in the world" in which to live. Me and the premiers, we go to China together as Team Canada, and we sign billions of dollars of contracts. I fly here and there and everywhere, and I get along with everyone. I crack up Bill Clinton and make Jacques Chirac smile. And I get along with the premiers. I keep all my Cabinet ministers in place. No scandals. My name isn't Mulroney. And the people love me. If you doubt it, check the latest Gallup poll. What, me worry?

The politics of sunshine, and government by management, formed a potent combination, the match of mood and moment. Now, however, the age of discontinuity, or of change that cannot be denied, is upon us, largely because of the October 30 Quebec referendum.

But the politics of sunshine is what Mr. Chrétien knows, so he showers his year-end interviewers with exhortations to Canadians to feel good about their country. Yet these noble and unquestionably genuine prime-ministerial sentiments are completely discordant—no, disquietingly discordant—with the *Maclean's*–CBC year-end poll. "In twenty years of analysing poll results," writes pollster Allan Gregg, "this year's set of findings is the blackest I have ever examined."

So who is kidding whom? Are Canadians not telling Mr. Gregg the truth? Are they so weary and wary that they deliberately mislead those who try to probe them? Is Mr. Gregg somehow misreading the raw data? Or, as is more likely, has the Prime Minister constructed a mental landscape, at least for public-relations purposes, inhabited by few of his fellow citizens?

Perhaps he feels, as optimists often do, that this bad temper will pass and that the genuine test of nerve, if you will, is to stay the course and cheer the troops while apprehension and doubt cover the mental flood plain of others. Floods do recede, and when they do, optimism can resume its connection between wish and reality.

The manager, however, now confronts forces that resist mere management and that escape the grasp of pragmatism. Debts are so great that governments must recast their role quite fundamentally. Programs built on different foundations cannot last. Thirty years of struggle between ethnic identification in francophone Quebec and the contrasting identification demands of the rest of Canada have reached a point at which a very large number of Canadians, inside and beyond Quebec, do not believe a synthesis is possible.

The traditional political culture of Canada cracked some time ago. The forces that cracked it are still shifting the foundations of the Canadian state, over which presides a manager of great decency, politeness and determination whose mental landscape suddenly seems oddly removed from that of so many of his fellow citizens.

PART 4 *Constitutional Follies*

THE CHARTER

Rule of the Courts *(May 7, 1986)*

VANCOUVER—Welcome to the new world of the Charter of Rights. Goodbye to the supremacy of Parliament.

Defenders of the Charter said it wouldn't happen, at least not right away, but some Canadian courts are using the Charter aggressively to strike down parliamentary laws.

In the process, some judges are turning to the United States for inspiration, grafting well-established American doctrines onto their decisions. The forecast is clearly for a more litigious society wherein courts take crucial decisions away from Parliament and the legislatures.

An illuminating case in point involves what British Columbia's lower courts are doing to the recently adopted law controlling street soliciting. Parliament adopted the law after extensive debate and prolonged agitation from residents in neighbourhoods in Vancouver and other Canadian cities.

Parliament decided that street soliciting was an important problem. But Judge Robert J. Lemski of the B.C. Provincial Court disagreed. "In my opinion, the overall importance of the problem of street prostitution is not that great. It is one nuisance among numerous nuisances that exist in Canada today," he wrote in a judgment declaring invalid one section of the law governing attempts to "communicate" for the purposes of prostitution.

Now Judge Lemski is obviously a most learned gentleman in the law. But his completely non-legal opinion on the relative importance of street soliciting is no more valid than yours or mine, and it certainly is worth less than the considered opinion of Parliament, whose members in theory are supposed to reflect public attitudes.

Judge Lemski continues: "Is it always necessary to drain the swamp to get rid of the alligators?" As this colourful phrase indicates, Judge Lemski obviously believes that Parliament used overkill, adopting legislation that infringes on basic freedoms. To reach this conclusion, he uses the "overbreadth doctrine," which stipulates that legislation which discourages citizens from exercising a guaranteed right amounts to a "constructive violation" of that right.

This doctrine, according to Judge Lemski, "is part of American jurisprudence now relevant to Canadian law." It means, to a non-lawyer, that judges who apply the doctrine will be always looking well beyond the meaning of a statute and into the social, economic and cultural issues surrounding the statute, which is precisely what activist American courts have historically done.

In another ruling, Judge Keith Libby declared invalid a section of the street soliciting law governing the place where soliciting could occur. He reasoned that "any place open to the public view" was too broad to tackle the problem of street soliciting.

Parliament wrestled with this definitional dilemma, as any reading of the debates will attest. Indeed, finding the proper language for the bill has been a persistent problem since the Supreme Court determined in the late seventies that soliciting had to be "persistent and pressing" before it would run afoul of the law.

That judgment effectively killed federal attempts to regulate street soliciting, forcing municipalities and provincial governments to tackle the problem. This they did with decidedly mixed results, and their setbacks caused Ottawa to try again with Criminal Code amendments.

Once again, the courts are making Parliament's task more difficult, this time using the Charter as their touchstone. In other Canadian cities, the law seems to be working well in removing soliciting from the streets. And courts are upholding the federal statute.

But the B.C. judgments, now under appeal, remind us that the Charter beckons judges into uncharted territory where the lines between what is legal and subjective are distinctly blurred.

The Irony of the Charter *(April 17, 1990)*

Scarcely a week passes without a Canadian court rapping governments on the knuckles, or being invited to do so by an interest group, for having contravened the Charter of Rights and Freedoms.

Last week, for example, the Quebec Superior Court ruled unconstitutional three sections of the 1986 Competition Act, a bill preceded by two decades of fitful and often fruitless debate.

The week before, the Supreme Court of Canada ended the so-called Patti Starr inquiry in Ontario. A few weeks before that, a Federal Court judge declared that the new refugee-screening process violated the Charter.

For better or worse, Canada now lives in the Age of the Charter, a radical change contained in the Trudeau government's constitutional package of

1981-82. Indeed, the Charter's impact on Canadian life and Canadian federalism eclipses anything contained in the Meech Lake constitutional accord.

The Charter was inspired by American traditions—a Bill of Rights, an activist judiciary, checks and balances. Not surprisingly, therefore, these American traditions transposed to Canada are doing more to Americanize Canada than any other recent development, including the free-trade deal.

Seymour Martin Lipset, the brilliant American political sociologist, caught the significance of the Charter in his book *Continental Divide*, published last year by the C.D. Howe Institute. After asserting that the U.S. and Canadian political cultures were fundamentally different, Mr. Lipset wrote: "Perhaps the most important step that Canada has taken to Americanize itself—far greater in its implications than the signing of the free-trade treaty—has been the incorporation into its constitution of a bill of rights, the Charter of Rights and Freedoms, placing the power of the state under judicial restraint."

Mr. Lipset believed the Charter "makes Canada a more individualistic and litigious culture, one that will place more stress on the enforcement of personal rights through adversary proceedings rather than government adjudication." He concluded: "By enacting the Charter, Canada has gone toward joining the United States culturally."

It's hard to contest Professor Lipset's wise observations; and yet, as always in politics, there is deep and abiding irony in the way we arrived at the Charter and its current impact. The irony of the Charter, with all its Americanizing tendencies, is that it was the brainchild of a prime minister who spent his entire career trying to diminish the American influence on Canadian life.

Pierre Trudeau, who calls the free-trade deal a "monstrous swindle," has just contributed to a book called *Towards a Just Society*, which explains, through contributions by him and many leading figures in his government, how the Liberals tried to curtail the Americanization of Canada. In energy and industrial policy, and in the cultural and foreign policy fields, Mr. Trudeau sought to create "counterweights" to the American presence in Canada.

Indeed, creating counterweights to dominant authority was the touchstone of Mr. Trudeau's entire political philosophy. Yet it remains the supreme irony that his enduring institutional legacy to Canada—one that will remain long after the Third Option, the Canadian Development Corporation, the public ownership of Petro-Canada etc.—will be the Charter, that most Americanizing of changes.

The Charter, modified only by the "notwithstanding" clause and certain other sections, is now the supreme "counterweight" to government action, a change that has weakened governments and political parties, emboldened interest groups and produced an increasingly litigious society.

These developments, coupled with others to be examined tomorrow, make Canada a harder place to govern. The result has been an erosion in Canadians' faith in government action, another ironic legacy for a prime minister who practised activist government.

Rights Are Rights and Equality Is Equality? Not in Canada *(May 21, 1992)*

The Charter of Rights and Freedoms reflects equality. It applies to all Canadians, and theoretically defends and enhances all freedoms, except where limits can be reasonably justified in a "free and democratic society."

This notion of pan-Canadian equality has turned the Charter into the country's most important national symbol. But the powerful symbolism of Charter equality is questioned from three directions, and each challenge reflects fault lines in the Canadian political culture.

The Quebec government demands that the province be considered a "distinct society" and that the Charter be interpreted with that in mind. Male aboriginal leaders demand either that the Charter not apply to their societies at all, or that it be applied by aboriginal courts according to aboriginal customs. During the Meech Lake debate, the whole country saw how unwilling Canadians outside Quebec were to accept the distinct-society clause. As a result, the federal government now proposes to define distinct society as meaning Quebec's language, culture and civil code.

Still, the distinct-society idea is widely unpopular outside Quebec, despite the apparent support from English-speaking political leaders these days. Indeed, the essence of turning Meech Lake, the "Quebec Round," into something now called the "Canada Round" is to coat the distinct-society pill with changes sought by other regions, such as Senate reform.

Native women have objected to removing their societies from Charter purview. But male Native leaders insist that the Charter, with its individualistic values, is inconsistent with aboriginal tenets of community.

Whether or not the Charter will apply to aboriginal communities, and in what way, is a major sticking point in the national constitutional debate. If public-opinion polls from 1988 to 1992 are any guide, a whopping majority of Canadians believe the Charter must apply to everyone, including Natives. Anything less—that is, any differential application of Charter rights—is anathema to Canadians' sense of the equality inherent in the Charter.

From a third direction comes a challenge directly to Charter equality. So-called equality-seeking groups, such as organizations promoting the rights of women, people of colour and the handicapped, seek something called "substantive equality," that is, equality of results or affirmative action.

Shelagh Day of the National Action Committee on the Status of Women puts the argument this way: "Provincial and federal politicians have apparently not grasped that equality is not a question of same treatment, or different treatment, but a question of whatever treatment is necessary to put a group which has historically been disadvantaged on an equivalent footing with the dominant group in society."

Ms. Day and dozens of other feminist lawyers and constitutionalists have developed the theory, articulated in the United States by such writers as Catherine MacKinnon and Iris Young, that real equality requires differential application of rights to favour women and disadvantaged groups.

Equality before the law is not only *passé*, it prevents disadvantaged groups from getting ahead. Instead of a formal model of equality, these groups seek "purposive" and positive use of the law to overcome inequality. Ms. Day, for example, thinks the Constitution should be rewritten to remove the sexual-equality provisions, to include only a goal of "advancing the equality of women." Susan Jackel of the University of Alberta proposes a Senate in which women would make up the same majority men enjoy in the Commons. The Canadian Philosophical Association has passed a resolution saying 75 per cent of all new hiring must be of women, despite the fact that only 20 per cent of current PhD graduates are female.

These are all manifestations of a different view of the Charter from that held by mainstream public opinion.

When Clifford Lincoln resigned from the Quebec National Assembly in protest against Bill 178, Quebec's sign law, he argued that rights were rights, the same for everyone. Neither the law, nor Canadian politics, is that simple.

Whether Canada, through its Charter, can accept differential application of rights is an argument at the heart of politics and constitutional change.

Parliaments, Not Courts, Should Decide the Rules on Selling Cigarettes *(January 20, 1993)*

Tobacco products, even in moderation, can damage health or kill. They cause annoyance to some who do not use them. They raise money for governments through taxes, but they also impose costs through avoidable health-care expenditures.

As such, governments have a legitimate interest in the sale and promotion of tobacco. Fortunately, the Quebec Court of Appeal agreed by a 2-1 majority last week that governments have such an interest, that the problem is national in scope and therefore warrants federal action, and that a proposed federal law restricting tobacco advertising is constitutional.

Tobacco companies will probably appeal this ruling to the Supreme Court of Canada, which is good news—provided the court rules the right way. Ruling the right way would be saying, in effect, that parliaments and not courts are best positioned to determine matters of public policy such as those raised in tobacco advertising.

In recent decisions, the Supreme Court has been giving legislators more latitude by backing courts out of some public-policy debates. That's good news for those who believe the Supreme Court went too far in the first years of the Charter of Rights and Freedoms in intruding on parliamentary prerogatives.

The Quebec Court of Appeal based its decision, in part, on recent rulings revisiting a 1986 Supreme Court of Canada decision in the Oakes case. Oakes was the court's first systematic attempt under the 1981 Charter to indicate how it would view governments' justifications of their infringements of Charter rights. (Section 1 of the Charter permits such infringements if they are "reasonable" and can be "demonstrably justified in a free and democratic society.")

The court, under then Chief Justice Brian Dickson, set forth an elaborate four-step analysis which in practice set a high hurdle for governments that wanted to cite Section 1. Because the court shied away from examining the ends of government policy, it concentrated on the means, insisting that these be proportional to the end sought.

The problem was that the assessment of means inexorably led the court to pass judgment on the ends of policy, which is more properly the business of legislatures.

More recently, the Supreme Court has been moving away from Oakes, showing somewhat more deference to legislative prerogatives and making it easier for governments to use a Section 1 defence.

In the tobacco case, the cigarette companies insisted there was no definitive link between tobacco use and the consequences and costs alleged by government to justify advertising restrictions.

Under the old Oakes test, this failure to provide a definitive link might have doomed the legislation, since the means of restricting advertising would not be proportional to the end sought. As Quebec Appeal Court Judge Louis Lebel wrote in the tobacco case, the old Oakes test seemed to require a legally proved link rather than reasonable political judgment.

Instead, Judge Lebel said (my translation): "The court must rather determine whether, on the basis of the information available, the choice adopted is part of measures which possibly, for a legislator acting reasonably, will

achieve the desired legislative objective." This lower hurdle gives governments more leeway than previous understandings of the Oakes test.

It also kicks the props from beneath the tobacco companies' insistence
that the standard of proof required in a criminal or civil trial should be
applied to the effect of advertising on consumption. Since nobody knows
categorically what that link is, the companies said, a Section 1 defence could
not be used to justify any infringement on their freedom of expression.

The Quebec Court of Appeal said there was enough evidence about the
health dangers associated with tobacco, and enough evidence that some link
existed between advertising and consumption, that reasonable legislators
were justified in passing a law restricting tobacco advertising.

A lower-court judge had thrown out the government's bill, and one judge
on the appeal court agreed with him. With the two other appeal-court
judges upholding the constitutionality of the law, the scorecard reads two
judges for, two against.

The Supreme Court will probably now rule. Let's hope the justices understand that the issue goes beyond tobacco advertising, important as that is, to
the sphere of action that should be reserved for elected politicians on matters of public policy.

MEECH LAKE

Trying for Harmony (May 8, 1987)

If the Meech Lake accord is accepted, we will, in the space of a few years,
have placed in the Constitution two sets of major changes that go in entirely
different directions.

The Trudeau changes of 1982 were an effort to reinforce the role of the
central authority, principally through the Charter of Rights. The Meech
Lake accord expands provincial clout by giving premiers new roles in
shaping national institutions (the Supreme Court and Senate), by enshrin-
ing an annual First Ministers' conference on the Constitution and by
expanding the powers of provinces to set their own agenda in the face of
national programs.

Basically, two dynamics produced the Meech Lake accord. The first was a
desire to bring Quebec into the Canadian Constitution, which required a
devolution of authority toward Quebec and guarantees such as a clause

affirming Quebec's "distinct society." The second was a granting to all provinces of what Quebec got (except the "distinct society" clause), because too much particular treatment for Quebec smacked of special status.

If you peer down the road a few years, you can see a federation even more challenging to operate than today's.

Suppose, for example, that we get an elected Senate. At that point, the question of who speaks for, say, Manitoba becomes intriguing. A major purpose of an elected Senate would be to weaken the role of premiers, since senators would speak for their provinces on national issues in Ottawa.

But the Meech Lake accord proposes to enshrine two annual First Ministers' conferences—one on the economy, the other on the Constitution. It would also give the premiers a direct role in appointing senators and Supreme Court justices. So the premiers' role isn't going to decline.

That means we will have members of Parliament, senators and premiers, all operating within national institutions and all democratically elected, claiming with justification to speak for their province.

This wouldn't be so difficult if jurisdictions were clear—if MPs and elected senators spoke on federal items and premiers on provincial ones. There is an internal logic in, for example, the West German system, where states are represented in the upper house, play a role in shaping national programs and have the administrative authority to operate programs; and in the American system, where states are weaker than our provinces and governors play no role in national decision making. But we may be heading toward a strange, unwieldy system wherein the lines of authority are blurred and the capacity to act fettered.

In a crucial sense, the Meech Lake accord gives constitutional effect to what has really been happening in Canada for twenty-five years, apart from the Trudeau attempt of 1982. Within that period, provinces became more powerful because the services they provided—health, education, training—grew more costly and were increasingly desired by the public. They wanted, and received, a greater share of overall government revenues and expenditures.

At the same time, Ottawa used its spending power to barge into areas of provincial jurisdiction such as social policy and natural resource management. The result was a mixture of gratitude and resentment. So the Meech Lake accord tries to achieve national harmony and improved decision making by recognizing the power of the provinces, whose ability to influence federal decisions is enhanced and whose own authority is protected.

The theory is simple: provinces with new constitutional protections for themselves and a new voice in federal institutions will act with Ottawa in the national interest and so provide a better reflection of the Canadian reality. We shall see.

The Role of Statesman *(May 9, 1987)*

Prime Minister Brian Mulroney can take pride in the Meech Lake accord.

It represented the culmination of a two-and-a-half-year strategy that displayed a steadiness of purpose and a sure grasp of tactics seldom, if ever, shown by his government. He knew what he wanted to achieve and how best to get there. And he understood how his sense of the national agenda and the pure politics of the issue could come together.

That he has the opposition parties on the run was demonstrated all week as the Liberals and New Democrats poked, prodded, but ultimately backed away from a frontal attack on the accord.

The accord stands on the high political ground of bringing Quebec to sign a revised 1982 constitutional document, the overarching objective he outlined in an August 1984 speech in Sept-Iles. Mr. Mulroney so carefully met the demands of Quebec Premier Robert Bourassa that the deal should fly in that province, a political reality which has kept quiet those English-Canadian politicians of every stripe who don't like the accord.

Nobody knows yet what political benefit will accrue to Mr. Mulroney in Quebec, to say nothing of the rest of the country, for having achieved his purpose. Good editorials and learned treatises seldom translate into votes. But for the first time since he became Prime Minister, Brian Mulroney looked like a statesman throughout. That image might start the process of rehabilitating his severely tarnished reputation.

The unsung heroes of the piece were Senator Lowell Murray and a civil servant, Norman Spector. Last summer Mr. Mulroney appointed the senator as minister responsible for the dossier and Mr. Spector as secretary to the Cabinet for federal-provincial relations. Quietly but surely they beavered away, helping to prepare the pieces for Mr. Mulroney to assemble at Meech Lake.

Both Mr. Murray and Mr. Spector are intelligent, bilingual English Canadians. Mr. Murray had the added advantage of having voted against the 1982 Trudeau package because it had been rejected by the National Assembly of Quebec. That meant he was working toward a deal with his intelligence, his political acumen and his heart.

The trick now is to translate the Meech Lake accord into reality as fast as possible. Two groups will gnaw at it: strong nationalists in Quebec who believe Mr. Bourassa got too little, and strong Canadian nationalists elsewhere who think Mr. Mulroney gave away too much.

Mr. Mulroney has probably neutered both groups. He gave Mr. Bourassa so much that those Quebec nationalists who remain federalists cannot justifiably work themselves into a lather. He gave the other premiers so much of what they wanted that they can hardly turn against him back home. And the federal opposition parties are too worried about losing support in Quebec to let Liberal Leader John Turner, and to a lesser extent NDP Leader Ed Broadbent, give vent to the full anger expressed privately by many of their English-speaking colleagues.

Mr. Mulroney delivered what he promised—a contented Quebec government participating more fully within Canada. He did it by the Meech Lake accord and by allowing the summit of French-speaking countries to go forward with Quebec's participation. When all the problems with the Meech Lake accord appear, chances are Mr. Mulroney will be gone from the scene. He will get credit for Meech Lake. Only much later will we find out whether he deserved it.

Hardening Hearts *(June 20, 1989)*

A country, by one definition, is a people with a shared sense of having done great things in the past and an eagerness to do more in the future. By this standard, Canada is dying.

Canada as we know it cannot exist without a desire by English- and French-speaking Canadians to do great things together. Never in my lifetime has that sense been weaker.

It is weaker in far more subtle and insidious ways than in the 1960s and 1970s. In those decades, when Quebec nationalism took a more virulent and threatening posture, it was possible to design institutional and even attitudinal responses—a new flag, bilingualism, French power, new federal-provincial cost-sharing arrangements, French-language immersion programs. And it remains possible to make further changes—la Francophonie, an updated Official Languages Act, and, of course, the Meech Lake constitutional accord.

But something has now snapped in the English-Canadian psyche, not because bigotry has appreciably grown. The hard-core anti-French elements are still there in the English-speaking population, but they are not the problem. Rather, the problem lies in hearts without malice which hunger for repose from the demands for accommodation.

National politics and, more precisely, the national political parties have always provided important bridges for French–English accommodation. Yet there is growing irritation in English-speaking Canada that those bridges are manned on both sides by Quebeckers.

The Tories piled up their majority last time by sweeping Quebec, just as the Liberals did under Pierre Trudeau. The Liberals are going to choose between two Quebeckers—Jean Chrétien and Paul Martin. The Meech Lake accord, which proponents in Quebec and beyond insist might be Quebec's litmus test for remaining in Canada, is Quebec's agenda. A space agency goes to Montreal. While English-Canadian parents place increasing numbers of their children in French-immersion programs, Quebec refuses to teach English before Grade 4, prohibits the use of English in external signs, and intervenes to oppose control by Franco-Albertans of their own school board. English Canadians, rightly or wrongly, see a double standard.

Quebec Premier Robert Bourassa is increasingly perceived as the most powerful politician in the country, having got the federal Prime Minister and the Premier of Ontario precisely where he wants them. He even has Liberal leadership hopefuls nervous about his capacity to influence events.

To list these perceptions is by no means to accept their grounding in reality. But a country is a matter of the heart as well as the mind, and the heart is seldom the place for rational discourse. Increasingly, English-Canadian hearts are hardening because there is a growing perception that in Quebec federalism is purely a matter for calculation, for the totting up of sums and losses, for a distinctly relativist approach without any deep-seated attachment to the common cause.

Free trade didn't help. The strongest opponents of free trade outside Quebec were generally speaking found among those Liberals and New Democrats who in the past had manifested, on other issues to be sure, the greatest openness to Quebec's aspirations. On the free trade that so exercised Liberals and New Democrats, they perceived (remember we are dealing with perceptions) that Quebec carried the day. They had stood with Quebec on matters they thought mattered to Quebec; on free trade, Quebec, acting naturally enough in its own interests, let them down.

Ten years ago, English Canadians generally manifested an almost desperate desire to see Quebec remain. Very few English Canadians desire that today. And fewer of them than a decade ago are eager for more accommodation.

Drifting Out of Touch *(June 21, 1989)*

All seems quiet on the surface of politics. The Prime Minister boasts a solid majority with plenty of seats in Quebec, Ontario and the West. Quebec Premier Robert Bourassa, a federalist of sorts, seems primed for re-election this autumn. The Liberals and New Democrats are in the early stages of going about the selection of new leaders. The deadline for the Meech Lake accord is a year away.

But the idea of Canada as we know it is dying on both sides of the linguistic divide. It is dying in many English-Canadian hearts, for reasons explored yesterday. And it remains in poor shape among French-speaking Quebeckers.

Among these Canadians, perceptions are almost completely at variance with those in English Canada, with one important caveat. The emotional attachment to the idea of Canada has seldom been as great in Quebec as elsewhere. The rationalist, calculating approach to federalism—*le fédéralisme rentable*, to use Mr. Bourassa's phrase—has frequently characterized Quebec's attitude to Canada.

What has changed, albeit in subtle and incremental ways, is Quebec's almost complete lack of interest in the rest of Canada. Again, there is a risk in overstating the case: Quebec has frequently shown little interest in developments elsewhere in Canada. When Jean Chrétien, speaking as a Quebecker, talks about "his Rockies," most French-speaking Quebeckers think of that as a quaint but quite inaccurate description.

The French-language newspapers, for example, still lack a single correspondent in all of English Canada (Ottawa excepted). Presumably, that persistent state of affairs reflects editors' and publishers' sense of where their readers' interests lie. Even the Ottawa coverage in the French-language media is frequently about whether Quebec got its "fair share" from this or that federal program.

No, what's changed has to do with economic and demographic shifts. The great surge of French-speaking Quebeckers into business has produced two phenomena. The world-class companies lead by Quebeckers (Lavalin, Bombardier, Laurentian, Power, the banks) have international horizons within which the rest of Canada fits as only a small part. And the English-Canadian companies which obtrusively or quietly departed during the turmoil of the seventies left behind Quebec regional offices whose interests do not extend beyond Quebec. In both cases, the importance of staying in touch with the whole of Canada has diminished.

Simultaneously, Quebec's demographics are changing. The declining birth rate among French speakers and the influx of immigrants is now poking at Quebec's insecurity. Losing linguistic control of Montreal, Quebec's metropole, provided the largest single impetus to the cultural fears of the sixties and seventies. Now, those fears are back again, lying underneath the prohibition of English on exterior signs, the determination to change the organization of school boards, the Meech Lake clause enhancing Quebec's control over immigration, and tax policies to encourage the procreation of more children.

These demographic fears, although seldom articulated this way, can be linked to membership in Canada as we know it. After all, it's the Canadian

Charter of Rights and Freedoms that must be overriden to prohibit English. It's Canada's immigration policy that produces the immigrant mix. It's English Canada's increasing distaste for the Meech Lake accord that frustrates Quebec's desire not only to be recognized as a "distinct society," but to increasingly act as one in the future. The pious concern for French-speaking minorities allows some English-Canadian bleeding hearts to criticize Quebec's treatment of its English-speaking minority.

In these circumstances, the interest in making accommodations is decidedly low.

Accord and Discord *(June 22, 1989)*

One of Canada's leading experts on public opinion was conducting a focus group interview in Saskatchewan on other subjects when he decided to ask about the Meech Lake constitutional accord.

Every respondent, in a province whose government had negotiated and ratified the accord, denounced Meech Lake.

The respondents could offer no specific reasons for disliking Meech Lake, or even express reasons for general unease, because not one of them knew what the accord was all about. They articulated only a vague sense that Meech Lake represented something for Quebec, and therefore should be rejected.

From the beginning, Meech Lake has been an issue for the elites. It was prepared in secret, negotiated in private, and ratified with surprising speed by eight of the ten provinces and the federal Parliament. Now it is stuck for lack of approval by Manitoba and New Brunswick.

The vast majority of Canadians reckon they have better things to do than to ponder Meech Lake. They have their own personal struggles and joys, and the Constitution seems remote from both.

And yet Meech Lake is a dagger pointed at the nation's heart, not because of its intricacies, about which the vast majority is and will remain unaware, but because it has the unique capacity in our current climate of insidious and subtle discontent to remind English and French Canadians of their growing lack of interest in, and mutual irritation with, each other.

As such, Meech Lake bids fair to become a clarion call for demons of the heart. Without knowing or caring much about its component parts, Canadians on both sides of the divide can read into Meech Lake their accumulated grievances.

In Quebec, Meech Lake will be seen as the irreducible minimum for further accommodation; in English Canada, or at least in large parts of it, Meech Lake has already become a maximal and therefore unacceptable demand.

The more Meech Lake is pressed upon English Canadians as something indispensable to Quebec, the greater the resistance is likely to become because there is a fatigue—where there is not hostility—with accommodating a part of Canada that manifests so little interest and conviction in the aspirations of the rest of the country. Conversely, the greater the hostility to Meech Lake, the greater the sense in Quebec that the rest of Canada remains implacably unwilling to accommodate the distinctiveness of Quebec within the federal system.

Meech Lake, then, is loaded down with two different sets of emotional baggage whose weight will grow as the deadline for ratification draws nearer (with apologies to Gordon Robertson, who argues Jun. 23, 1990, is not a deadline). That weight grows with each declaration of the dire consequences for rejecting Meech Lake.

Each time a leading politician puts the argument in terms of Meech Lake or disaster, Quebeckers are reminded that Meech Lake will be the one and only litmus test of English-Canadian accommodation, and English Canadians recall that Meech Lake is the latest in a series of what many of them consider endless and profoundly fatiguing demands for accommodation coming from the same place.

Meech Lake might yet be saved, for better or worse, if English Canadians believed its acceptance would truly mean that Quebec would become psychologically a more committed part of Canada, instead of believing that the accord will consecrate constitutionally the already widespread indifference in Quebec to the rest of Canada.

Meech Lake cannot be wished away. It is the receptacle for conflicting national visions and gnawing mutual irritations. These visions and irritations, lying just beneath the surface of public discourse, carry the seeds of abrasive discord.

Meech Lake Visions *(June 23, 1989)*

The Meech Lake constitutional accord, Canada's most boring and explosive subject, represents the minimum constitutional demands the rest of Canada will likely receive from a Quebec government.

Anyone even vaguely familiar with Quebec during and since the Quiet Revolution of the sixties knows previous Quebec provincial governments have demanded more.

This comparison is not intended to commend Meech Lake, merely to describe it. Meech Lake may be a minimalist set of demands from a historical perspective, but that provides cold comfort for the growing number of English Canadians who dislike it. If yesterday's Gallup poll is accurate, a sharp deterioration in support for Meech Lake has occurred in English Canada since the beginning of 1989. Why?

The simple explanation might be that more English Canadians have bought copies of the accord, studied it, and decided they don't like it. But that presumes thousands of people are like retired judge Marjorie Bowker who made a splash during the election campaign with interviews and writings against the free-trade agreement. To state the possibility is to laugh.

Nor have Canadians read much about Meech Lake in the media, which has relegated the issue to the back burner for lack of any recent, dramatic developments. After all, Gallup showed 40 per cent of respondents without the foggiest idea of what Meech Lake is all about.

No, the souring of English-Canadian opinion toward Meech Lake is part of a more subtle and insidious irritation with anything that smacks of Quebec. But it's also part of the vacuum that surrounds Meech Lake's chief federal proponent, Prime Minister Brian Mulroney.

Mr. Mulroney has certainly been delivering speeches about Meech Lake, encouraging Canadians to accept the accord. So far, however, his exhortations have produced nothing but sullen resentment.

Mr. Mulroney may believe deeply in Meech Lake, but plenty of people don't believe his sincerity. To be more precise: they may accept that he believes in Meech Lake, but for the wrong reasons.

There's a widespread feeling among the disenchanted that Meech Lake represents another Mulroney bow toward Quebec rather than an integral part of a coherent vision of Canada. True, Mr. Mulroney pleads with English Canadians that alienating Quebec from the formal constitutional arrangements is unfair and dangerous. But increasingly the question is being asked: if Meech Lake passes where will it lead?

What a campaigning George Bush, admittedly in another context, called the "vision thing" now enters the Meech Lake equation. Adore or revile him, Pierre Trudeau had a vision of Canada and Quebec's place within it. Mr. Mulroney knows he wants Quebec in Canada—no one can gainsay his desire—but for what purposes?

Meech Lake is rooted in the past practices and intellectual approaches of "co-operative federalism," or what former prime minister Joe Clark called governing a "community of communities." It's the kind of federalism—indeed, the only kind—Quebec provincial politicians have ever demanded. The response to those demands has been either to accommodate them or to blunt them, as Mr. Trudeau did by appealing over the heads of the provincial politicians and their supporters directly to Quebeckers.

"Community of communities" did Mr. Clark political harm in his contests against Mr. Trudeau. But at least Mr. Clark tried to articulate a "vision."

At the moment, Meech Lake bespeaks only one vision to many English Canadians: yet another accommodation to Quebec. If they could be persuaded Meech Lake is really about conflicting visions of federalism in which all regions should be interested, then the debate would be fully joined about the "vision thing" and Meech Lake might stand a chance.

His Feelings Then, His Remarks Now

(January 4, 1990)

The start of a new year is as good a time as any to implore Prime Minister Brian Mulroney to stop his outrageous and untruthful distortions about the constitutional reform of 1981-82.

For the past year, while the Meech Lake debate heated up, Mr. Mulroney repeatedly complained about the 1981-82 patriation package because it proceeded against the wishes of the Quebec government and National Assembly.

In his year-end interview with the CBC, he said of the package, "The exclusion of Quebec and the inclusion of the 'notwithstanding' clause were two fundamental flaws that should, in my judgment, have prevented it from going ahead at that time."

When the Prime Minister gets going on what happened in 1981-82, his rhetorical juices start flowing. He describes Liberals wearing tuxedos, popping champagne corks, congratulating themselves on having shoved something down Quebec's throat. In the CBC interview, he gave a milder version of the same rhetoric: "If Queen's Park and the people of Ontario had said, 'We don't want this constitution,' do you think the Queen would have come over here and there would have been a big party in front of Parliament Hill with everybody in striped pants celebrating a constitution without the industrial heartland of Ontario? The answer is clearly no."

Now, just a minute here. For better or worse, I keep confidences. But this outrageous distortion is too great to let go unchallenged.

I remember as if it were yesterday a long lunch at the Mount Royal Club in Montreal in January 1981, with private citizen Brian Mulroney, in which he went on at great length against the "community of communities" approach to Canada of then Conservative Leader Joe Clark. In the course of that animated soliloquy, Mr. Mulroney said emphatically that Prime Minister Pierre Trudeau, faced with a separatist government in Quebec, would have no choice but to bring home the Constitution over Quebec's objections.

Later on, when the patriation debate heated up, Mr. Mulroney again said privately that he supported what the Liberals were doing, given the circumstances that presented themselves at the time in Quebec. For Mr. Mulroney to say now that the whole exercise was done by people celebrating "in striped pants" is a gross perversion of his own attitudes.

The historical revisionism of his own attitude toward the patriation package introduces an unfortunate element of partisan politics into what should be a non-partisan debate. After all, Mr. Mulroney was greatly helped in the early days of Meech Lake by the support of Liberal Leader John Turner.

The partisanship hurts, too, because the more Mr. Mulroney indulges in revisionism, the more he bids people to believe Meech Lake is just that: a partisan exercise. It's hard enough selling Meech Lake these days without asking Canadians, three-quarters of whom are telling pollsters they don't support the government, that it's part of a Conservative Party strategy.

Who knows? Maybe Mr. Mulroney is trying to prepare the ground for a debate with Jean Chrétien should the former Trudeau minister and major player in the patriation battle become Liberal leader. Maybe Mr. Mulroney thinks he can wipe the floor with Mr. Chrétien in Quebec by reminding people of the bad old days of 1981-82. If so, he is making a serious mistake, because whatever the partisan opportunities may be in that province, Meech Lake is in trouble in English Canada, not Quebec.

New Year's is a time for resolutions of improved behaviour. Mr. Mulroney should resolve that every time he feels the urge to engage in another bout of revisionism, he should bite his tongue.

As the Meech Clock Ticks *(April 3, 1990)*

New Brunswick Premier Frank McKenna finally blinked.

After a long period of riding the Meech Lake tiger, Mr. McKenna suddenly discovered that he, and the country for that matter, might wind up inside. So his "compromise" proposals designed to "save" Meech Lake are now before his own legislature and a Commons committee. The proposals have been justifiably praised by those who wish to save the constitutional accord, and predictably damned by those who dislike the accord.

If Meech Lake fails, Mr. McKenna's "compromise" effort notwithstanding (dare I use the phrase?), the burden of failure must rest heavily upon the Premier's shoulders. Lest we forget, it was Mr. McKenna, more than any other politician in the months following the negotiation of the accord, who derailed the momentum toward ratification.

Meech Lake was signed by Mr. McKenna's predecessor, Conservative Premier Richard Hatfield, a veteran of constitutional negotiations. The signatories of Meech Lake agreed to seek legislative ratification "as soon as possible." But Mr.

Hatfield's star was waning badly, and within a short time Mr. McKenna won a provincial election fought, in part, on his opposition to Meech Lake.

From the day of his election, the Meech Lake ball of string began unwinding. Well does a wandering columnist remember being in Fredericton six months or so after the election, listening to the defiant words of Mr. McKenna and his aides: we've got five years in power, constitutional amendments require unanimity, the population is on our side, Ottawa and the other provinces must come to us.

They were brave, cocky words, and they ring hollow. The words, then as now, are true, but they are not wise. Like Meech Lake, the country's ball of string has unwound in the meantime, and now, with his Acadian population supporting Meech Lake, Mr. McKenna offers his compromise. Finally, after so much speech-making, so many interviews, so many meetings, the Premier has put his ideas on paper.

Mr. McKenna and those who helped craft his package have grasped the only reasonable formula for a Meech Lake compromise. Boiled down, his package contains three parts. First, a series of reassurances for groups that feel their rights would be abridged by Meech Lake. Second, a firmer commitment (presumably to evolve through the Commons committee's report) to an elected Senate. Third, a reassertion of the federal government's role in protecting official-language minorities.

True, there are some clever and useful add-on bits about letting the territories eventually become provinces without unanimous consent and getting the infernal fisheries dossier off the constitutional negotiating table, where it should never have been. But the essence of the McKenna package remains the three core elements.

Buying into this package will require compromise from Quebec and Manitoba. Premier Robert Bourassa, spooked by polls and the Parti Québécois, would have to accept Ottawa's ability to "promote" official languages, including English in Quebec. Premier Gary Filmon and one of the opposition leaders in Manitoba will have to accept that they get half a loaf. They get reassurances for worried groups (especially important for the New Democratic Party), a stronger affirmation of Ottawa's role and, presumably, a forthcoming commitment to Senate reform.

But in the hardened climate of the times, compromise brings risks. These are politicians worried about re-election, busy jockeying for position and preoccupied with fiddling while the country burns.

Consider Gary Doer, the NDP leader in Manitoba. Mr. Doer raced into the television studios, one eye on the camera and the other on local politics, to denounce the whole exercise. No compromise there.

A small man on a small screen in a country growing smaller by the day.

The Climate of Indifference *(April 19, 1990)*

A political meteor called Pierre Trudeau recently flashed again across the Canadian political sky, leaving a more dazzling impression in English Canada than in French Canada.

In lambasting free trade and the Meech Lake accord, the former prime minister made common cause with many English Canadians. In French Canada, his criticisms fell on barren ground.

For an entire generation of English Canadians, Pierre Trudeau defined what French Canadians "wanted," or at least what they should want and receive. Thousands of English Canadians bought his vision of Canada and the solutions he proposed to the "Quebec problem."

Five years after he left office, Mr. Trudeau's persona still excites interest everywhere—even in Quebec, where his rare public appearances receive extensive media coverage. But while the vision still lives in parts of English Canada, it only flickers in Quebec—perhaps because no prominent French-Canadian politician defends it any more. Once Jean Chrétien becomes Liberal Party leader, this might change. That's what the Trudeauites and Chrétien supporters believe.

Unfortunately for Mr. Trudeau, some of his former Liberal Cabinet colleagues and MPs from Quebec don't agree with his Meech Lake criticisms. Marc Lalonde, Donald Johnston and Mr. Chrétien are on side; Francis Fox, Monique Bégin and André Ouellet are not. That Mr. Trudeau cannot even carry his former colleagues *en masse* speaks eloquently, if sadly, to his marginality in his home province.

That marginality speaks to a change of perhaps historic proportions in Quebec. For generations, from Louis-Hippolyte LaFontaine through George-Étienne Cartier, Wilfrid Laurier, Ernest Lapointe and Louis St. Laurent to Pierre Trudeau, French Canadians used their extraordinary political sophistication to elect both nationalist premiers and federal politicians who would make common cause with sympathetic English Canadians to defend French Canadians' interests in Ottawa and throughout Canada.

Meech's rejection, and the debate so far, has made making common cause seem a dubious bet to French-speaking Quebeckers. A federalist politician in the LaFontaine–Laurier–Trudeau mould now seems less important. Brian Mulroney doesn't fill the bill, because he has made common cause with nationalists such as Environment Minister Lucien Bouchard, who sees his role as representing Quebec in Ottawa rather than Ottawa (and Canada) in Quebec. Perhaps Mr. Chrétien's arrival will alter public attitudes. Perhaps.

Quebec has never understood English Canada, because of either profound indifference or the stereotype that English Canada is a homogeneous entity. A majority of Quebeckers could rally behind free trade and Meech Lake. English Canada—a collection of ethnicities, regions and ideological currents—was torn up by both.

Quebec's sophistication, the natural outgrowth of a minority's instinct for maximizing leverage, infuriates English Canadians who cannot themselves act in a similar fashion. Assuming that Mr. Mulroney and Mr. Chrétien fight the next election—and that the next government lasts until 1998—Canada will have had prime ministers from Quebec for thirty years, except for the Joe Clark and John Turner hiccups.

This grates on many English Canadians. Imagine, for example, the reaction in the American South or far West if for thirty years every president had come from New York State or the Boston–New York–Washington corridor.

The sad fact these days is that Quebeckers aren't interested in federalists eager to make accommodations with English Canadians, and a growing number of English Canadians aren't interested in accommodations anyway.

The State(s) of the Nation(s) *(April 20, 1990)*

Asa Meech, an American Congregational minister, left his homeland near the end of the eighteenth century, disgusted by the bickering among constituent parts of his country.

Seeking peace, Mr. Meech settled near a hamlet called Ottawa on a lake that now bears his name and that of a constitutional accord straining the Canadian fabric. On his tombstone are chiselled ironic words: "I ask not to stay where storm after storm rises o'er the way."

If old Asa could rise from the grave, he would see nothing but "storm after storm" these days. And he would hear John Buchanan, Premier of Nova Scotia, mentioning aloud the politically unthinkable—that his province, and others in Atlantic Canada, might have to join Asa's former country, the United States, should Canada fail.

Of course, Mr. Buchanan is way ahead of himself. He may even have been consciously contributing to the strategy of raising the national temperature so that a last-minute compromise on Meech might be forged.

Canada isn't done yet. Quebec sovereignty isn't a sure thing, although an astonishing number of English Canadians are talking themselves into accepting independence as a foregone conclusion. A recent poll for *L'Actualité*, the Quebec *Maclean's*, does show an upsurge in support for independence, although the same poll demonstrates that economic uncertainties associated with independence still make French-speaking Quebeckers wary.

But if it should come to Quebec independence, then Mr. Buchanan is right. Nova Scotia, and the rest of what remained of Canada, would have to consider three options, one of which would be joining the United States.

Canada *sans* Quebec could keep going like East and West Pakistan, a totally unnatural country that eventually split into Pakistan and Bangladesh. Or, it could split into a series of quasi-independent states loosely joined in a common market with a common currency, something like AtlanticCan, Ontario and WestCan. Or, parts of what remained of Canada could throw in their lot with the Americans, provided the Americans would have them.

There are, of course, variations on these three options. But at the very least, Quebec's departure would force what remained of Canada into agonizing debates about its future.

In the Quebec referendum of 1980, the Parti Québécois government asked for a mandate to negotiate "sovereignty-association." The PQ's white paper preceding the referendum spoke at length about continued economic ties with Canada. Quebec Premier Robert Bourassa has recently ruminated about an "economic superstructure" between Quebec and the rest of Canada.

"Sovereignty-association" and "economic superstructure," whatever their economic merits, are political attempts to reassure Quebeckers that political change would mean limited economic dislocation. That's fine for Quebec. But an idea that has seemed axiomatic in Quebec—a continued strong economic link with Canada—would be hotly debated in Canada.

Before the referendum, for example, many English-Canadian premiers insisted they would not necessarily be interested in a tight economic association with an independent Quebec. Maybe they were bluffing, since to have said otherwise might have helped the secessionists.

It isn't axiomatic that what remained of English Canada would rush to embrace a sovereign Quebec. Ontario might be so inclined, but it would find itself pulled between Quebec and the West. In Western Canada, citizens might see their economic and political future elsewhere, either with the United States or as an independent confederation.

Mind you, with free trade a reality between the United States and Canada, Quebec might not be quite so eager for economic ties with Canada. And maybe the rest of Canada, where at least one premier has spoken the unthinkable, wouldn't be too interested in tight economic ties with Quebec.

Among the Guilty Parties *(May 23, 1990)*

Atta boy, Clyde. Way to go, Sharon. Nice reasoning, Frank. Well done, Gary and Gary. You're now reaping what you sowed, a whirlwind in Quebec.

Polls show a majority of Quebeckers for sovereignty. The Parti Québécois can't believe its good fortune. Three Quebec Tory MPs, including Environment Minister Lucien Bouchard, have resigned, and more will undoubtedly follow.

All this, and more, could easily have been predicted by those with the wit and heart to understand the country and Quebec. But Newfoundland Premier Clyde Wells, New Brunswick Premier Frank McKenna, and Manitoba politicians Gary Filmon, Sharon Carstairs and Gary Doer decided Quebec's minimalist demands in the Meech Lake accord were too much.

They were told, by English Canadians of good faith and superior under-standing of Quebec, and by French-speaking Quebeckers what would likely happen. But they did not listen.

Their opposition sent a clear signal to moderate Quebec nationalists, and those of stronger stuff, that Canada could not reconcile itself to contemporary Quebec. Their opposition signalled that a reconciliation would not occur on reasonable terms asked for by Quebec, but on terms dictated by Canadians elsewhere.

Whether Meech Lake passes now or not is almost—not totally, but almost—irrelevant. Huge and probably irreparable, damage has been done to the national fabric. The English-Canadian tribal drums beaten by the recalcitrant provincial politicians are now being met by tribal drums in Quebec. If Meech Lake yet passes, it will give federalists at least a tattered flag to wave in Quebec; if it fails, they will be waving the white flag.

The tragedy of our current discontents, especially of Quebec's retreat into tribalism, is that English-Canadian reaction has been the root cause.

In the mid-1980s, Quebec nationalism was quiescent. The referendum had drained Quebeckers and deflated the *indépendentistes*. The PQ had split into warring factions, and the Liberals returned to power, offering Canada a modest set of constitutional demands.

At the time, what became the Meech Lake accord excited little interest in Quebec. The modest package seemed to fit perfectly the mood of "depoliti-cization," or disinterest in things political. The overwhelming mood in Quebec in those now faraway days was simply: let's put the constitutional issue to bed, make peace with ourselves within Canada, and get on with other matters.

First, newly elected Premier Frank McKenna, then the New Democrats of Manitoba, then all the parties of Manitoba, then Newfoundland Premier Clyde Wells—and English-Canadian public opinion—turned thumbs down on Meech Lake. They had their own visions of Canada, their own provincial electorates to placate, and, for the Liberals, the prospect of a new federal leader, Jean Chrétien, to demolish Meech Lake, banish the Tories and put Canada back together again.

Similarly, Quebec's language legislation outlawing English on exterior signs dealt a crippling blow to moderate English-Canadian opinion. English-only resolutions in Sault Ste. Marie and Thunder Bay added logs to the fire. All the other problems of the Mulroney government—the GST, western alienation, deficit reduction—eroded its credibility in the country.

Meech Lake, then, began as a modest constitutional settlement. It has now become a monster, shattering a government, driving Canadians apart, and leading inexorably to the end of Canada as we have known it.

History will judge Clyde Wells, Sharon Carstairs, Gary Filmon, Gary Doer and Frank McKenna with the utmost severity.

CHARLOTTETOWN ACCORD

Ottawa Tries to Find Halfway-House Solutions to an Insoluble Problem (February 5, 1991)

Yogi Berra, the renowned American philosopher ("It ain't over till it's over"), has become the federal government's guru. Understandably reluctant to admit the obvious—that Quebec wants out of Canada except on unacceptable terms—the government now draws inspiration from Yogi's aphorism.

Yogi, who ought to know, witnessed a few late-inning miracles during a life of baseball. But he also knew, without coining a phrase to crystallize the thought, that heroics are a poor strategy for winning pennants. Commitment and talent count for more during a long season.

Yogi understood the mechanics of the curve ball and the tricks of a spitter, but he never learned much about asymmetrical federalism, paramountcy and concurrency. In trying to save Canada (and their jobs), ministers in the Mulroney government and senior civil servants are playing seriously with these ideas.

The Mulroneyites look at the constitutional impasse and see two irreconcilable visions. Outside Quebec, most citizens believe all provinces must be treated equally by the Constitution and the law—that is, *de jure*. Inside Quebec, the majority thinks Quebec is different and should be allowed to express that difference by exercising powers other provinces don't have.

Meech Lake smashed against the first of these visions—equality of the provinces—because too many people feared the "distinct society" clause would give Quebec special legal status, a political no-no elsewhere. Meech

Lake also failed, among other reasons, because too many people elsewhere feared an excessive weakening of central authority.

So now the Mulroneyites, reflecting on the demise of Meech, are ready to give every province the massive decentralization of powers it thinks Quebec must have to remain part of something called Canada. Not every province, of course, will want those powers, so here's where Yogi and the rest of us must brush up on concurrency and paramountcy.

Ottawa's thinking now runs like this: offer large swaths of federal jurisdiction to every province. They will all therefore be legally the same. *De jure* equality! No special status! No Meech Lake problem! Whew!

These powers will be considered concurrent ones—are you listening, Yogi?—which can be exercised by Ottawa or by the provinces, although the provinces will have first call on them. That's paramountcy, Yogi.

Quebec will take everything on offer. Other provinces will take some of what's offered. Little provinces will likely take nothing, preferring that Ottawa keep running things. This gives Quebec the decentralization it seeks, offers flexibility for others and reassures those who want a strong central government that they will retain one. *De jure* equality; *de facto* asymmetry, or special powers. Neat, eh?

The whole exercise runs along the lines of Queen's Professor Thomas Courchene's latest thinking, which he called a "community of Canadas" for his presentation to the Bélanger–Campeau commission. A few other academics have bought into the broad lines of this thinking. The Quebec Liberal Party's Allaire report hints at extensive concurrency and provincial paramountcy. Mulroney ministers are already touting the idea as the only one that can keep Quebec in Canada on terms acceptable elsewhere.

Yogi, the whole idea is a crock. It's a fancy recipe for a checkerboard Canada far more mixed up than anything that we have now or that could be workable in a country worth the name. It raises the question of what role Quebec MPs will play when matters arise in Ottawa over which Quebec has jurisdiction. It's a recipe for two classes of MPs, and resulting confusion.

If a country is a country, it must have some sort of national standards. This proposal offers none, save what provinces might agree to among themselves. And we know how they like to co-operate: the Maritimes and Newfoundland over fish, Ontario and Quebec over construction, Quebec versus the rest over medical fees, all of them over beer, professional regulations, out-of-province tuition fees etc. etc. etc.

Where would the sense of citizenship, or belonging, be in such a crazy-quilt country? Without that sense of belonging—and the lack of that sense is why Quebec has already separated psychologically—a country will be internally torn up.

What the Mulroneyites are cooking up won't fly, or shouldn't fly, in the rest of Canada, and it will probably be treated with the greatest suspicion in Quebec. It's a halfway-house, over-intellectualized non-solution to an insoluble problem: the gap between what a psychologically separated Quebec demands and what Canada is prepared to concede.

A Hyra-Headed Monster of a System Is in the Works *(May 22, 1992)*

The constitutional deal now being negotiated, and perhaps later submitted to a national plebiscite, will produce the world's most complicated system of government.

If it ever becomes law, it will make effective government next to impossible. National programs will be extremely difficult to conceive, let alone implement. Governments will be checked and balanced and checked again.

What is emerging is a neo-conservative's dream and a social democrat's nightmare. Anyone who wishes to use creatively and actively the Canadian state for whatever purposes should draw a deep breath before signing on to this deal.

The system now has some checks and balances to parliamentary supremacy. These include, of course, the opposition, occasional outbursts of activity from an appointed Senate, the common law, the force of public opinion and the activities of interest groups.

Starting in the early 1980s, with the Charter of Rights and Freedoms, a new obstacle was put in the way of parliamentary majorities. The Charter greatly expanded the scope for judicial review and encouraged interest-group formation and activity. Matters that once were considered political questions now regularly come before the courts.

And now, after the dramatic changes heralded by the Charter, comes the emerging constitutional deal. It includes devolution of power to provinces, aboriginal self-government and Senate reform.

All three changes are designed to make government more accountable, representative and fair. They may well accomplish these objectives but, coupled with the Charter, they will erect large roadblocks in the way of creative, national government.

Start with the Senate. Its powers are considerable, but they are seldom used, because the appointed senators, despite periodic friskiness, realize their lack of political legitimacy.

An elected Senate would have no problems of legitimacy. The new Senate would use its powers. On paper, these might be fewer than those of the existing Senate; in fact, they would be used more frequently.

The chances are excellent, given the history of counter-cyclical voting in Canada, that the Senate would be dominated by parties other than the majority one in the House of Commons. At the very least, therefore, getting a bill through Parliament will become more difficult; at worst, deadlock will arise.

As for the devolution of powers, discussed this week in Montreal by federal and provincial representatives, the negotiations are a one-way street. Ottawa is proposing to give, the provinces to take. Rather than a careful consideration of which level of government can best do what, the negotiations are essentially about how much to give to Quebec and/or the other provinces.

The more devolution in what is already the world's most de-centralized federation, the less likely that national initiatives will be possible. Couple devolution with an opting-out provision for provinces when Ottawa acts in areas of provincial jurisdiction, and another significant obstacle has been placed in the way of federal action.

Aboriginal self-government, however it emerges, will be a variation on the devolution theme: more power and money from Ottawa to a new level of government. Native self-government may be desirable in and of itself, because previous states of affairs have failed to satisfy aboriginals, but the effect on national policies will be to diffuse them in a welter of new inter-governmental arrangements.

The Charter, Senate reform, devolution and aboriginal self-government represent four new institutional changes that, taken together, will give Canada a complicated, highly bureaucratic, extremely expensive and exceedingly inefficient form of government. A hyra-headed monster of a system is in the works.

What the constitutional changes have indirectly in common is a distrust of the exercise of power by parliamentary majorities controlled by Cabinets and the Prime Minister's Office. Dissatisfied with the existing checks and balances, Canadians are about to implant new ones in their system of government. Only later will they see how difficult this will be to operate, because the balance between effectiveness and representativeness has been tipped too far one way.

Those who dislike activist government will rejoice, except for the costliness of the new system. Those who want creative, vigorous government will eventually weep.

It May Sound Good, But a Triple-E
Could Be Double Trouble *(June 2, 1992)*

Plenty of Canadians, when asked about a triple-E, will respond that their shoe size is double-B or just plain C. Like a triple-E shoe, a triple-E Senate will be too big for comfort, and those who sit there will soon become too big for their britches.

The tiny minority of Canadians following the current constitutional negotiations will know that Senate reform has become a reef on which the talks are stalled and may yet founder. The country, however, has been on the reef before. In the conferences that preceded Confederation in 1867, delegates spent more time thrashing out the form and powers of the Senate than any other issue.

Nor is an elected Senate something new. When the Fathers of Confederation chewed over alternatives, a minority favoured electing senators, as a few provincial assemblies did in pre-Confederation days. Eventually, the appointed method won out, and Canada has been saddled with nominated senators ever since.

Now the appointed Senate is completely discredited and the cry is up for an elected replacement. That very fact—the election of senators—will give the body credibility and legitimacy. Election, in turn, will embolden senators to use such powers as they have.

Those pressing for an "effective" Senate want considerable powers for it: not just 180-day periods of delay, but real blocking power over most of what emanates from the House of Commons. Indeed, the whole logic of an elected Senate in a parliamentary system—as opposed to a division-of-powers system in which senators can initiate independent legislation—is to block, thwart, modify or alter what the government has managed to get through the House.

Listening to the debate about the triple-E Senate and its watered-down alternatives, the message is clear. An elected Senate would stop nefarious policies from being imposed on recalcitrant and usually small provinces. The National Energy Program, the Goods and Services Tax, and federal reductions in provincial transfers are often offered as examples of dangerous, iniquitous policies that never would have passed an elected Senate.

But coins have two sides, of course, and power can be used in unexpected ways. The blocking power of an elected Senate will prevent undesirable results, and thereby offer some regional protection against the "tyranny of the majority." But depending upon the coalitions and parties, it will also prevent results eagerly desired by the very regions keenest on an elected Senate.

Take, for example, free trade with the United States, a policy devoutly desired by Alberta, champion of triple-E. Had the free-trade agreement been submitted to a triple-E, it probably would have been defeated. Why? Because electorates in at least seven provinces were opposed in the majority to the deal. The Ontario electorate was sharply divided. Only two electorates—Quebec and Alberta—were strongly in favour.

Or take something such as transportation de-regulation, another policy thrust sought for decades by Alberta. That, too, would have been questioned by the four Atlantic provinces, Ontario, Quebec and perhaps other western provinces.

Rare are the governments that enjoy mid-term popularity. Yet many Senate elections will be held at mid-term, under the various proposals being considered in the constitutional talks, thus increasing the likelihood of an upper house controlled by parties opposed to the government.

Therefore, an "effective" Senate is almost certainly destined to produce continuous quarrelling and deadlock between the two houses of Parliament. For an example of what lies ahead, just look at the U.S. system. There, periodic bouts of activist government, usually following a presidential sweep, are followed by prolonged periods of inactivity arising from the inability of the administration and Congress to work together.

In Japan these days, the Liberal Democratic Party's loss of control of the upper house has all but paralyzed the government on such crucial issues as world-trade negotiations on agriculture and committing Japanese troops to peacekeeping.

A triple-E Senate, or variations thereto, may well prevent dastardly things from happening in Ottawa and therefore be an improvement in some eyes on the existing system. But a fundamental question is whether a pure or modified triple-E Senate might prevent anything from happening in Ottawa.

Just Take an Anti-Constitutionalitis Pill and Lay Off the Amendments *(October 20, 1992)*

If the No side prevails next Monday, those who defeated the Charlottetown accord will offer a variety of suggestions for what to do next. Chances are, all will be wrong.

Interest groups will claim the process did not include them. Change the process, let us in, and constitutional amendments will work. Indian leaders will offer similar arguments. If Charlottetown had been written differently, it would have passed.

Defenders of the status quo, mostly disciples of former prime minister Pierre Trudeau, will reshape his assertion that the changes he wrought in 1981-82 were set to last for a thousand years and should not be altered.

Still others will insist that the Constitution is inherently so divisive that the status quo should be left alone. Reform Party Leader Preston Manning's call for a five-year moratorium on constitutional talk will resonate loudly after October 26.

As a matter of political fact, nothing will happen on this front in the months after October 26. The next federal election must be held by the autumn of 1993, and no constitutional amendments could be negotiated by then. The process is too time-consuming and complicated.

Similarly, if the No side wins, Prime Minister Brian Mulroney will have twice failed in his objective of changing the Constitution. The country will not offer him a third chance. Canada needs fresh leadership—in Ottawa, in Quebec and perhaps in other provinces and in aboriginal organizations—before debate resumes.

So the country will have an opportunity, imposed by electoral circumstances, to stand back from the constitutional fray. It should seize the chance to rethink completely the assumptions of the past twenty-five years, during which Canadians have failed six times to change the Constitution to the satisfaction of all players.

Canada has caught a bad case of constitutionalitis, a disease that can be fatal if not treated properly but is controllable with the correct remedies.

The disease has its roots in the widespread assumption among political elites (aboriginal and non-aboriginal) and interest groups that the pressures for change in Canada can best be dealt with by formal constitutional amendments. That assumption cannot easily be uprooted.

The Charter of Rights and Freedoms, now the country's most important national symbol, has spawned a panoply of groups who talk of "rights." They look to the Charter and the courts to affirm and expand their rights. By definition, since the Charter is part of the Constitution, they play politics by legal means.

Aboriginals have invested their dreams in constitutional recognition of their rights in order to put their relations with other Canadians on a new footing.

Quebec nationalists seek constitutional changes to give symbolic and practical effect to their aspirations. Secessionists want complete change: the creation of two sovereign states in the northern part of North America.

Politicians, too, have sought the holy grail of amendments for their purposes: more power for the governments they run, reinforcement of economic and political objectives (a social charter, economic union, equalization), and an effective response to the place of Quebec and Western Canada in Confederation.

The detoxification of these groups and individuals will not be easy. They are hooked on the Constitution, and many will not interpret the defeat of Charlottetown as further proof that amendments tear the country apart. They will not understand that the inherent divisiveness of such amendments has been increased by two new precedents.

The first is that the number of participants in constitutional reform has grown from eleven first ministers to include aboriginal and territorial leaders. Indeed, the Native Women's Association of Canada will claim it must be included if there is a next time, thus bringing the participants to eighteen.

The second precedent is the referendum. Although not required by law, the fact that a referendum is being held on the Charlottetown accord will make it politically impossible for any future national government not to hold one when it seeks constitutional changes.

These difficulties, old and new, should convince Canadians to fight the disease of constitutionalitis, even if some groups remain so hooked on the process that they continue to press for further changes.

A Country of Tolerance and Compromise, or Seething Passion and Resentment?

(October 23, 1992)

Those who negotiated the Charlottetown accord believed they had accomplished the impossible. Elite accommodation had triumphed. First ministers and aboriginal and territorial leaders had almost miraculously agreed among themselves. That agreement was then approved by the federal Liberals and New Democrats, most of the provincial opposition parties, the bulk of the nation's newspapers, business and labour leaders.

The elites had money, access to the media and organizational talent. They covered almost the entire formal political spectrum, from the Canadian Labour Congress to the Business Council on National Issues, from the New Democratic Party to the Conservatives. Probably not since the decision to enter the Second World War had Canada's institutional elites been so united on a vital national issue.

Arrayed against this elite consensus outside Quebec were puny political formations: the Reform Party, running fourth in national polls in English-speaking Canada; the second and third parties in British Columbia (Liberals and Socreds); the third party in Manitoba (Liberals); a smattering of media voices; and several vocal but not very representative interest groups, such as the National Action Committee on the Status of Women.

In Quebec, the balance of forces was almost even as the campaign began. The provincial political and media elites were split. Most business people were pro-Charlottetown; all major union leaders were opposed. The mass of the artists and intellectuals were committed secessionists and therefore hostile to Charlottetown.

So in Quebec, a fierce battle beckoned. But elsewhere, the elites had so many overwhelming advantages that it was easy to lose sight of one overwhelming liability—that the elites themselves were resented.

Elites kept talking about Canada as a country of tolerance and compromise, putative national characteristics reflected in the elite consensus at Charlottetown. The trouble was that this view misunderstood the real country, where tolerance and compromise had long since yielded to a seething mass of regional, class, ethnic and linguistic passions usually directed against other parts of Canada.

For example, the palpable resentment outside Quebec that the province was the spoiled child of Confederation met the equally rooted belief in Quebec that the rest of Canada did not understand its ambitions.

Many in the rest of Canada thought, rightly or not, that they understood those ambitions perfectly well—namely, to continue wringing concessions from federalism without yielding anything in return. Only if Quebec's caterwauling, bellyaching and blackmailing were firmly resisted could Canada's unity be assured.

When former prime minister Pierre Trudeau described his province's attitude as "gimme, gimme, gimme," whoops of agreement resounded throughout the rest of Canada, even from those who had disagreed with almost everything Mr. Trudeau had done as prime minister.

This kowtowing to Quebec, as it was seen by many outside the province, had been part of elite preoccupations for a generation. And now with the Charlottetown accord, as with Meech Lake, the rest of Canada seized a perfect opportunity to draw a line in the sand. The elites might be in an accommodating mood, but that was their problem. The elites might claim dire consequences if accommodation failed, but that too was their problem.

Most No supporters did not accept the legitimacy of Quebec's beefs, did not see a link between their vote and either economic or political instability, resented the attention lavished on constitutional matters, preferred the insistence on their own view of Canada over any other, and took their revenge on all the elites who seemed to know better.

Then, too, there was the fierce anger directed against Prime Minister Brian Mulroney for a multitude of reasons, and the more diffuse anger directed against all politicians, regardless of stripe. The political elites sensed their unpopularity and tried to deflect it by appointing eminent "ordinary Canadians" to carry the Yes banner.

But the media kept lavishing attention on political figures who, let it be said, knew the constitutional file better than most of the eminent "ordinary" Canadians, partly because the politicians had been mixed up in the Constitution for much of their careers.

The elites—political, business, labour, press—led. Alas for them, their own standing meant that not enough of the people followed.

Who Would Be an Elected Politician in This Corrosive, Mean-Spirited Age?

(October 28, 1992)

No means No. For some, it means No to the Charlottetown accord. For others, it means No to Brian Mulroney's leadership, or No to the political elites. No to Quebec's demands outside the province; No inside Quebec to the vision of the province beyond its borders.

No means No to formal constitutional negotiations for a very long time. No to putative betters telling the masses how to think. No to any tampering with Canadians' beloved Charter of Rights and Freedoms. No to aboriginal self-government enshrined in the Constitution, a No abetted by the Indians' own internal divisions about Charlottetown.

No means No to any link drawn between constitutional debate and economic or political uncertainty. No to constitutional compromise. No to any equation between constitutional reform and the country's future. No to special status for Quebec; No inside Quebec to equality of provinces.

No means Yes, however, to interest groups and factionalized parties outside Quebec. No means Yes to the Association for the Preservation of English in Canada, the Confederation of Regions Party, the Reform Party, the National Action Committee on the Status of Women, the Native Women's Association of Canada, the Committee for an Independent Canada, arts lobby groups, instantaneous and issue-specific groups whose great victory will quite reasonably embolden them to believe they speak for the Canadian public.

And who can deny them their triumphal interpretation, for they met the established political order on the field of constitutional combat and won hands down? Who of repute now contemplating a career in public life would opt for the realm of elected office when such triumphs lie in store for those who join and finance interest groups?

An old saw suggests we get the government we deserve. Never will this be more apparent than in the wake of the shattering rejection of the political leadership.

The rejection was total, extending far beyond Mr. Mulroney. NDP Leader Audrey McLaughlin could not even carry her own Yukon constituency; NDP Premiers Mike Harcourt of British Columbia and Roy Romanow of Saskatchewan were crushed in their own provinces. Ontario NDP Premier Bob Rae saw a twenty-point lead evaporate in his province. Trade-union leaders and the NDP in Ontario said Yes to Charlottetown; their own supporters said No.

It is not even clear that Mr. Mulroney's departure from the political scene would purge the public's anger, though it would certainly help. There is no guarantee that Liberal Leader Jean Chrétien, Ms. McLaughlin or Mr. Mulroney's successor would win the people's confidence.

Provided that a No vote is properly interpreted as a No to formal constitutional amendments but not to non-constitutional changes, a No victory is perfectly defensible. It may even be the catharsis the country needs to kick the mania for constitutional reform, and to return to political debate what, in the Age of the Charter, should never have been taken away.

The Charter has spawned a generation of rights-hungry but responsibility-wary citizens for whom the old totems of Canadian federalism—federal-provincial negotiations, intergovernmental compromise, French–English accommodation—mean next to nothing. Worse, in their eyes these are totems of oppression, subjugation and stagnation, which symbolize that the demands of governing allegedly superseded the rights of citizens.

The Constitution passed into the hands of the people after the Charter, but since then politicians have tried to change it to their satisfaction. There has been zero tolerance for their efforts; now they have been told that No means No.

From this No does not emerge any coherent Yes, since no such coherence exists in the Canadian body politic. Much derided in its day, the Keith Spicer task force into the nation's psyche did provide the shrewdest examination of contemporary Canada, a seething mass of resentments and grievances wherein the virtues of compromise and tolerance lived only in the chairman's poetic imagination.

The country can survive a No, and even profit from it. What it cannot survive is the constant vilification of and mean-spiritedness toward all elected politicians, exceeding the bounds of healthy skepticism. So corrosive is this mood that those who risk public life will be largely those who cannot think of anything better to do with their time and who, if elected, will earn more money than in any other job they might ever have.

PART 5 *Politics*

ELECTION 1988

His Best Hour *(October 26, 1988)*

Liberal Leader John Turner exorcized the ghosts of the 1984 debates last night, but he didn't conjure up any new ones to scare Conservative Leader Brian Mulroney.

Mr. Turner was offered the perfect opening question last night to lambaste the Mulroney government's record on ethics and patronage. But he let the opportunity slip by because the Prime Minister, obviously primed, overwhelmed him with verbiage, sanctimony and an acknowledgment of errors early in his term of office.

After that, Mr. Turner comported himself well, vastly better than in 1984. And because the expectations held for him by the public before the debate were so low, he can be declared to have prospered from last night's encounter. But—and this is the critical point—Mr. Turner needed to flatten Mr. Mulroney, more than that, to squash him. And he didn't do it, despite his most persistent efforts.

In one absolutely riveting exchange during the last hour of the debate, Mr. Turner and Mr. Mulroney literally stood toe-to-toe and waged about the most intense debate on free trade imaginable. Because he was the attacker, and because he waved the flag, this bristling exchange on a medium that is so given over to emotion was won by Mr. Turner.

Mr. Turner was particularly tough on New Democratic Party Leader Edward Broadbent's defence policy, blasting it for leading Canada toward more costly, insular and ineffective defence arrangements. Mr. Turner was particularly effective in challenging Mr. Broadbent to spell out the costs of an independent defence policy. Indeed, every minute spent discussing NATO and NORAD did Mr. Broadbent damage because the party's position is manifestly unpopular with the Canadian public.

Last night, Mr. Broadbent was like a new man in comparison with his struggling performance in the French-language debate. At ease in his native language, and experienced in televised debates, he badgered Mr. Mulroney remorselessly on women's issues and free trade. He cleverly offered selected quotations from businessmen warning about harmonization of social programs.

Naturally, Mr. Mulroney was placed on the defensive all night by virtue of having a record to defend. He did as well as he could, but the general impression left was of a Prime Minister trying the difficult task of looking prime-ministerial and partisan at the same time.

Leading in all the public-opinion polls, Mr. Mulroney needed only to escape from the two national debates without a serious blunder. This he did. He left no new hostages to political fortune, nothing new that the opposition parties could use during the campaign. Mr. Mulroney's advisers will clearly be pleased that he escaped. He drew no blood from the others, but only a bit was drawn from him.

Of course, the Mulroney–Turner clash dominated the debate, but the most interesting sustained debates were those between Mr. Broadbent and Mr. Turner.

Obviously, both know that unless something dramatic happens in the next three weeks, the real battle in the campaign lies between the NDP and Liberals for second. Their exchanges were bitter, lacerating and distinctly personal. They shed some light, much heat and considerable animus on debates between the NDP and the Liberals.

Over all, Mr. Broadbent was tough throughout and clever, and he had never been so severely criticized in a national debate. That he could take as a compliment on his party's standing.

Mr. Mulroney escaped, which was his overriding objective. He didn't do much damage to either of his opponents.

Mr. Turner, for whom the debates were so critical, seized the moment. If there is any life to be breathed into his campaign, he did it last night. It was his best hour.

Mr. Turner's Issue *(November 15, 1988)*

VANCOUVER—What Liberal Leader John Turner needed more than anything else during his pre-election months in political purgatory was an issue, almost any issue, that he could clutch and make his own.

At first blush it seemed improbable that Mr. Turner could make free trade that issue. Here was someone, after all, who had severely chastised the Trudeau government for souring relations with the United States. He had sent his children there for their higher education (Stanford, Princeton). And the conservative business orientation of his mind suggested that he might favour free trade with the United States.

But he needed an issue desperately to make people pay attention to him. And free trade turned out to be a winner—starting with the gambit of instructing the Senate not to pass the agreement, and continuing through the election and the television debates. It may have been hyperbolic, even slightly demagogic, but Mr. Turner's self-styled Crusade for Canada has brought the party into the electoral competition.

Free trade did two things for Mr. Turner. First, it demonstrated that he believed in something, which was crucial to the way the public perceived him. Before his crusade against free trade, he had not been identified with an issue or a set of core values.

Second, the crusade brought together most of the Liberal Party. Ever since the television debates, the Liberal rats who had deserted what they believed to be a sinking ship have been swimming back. Those who had decided to give the campaign a pass got active; those who were participating in a desultory fashion picked up their pace.

The return of the reluctant Liberals is the major development of the election campaign. By reuniting most of its members, by making them comfortable again with calling themselves Liberals, the party has renewed its enthusiasm at the grass roots and made itself content with the leadership. Yes, there remain disaffected Liberals among those who support free trade. But they are at the margin of a party that is now strongly nationalist and interventionist.

The Liberals' return sets up a fascinating post-election scenario. Despite the turmoil of the past four years and the carping about his leadership, Mr. Turner has pulled the party back by his own efforts before and during the campaign. He owes no debts, except to a handful of backroom people and a few caucus members, such as Raymond Garneau, who stuck by him throughout.

As for Jean Chrétien and his supporters in the party, they are done like dinner, because they are perceived as having had their own agenda. That agenda—to make Mr. Chrétien leader after Mr. Turner stumbled—is now in tatters, assuming the Liberals make a respectable showing on November 21.

Mr. Turner had plenty of knives stuck in his back before the campaign and during its early stages. Chances are he knows whose hands grasped each knife, and he has a long memory.

His only peril as he enters the last week is that his campaign may have peaked a week ago. He is still in considerable pain from a bad back, and he is terribly tired. Perhaps that's why he has turned down what the other party leaders accepted—a full-length interview on *The Journal.*

The Liberals have been hammering at one note—against free trade—since the third week of the campaign, and after a while it's hard to sustain the voters' attention. But this is the issue that made the Liberals competitive and restored some political esteem to a battered John Turner. That's why they are likely to keep hammering away until election day, hoping they can form a minority government.

Standing Back on Top   *(November 22, 1988)*

Two years ago, Brian Mulroney was given up for lost, a footnote in Canadian history. Last night, he stood atop the Canadian political world again, the first prime minister in three-and-a-half decades to win back-to-back majority governments.

Nobody can gainsay his second victory, although his party suffered large losses. These were entirely predictable, because the 210 seats of 1984 represented a political fluke, a once-in-a-generation happening.

With the exception of Atlantic Canada, the Tories won a majority of the seats in every region of Canada. That will utterly undercut any post-election arguments that the government lacks a mandate to proceed with the free-trade agreement with the United States.

Mr. Mulroney will now reconvene Parliament in mid-December and push the free-trade bill through the Commons. The Liberal majority in the Senate will lie down and respect the results of the election. Tory insiders also say the government will push through the child-care legislation that died on the order paper.

After free trade and child care, the Tory plans call for a long parliamentary recess, perhaps as long as two months. During that period, the Prime Minister will overhaul his Cabinet.

Mr. Mulroney also faces some personnel decisions, notably a replacement for his chief of staff, Derek Burney, who will become Ambassador to Washington on January 1. Peter White, who is principal secretary, might like the job, but almost every senior Tory wants somebody else. Changes are also in order for some senior civil-service positions.

The recess will also be used to prepare the new government's first budget. That budget will be almost completely at variance with the airy campaign rhetoric, since a combination of spending cuts or tax increases is clearly on offer with the federal deficit high and rising.

Mr. Mulroney's most singular accomplishment was to win again—and win big—in Quebec. By so doing, he cemented the bridge between French- and English-speaking Canadians via the Conservative Party.

The Liberals, by contrast, wound up on the wrong political side of free trade and received absolutely no credit for supporting the Meech Lake constitutional accord.

Perhaps the biggest non-federal winner of the evening was Quebec Premier Robert Bourassa, who did everything possible to assist the Conservatives. He wanted free trade and Meech Lake and he will get both if New Brunswick and Manitoba fall into line. He will also want some federal preferences for Quebec, and he may get them, too, starting with the designation of Montreal as the headquarters for the space agency.

A loser must be Premier David Peterson of Ontario, who joined the federal Liberals in opposing free trade. But neither he nor the federal Liberals could turn Ontario. Winning a majority of Ontario's ninety-nine seats was the bare minimum the Liberals needed to prevent a Conservative majority. When they couldn't sweep southwestern Ontario and Metropolitan Toronto, the Liberals were finished.

Clearly, the Liberals could not sustain their anti–free-trade crusade to the end of the campaign. They faded badly in the final ten days, partly because they had nothing else on which to campaign and partly because their past four years caught up with them. Too many Canadians harboured too many doubts about Mr. Turner and his party to give the Liberals more than the moral victory of about twice as many seats.

Mr. Mulroney, having won two majorities with strength in all regions of the country, is now the most successful Conservative leader since Sir Robert Borden.

Given where his party stood two years ago, Mr. Mulroney's victory last night is a remarkable personal testament.

ELECTION 1993

Tories Failed Their Own Test *(October 23, 1993)*

A poor campaign, the leader's gaffes and the accumulated baggage of nine years in office contributed to what now appears certain to be a decimating of the Conservatives. But these factors, important as they are, still do not adequately explain the magnitude of the Conservatives' electoral disaster and the further shattering of Canada's traditional political culture reflected in the election campaign.

The Progressive Conservatives are being crushed—and new parties are rising—because the previous government of Prime Minister Brian Mulroney failed the two tests of leadership established by the party itself for the unwieldy coalition Mr. Mulroney assembled. These were: deficit reduction and a reconciliation of Quebec nationalism to federalism.

The deficit and Quebec anti-nationalism are not central to the voting intentions of people on the political left, but they are the litmus tests for conservatives. And when the Conservative Party flunked both tests—the deficit remains staggeringly high and all attempts to negotiate a new constitutional deal for Quebec failed—the result was a radicalization of options within the former Mulroney coalition. Hence, the rise of the Reform Party and the Bloc Québécois—both born of disillusioned Conservatives.

Deeper still, however, the search for the election's significance might acknowledge the widening fault lines in Canadian society, especially the one between Quebec and the rest of Canada, that increasingly threaten the country's ability to remain united.

Not only do the Reform Party and Bloc Québécois represent the political radicalization of disaffected Conservatives, they also represent a reaction to each other. Each party's strength partly arose because of a growing awareness of the tribalist forces that had spurred the others' growth.

The Reform Party, for its part, always appealed to those fed up with what they perceive as Quebec's privileged place in Canada. The more restless and demanding Quebec became, the more powerful became Reform Leader Preston Manning's inferential message that only his party—without candidates or aspirations in Quebec—could defend the interests of the "rest of Canada" in whatever showdown loomed with Quebec.

The Bloc Québécois, for its part, reflected the sense of rejection felt in Quebec after the defeat of the Meech Lake accord and the belief that a growing hostility toward Quebec's aspirations in the rest of Canada, epitomized by the Reform Party, called for a more radical expression of Quebec's self-interest at the federal level.

The Bloc's success was both unique (as being the first expression of secessionist opinion in federal politics) and deeply traditional. It has long been quite wrongly assumed, as indeed it was in this election by Liberals and Tories, that Quebeckers vote for something called "power" and that, shown the direction of political momentum elsewhere in Canada, Quebeckers would hustle to join the flow. Indeed, this was the message constantly delivered to Quebeckers by the Conservative and Liberal campaigns: don't waste votes by supporting a party destined for Opposition.

But this strategy misunderstood their motivations. If they could vote for a party that won power, fine; but what they really searched for was the leader who could best articulate and define their interests among those on offer in any election. In this campaign, the choice was clear. Among a Quebecker (Jean Chrétien) who had actively opposed the entire nationalist thrust of Quebec for thirty years, a Prime Minister whose French was awkward, and Lucien Bouchard, Quebeckers are opting for Mr. Bouchard. They are not reaching for power; they are reaching, as they always have, for their interest—and power and interests are not always synonymous.

The Bloc Québécois surge radicalizes politics in Quebec because it offers further evidence that after a quarter of a century of searching for some "middle ground" between status-quo federalism (or that federalism as amended in his own idiosyncratic way by former prime minister Pierre Trudeau) and secession, the choice has come down to "in or out." That has been, after all, the consistent message delivered by the rest of Canada through all the constitutional changes (women's rights, Senate reform, aboriginal issues etc.): that it is not remotely interested in the devolution of power sought by Quebec governments through a variety of guises. As gamblers would say, *les jeux sont fait,* as between the existing federal system with whatever flexibility remains therein and secession, pure and hard.

The rise of the Bloc Québécois, coupled with the support the federal Liberals maintain in the province, clarifies the options at hand and undermines the efforts extending back many years by Quebec politicians and those interested in national unity outside Quebec to find some way of escaping the forthcoming moment of truth.

Plenty of people who support Reform—and this could be easily ascertained by attending party meetings and talking to the rank and file—believe in the inevitability of the forthcoming showdown. Indeed, in many cases they welcome it, believing either that Quebec will be humiliated and hurt or simply that the rest of Canada would be better off without this Frenchified sore festering and enfeebling the rest of Canada. So, too, many who will not vote Reform are plagued by the same gut-wrenching fear that maybe the fault lines within Canada, especially the Quebec/rest-of-Canada one, are now so wide that they cannot be bridged, and that all the future offers are further painful, but doomed, attempts to hold together what ultimately will break apart.

This kind of possibility is dismissed, of course, as "hyperbole" by wise men and women (a recent essay by Eric Kierans comes to mind) who apparently remain convinced that the divisions in the country, although real, do not have the power to shatter the traditional political culture and indeed the country. Perhaps their insouciance will be borne out. But the explanations of the election by the insouciant among us will have to be wondrously concocted.

It was, of course, not supposed to work out this way when Mr. Mulroney and his wife basked in the adulation of the crowd that electoral night in 1984. Less than a decade later, the Conservatives have descended from the largest number of seats in the history of Canada to the eve of a shattering defeat, a defeat that may end their standing as a national party in a country increasingly retreating to tribal entities.

Mr. Mulroney left the Conservative Party in desperate shape, despite his vainglorious attempts as he left office to portray his years in a better light. But the conventional media yardsticks of the party's desperation—18 per cent in the polls, a popular disgust with Mr. Mulroney, a widespread dismay at the moral and ethical tone of the federal government—were not the most important reasons for the desperation.

Rather, these were the failures by the Conservative government, despite its ministers' and MPs' good intentions and best efforts on the way, to produce results on the two issues of greatest importance for the Conservative supporters who had come together in 1984 and remained faithful to the party in 1988.

To those for whom the deficit/debt problem was the country's most acute economic one, after nine years in power the Conservative government could only deliver a deficit of $34-billion—lower as a percentage of gross national product or total government spending than in 1984, but still astronomically high.

The failure, despite good intentions and many revenue-raising and expenditure-reducing measures, spoke of a more generalized inability to cope with the severe structural adjustments in the Canadian economy.

Thus the Conservatives of the 1980s and early 1990s increasingly resembled the Republican Party of the 1960s in the United States: a party apparently unable to ride events rather than be buffeted by them and therefore prone to an internal revolt by those who wished a change of direction.

In the Conservatives' case, as in the Republicans', the erosion began at the grass roots rather than in the party establishment. The grass roots, angry over the accommodations with Quebec and alarmed by the failure to attack government spending, began drifting to the Reform Party, at first in Alberta, then in the other Tory strongholds of British Columbia, the Prairies and even rural and small-town Ontario. The Conservative Party establishment, studying the polls, began to adopt certain policies designed to woo back these disillusioned and increasingly radicalized Conservatives, but instead of the Conservatives subsuming Reformers, Reformers overwhelmed Conservatives.

In Quebec, many of those who supported the Conservative bandwagon in 1984 were fiscal conservatives, including small businessmen and farmers. Despite having grown up in a province accustomed to government intervention in the economy through grants, loans and subsidies, they wanted fiscal rectitude in all areas but those that affected their own spiggots to government. Mr. Bouchard himself, despite the penumbra of social democratic rhetoric with which he occasionally covers himself, is quite typical of the breed of Conservatives circa 1984. He is *petit bourgeois* in every sense of the term. Indeed, one of his best arguments against the federal system is the incredible fiscal mess in which Ottawa finds itself. (Mr. Bouchard, however, is like so many other fiscal conservatives in Quebec: cut spending but not if it affects Quebec.)

The special twist for the Conservative vote in 1984 in Quebec was, of course, its nationalism. Old-style Quebec blues had always been more nationalist than the federal (or provincial) Liberals. From this small cluster of federal Tories, Mr. Mulroney widened his party's appeal by overt appeals to Quebec nationalism, buttressed by special early decisions of his government (to subsidize industries such as Domtar and Hyundai in Quebec) and by promises to negotiate a new constitutional deal for Quebec within Canada.

After nine years, Mr. Mulroney's failures on deficit/debt and constitutional reform had disillusioned and thereby radicalized opinion in Quebec among those who had supported him in 1984 and 1988. This disillusionment, coupled with the arrival of an anglophone as party leader and the general economic discontent felt in Quebec, as elsewhere, destroyed the Conservatives in Quebec and produced an opening brilliantly exploited by Mr. Bouchard.

For those who believe that Canada's traditional political culture is breaking up, the results of the election on Monday will therefore not be at all surprising. There are still many elements of the old culture of accommodation that remain and these will coalesce in a strong vote for the Liberals, especially in Ontario, the part of Canada most wedded to the maintenance of the country's unity, and in Atlantic Canada, the region so dependent upon the federal government. The elements of the new culture of confrontation and tribalism, elements that reflect disillusionment, anger and a sense that the future must be radically different from the past, destroyed the Conservatives and left the interplay between the forces of the declining old political culture and the burgeoning new one to play themselves out in the next few years.

REFORM/CONSERVATIVE

A Few Things a True Conservative Should Remember About Canada *(August 18, 1995)*

Party Leader Jean Charest, scrabbling around for new, gimmicky Conservative ideas, would be better advised to ask what enlightened conservatism has meant and go from there.

A conservative, after all, should have a sense of history, and draw inspiration from the best of the past for an assault on tomorrow's problems. A conservative with a sense of history recalls, for starters, that Canada is the world's second-oldest federation. It is a success by any absolute or comparative standard in the families of nations, and especially federations.

A conservative should therefore be proud and patriotic, without being boastful or chauvinistic. This country has its own history, derivative in parts, distinctive in others. A conservative should remember that a country is more than an agglomeration of individuals seeking their own satisfactions and fulfilments but also a collective enterprise of people who have done great things together and wish to do more together in the future.

A real conservative, as opposed to a nineteenth-century liberal who is called a Conservative, believes that society has an organic element that mixes collective and individual aspirations. An organic society is one that marries rights and responsibilities, because the individual should recognize that his or her rights and liberties depend upon the exercise of limits.

The British North America Act, now eclipsed in the public's mind by the Charter of Rights and Freedoms, spoke of "peace, order and good government." These are probably heretical words to many people today, but they speak to a conservative conception of society whereby liberty is best enhanced through order. These words also speak directly to the role of the state in securing liberty through "peace, order and good government." The state thereby can be the friend, not the enemy, of liberty.

A conservative therefore does not take as a starting point that government is bad *per se*, or the root of all evils. A conservative does not believe, as do right-wing populists, that the people are being oppressed by government but rather that government, properly structured and financed, can assist society in achieving collective goals which will in turn enhance individual liberty.

None of this kind of analysis has appeared in Mr. Charest's pronouncements, which read like Reform Party speeches redux. Instead of what he has been saying, how about something like this?

"Canada, my friends, is more than the sum of its parts, more than a community of communities, and the federal government is more than a broker for the provinces. There are provincial constituencies and regional pride throughout Canada, and there is a distinctiveness in Quebec that stems from its history, culture and language. And among aboriginal groups too. But there is also a greater Canadian whole, a success story that as prime minister I will defend and enhance.

"I also believe, as a Conservative, in responsibilities and collective action. For example, a clean environment is a collective good that enhances the individual liberties of everyone. We may therefore have to take radical collective action in environmental areas to secure individual enjoyment of our heritage.

"I believe, too, that an organic conception of society includes concern for all members, especially those least able to care for themselves. In a conservative society of mutual responsibilities, I will be asking those most favoured by fortune or family to pay more to assist those less fortunate. Our society will be therefore more orderly and just, and thereby our individual liberties will be enhanced.

"In speaking for the whole country, and conscious of our history, I will seek to expand Canadians' ability to speak to each other. I will therefore promote vigorously Canadian culture as an expression of the whole nation in the multichannel universe. I will not denigrate the state, through which Canadians debate and resolve collective matters, but seek to reshape its programs to meet modern requirements. And I also believe in representative democracy, not direct democracy, because I freely admit as a conservative that it has stood the test of time as a superior deliberative mechanism to the fevers of the moment and blatant self-interest that infect direct democracy."

That's conservatism, modern-style, not warmed-over Reform Party or imitation Mike Harris.

Considering the Desirability of a Reform and Conservative Merger *(April 4, 1996)*

Are we witnessing the death throes of the federal Conservative Party? Quite probably, unless the Conservatives give Canadians a plausible reason why the party should exist. And ever since the humiliation of the 1993 election, Conservatives have offered no such reason.

Nostalgia never took a political party very far, and in the Conservatives' case, a backward glance at immediate history reminds them—and the electorate—of the Mulroney years. But a sense of the party's most honourable moments can help a party explain to itself, and to the country, why its existence counts.

Talk of a merger of the Reform and Conservative Parties is now aloft in the political air. At the grass roots level, and in the mouth of Alberta Premier Ralph Klein, an exploration has begun about the desirability and modalities of some sort of union on the political right.

Those floating the idea are displaying admirable pragmatism: a divided right-of-centre alternative to the Liberals means a continuation of Liberal rule. And if Conservatives cannot think of anything better to offer than what they have put forward since 1993, they might just as well strike the best deal possible with Reform. Nothing is immutable, after all, in the history of political parties, as is demonstrated by the "strange death" of the British Liberals, the extinction of the American Whigs and the disappearance of certain French conservative formations.

Conservatives can mull over tactics and strategy all they like, to no particular avail. They should spend more time on first principles, and if they find these to be similar to those of Reform, they could proceed with a merger. If not, say why.

There can be major differences on first principles between Reform and Conservatives, depending on how Conservatives define themselves. Many of these potential differences flow from diverging notions of state and society.

A Conservative could argue that society is organic, that it is more than an agglomeration of individuals, which is the Reform view of society. Reform is essentially an updated set of ideas from the rugged individualism of the United States and the nineteenth-century British liberal school.

Reform distrusts the state for its restraint on liberty; Conservatives can see the state as the defender of liberty. Reform prefers governments that govern least; Conservatives can prefer governments that govern wisely, which does not always mean least.

Reform is hard-pressed to envision the state as articulator and defender of a collectively defined national interest, hence its preference for that agglomeration of individuals it calls society to express itself wherever possible in referendums. Conservatives can see the institutions of the state as definers of the national interest, central to which is Parliament.

Reform, as its foreign-policy declarations have shown, is skeptical of Canadian engagements abroad, in part because the party remains skeptical of the state and its costs; Conservatives, willing to use the state to help define the national interest, can see a persistent international engagement by Canada as an expression of its values and interests.

Reform, perceiving society as an agglomeration of individuals, places extraordinary emphasis on the "rights" of individuals, including property rights; Conservatives, while upholding individual rights, could also emphasize responsibilities that we owe one another through the state and its laws. The recognition of responsibility—of what we owe one another—can enhance social cohesion, which should be a Conservative's abiding concern. An approach that balances rights and responsibilities—a direct attack on today's prevailing discourse of "rights talk"—would be consistent with a Conservative view of an organic society.

Reform, disapproving of the state, wishes a massive decentralization of power from Ottawa to the provinces to bring government "closer to the people"; Conservatives, while accepting some decentralization for reasons of efficiency, would be more inclined to defend the national interest as the expression of the organic nature of Canadian society.

Conservatives can choose. They can articulate a different vision from that of Reform of Canadian society, and government's role within it, and fight in the ring of public debate to remain alive. Or they can accept Reform's definition of modern conservatism and pass unlamented from the scene.

Having a charming leader and a group of *apparatchiks* with nothing important to say is a poor excuse for a party.

PART 6 *Parties*

TORIES IN OFFICE

Tories in Trouble *(February 3, 1987)*

Tomorrow, the Mulroney government reaches the theoretical midpoint of its term. It is still hanging in there, but just barely. It has consistently returned to its corner of the ring, promising to turn things around, only to get beaten up again in the next round.

On form, the government should not be in such horrible shape. Conventional wisdom and that of many pollsters used to suggest that the economy, more than any other issue, dictated the government's fortunes.

So what have we got? Uneven regional economic performance, to be sure, but we have always had that in one form or another. It may be somewhat more acute these days, which might largely explain the unhappiness in places such as Atlantic Canada and Alberta. But how do you account for the fact that booming Ontario and nicely percolating Quebec are so sour on the Conservatives, or that Manitoba was sour on them even before the CF-18 decision?

Interest rates, which crippled the popularity of the last Liberal government, are at their lowest level in nearly a decade. The national unemployment figures are down. Inflation is low. Business attitudes, at least in central Canada, are reasonably bullish. The federal deficit is drifting downward. Generally speaking, the economic numbers aren't bad. But all the Conservatives' polling numbers are.

The Conservatives, scratching their heads, blame poor communications. In part, they're right.

The Conservatives began by fighting the public service. Maybe they suspected the service's loyalty. Maybe they wanted to put a political spin on everything. Whatever their assumptions, they were wrong.

Muzzling the public service was dumb. Public servants don't want to get the government into trouble. Most of them want their ministers to succeed and, rightly or otherwise, they have a credibility with the media which politicians often lack. Muzzling the public servants cost the government credible allies.

The government worried so much about what came out of the communications pipeline, including the right photo opportunities for Prime
Minister Brian Mulroney, that it forgot about what went in; it didn't explain
what it was doing before it did it. The softwood lumber export tax was a
perfect example: ministers and officials scrambled around after the fact
explaining what was going on.

Everyone in the government knew about the Prime Minister's preoccupation with the media. So they took their cues from him and those around
him, fearing the fallout that would come if they got into trouble. Mr.
Mulroney, of course, had little confidence in the political judgment of many
of his senior colleagues. That may have changed, since many of them are
now in better political odour than he is.

All the silly trappings of presidential authority became a subject of
ridicule. So did the flowery phrases, the exaggerated promises (such as the
one to do much more for the oil industry during the Prime Minister's last
visit to Calgary), the light airs of cliché that enveloped so much of what he
said—in short, the lack of straight talk.

So inordinately did the Prime Minister dominate the public presentation
of his government's case that his ministers, including the presentable ones,
seemed faceless, if not nameless. How can it be that such ministers as David
Crombie, Flora MacDonald, Jake Epp and Ray Hnatyshyn have disappeared
into the insularity of their local bases, unknown to all but the client groups
of their ministries?

The Prime Minister has tried fitfully to lower his profile. But it is a demonstrable fact that all the perceived liabilities of this government stick to him.

Tories in Trouble (2) *(February 4, 1987)*

Voters judge politicians and governments in different ways: on policies, attitudes and values.

A voter's policy judgment, pro or con, can be altered. The government
can modify the policy, explain it more clearly, abandon it or carry on, hoping at least to win grudging respect. It always has a chance to recover popular esteem.

A voter's judgment about attitudes—the general sense of where the government is going, which groups it represents—is much harder to alter,
because attitudes are more durable and less tied to a specific policy decision.

Hardest of all to change is the judgment about a politician's or government's values. Value judgments involve questions of trust, integrity, commitment and patriotism—matters of the heart and soul. What has happened to

the Mulroney government, I think, is that a lot of voters have started judging the government on its attitudes and values, and too many of them don't like what they see. It is an enormous, perhaps insuperable problem for a government to turn such judgments around.

Consider the reverse situation south of the border. There, by all accounts, a number of people who didn't buy many of President Ronald Reagan's policy options voted for him anyway. Why? Because he incarnated, or at least spoke to, values that Americans admired: deep patriotism, self-confidence, integrity, a sense of optimism. Many also admired his attitudes—less government, a strong military, a lighter tax burden—even if they disagreed with a particular policy.

The result has been a remarkable forgiveness of gaffes and policy somersaults. The Iran-contra affair may be testing that forgiveness, partly because it tarnished the positive judgment of the President's attitudes and values. After all, the affair raises questions that reflect on his truthfulness, integrity and competence.

In Canada, the negative judgments about the Mulroney government's values are based on at least three perceptions; and whether those perceptions are grounded in reality is only marginally relevant to their political impact.

The first relates to the Prime Minister's values. Many people aren't sure what they are; others think they know and don't like what they see. His reliance on old friends, his inflated rhetoric, his propensity for making promises, his blend of sanctimony and partisanship—these practices raise too many questions about what's inside the man. This uncertainty, which breeds a certain mistrust, means that, unlike the example of President Reagan, the gaffes of Mr. Mulroney's government all stick to him.

The second perception has to do with the government's competence. There have been too many screws-ups, too many surprises, too many ministers in trouble to give enough Canadians confidence in the Conservatives' ability to run the ship, a politically dangerous perception for the party of the outs.

The third—and in my view quite unfair—perception is a sense that Ottawa is not interested in treating everyone equally. The government, with its huge mandate, is riding uneasily the tiger of regional discontent; almost every region feels Ottawa is not doing enough about its problems. So, too, a great many Canadians still think of the Tories as the party of the privileged, within which lobbyists and those with money and influence get a fairer shake than the rest of us.

If it were just a matter of adjusting a few major policies, the Mulroney government could redeem itself. Instead, faced with a negative judgment about its attitudes and values, the government is in deep political trouble.

Tories in Trouble (3) *(February 5, 1987)*

The Conservatives' election campaign left scattered across the political landscape too many hostages to fortune.

Not surprisingly, these are coming back to haunt the government. The weaker the government's political standing, the more insistent the demands will be that the government make good on its promises.

Brian Mulroney's campaign was a happy, even joyous, affair full of *bonhomie*, smooth words and an apparently endless litany of promises. Even in the final weeks of the campaign, with the election in the bag, the promises rolled on.

A party accustomed to opposition could not resist the temptation to smash the Grits and scoop up as many seats as possible. Now the Conservatives find themselves whipsawed by the inflated expectations raised in part by their own campaign and the astonishing size of their majority.

Some early critical assumptions and decisions sowed the seeds for future trouble. The decision to subsidize the Domtar plant in Quebec let everyone know that it was business as usual in providing grants to save jobs, even if the company was financially healthy. That precedent established, the government was hard-pressed to say no to anybody else. When it did say no, those in disagreement could point to many cases where the answer had been yes.

The Shamrock Summit, by its very effusiveness, contributed to a great overselling of the practical possibility of warmer ties with the United States. And decisions which had as their direct or indirect intention the pleasing of the Reagan administration left the government vulnerable to charges that it received little, or nothing, in return.

The idea of de-indexing pensions irritated a bastion of Conservative support—senior citizens. The subsequent retreat largely closed off any social-policy debate on reordering spending.

Because the Conservatives ran such an effusive election campaign, they would have had to expend some short-term political capital after the election if they wanted to dampen expectations. But that wasn't Mr. Mulroney's style; nor was it his political judgment about how a minority party such as the Conservatives could win enduring public confidence. So the expectations were allowed to billow, with the result that the government found itself continuously on the defensive when it could not deliver. (In fairness, when it did deliver on a policy—such as tying energy policies to the market—the delivery came just as prices tumbled.)

The Conservatives arrived after years of Liberal governments, during which massive amounts of money were thrown at every conceivable interest group. Not surprisingly, the population had come to expect Ottawa to solve every problem, to finance every program, to meet every demand regardless of the economy's ability to sustain such spending. The vicious circle of relentless expectations entrapped the Conservatives, just as it would have grabbed a Turner Liberal government by the throat. And since the game of Canadian politics as played by the Liberals, Conservatives and especially the New Democrats consists largely of smooth promises, the public expectations of what governments can reasonably do and finance may easily ensnare any government faced with a huge deficit.

John Turner knew this; that's why he tried to dampen expectations by pledging to cut the deficit in half over a period of seven years. But he learned what the Conservatives already knew—that bad news doesn't sell, and smooth talk does.

It is a bitter irony of the Mulroney experience that he is being criticized for a lack of straight talk, when there is absolutely no evidence that the public prefers this kind of talk to the smoother, satisfying variety.

Tories in Trouble (4) *(February 6, 1987)*

Most analyses of the Mulroney government forget that the Conservatives are the country's natural opposition party and that the 1984 election was a fluke.

Plenty of observers, including this one, went a trifle overboard in 1984, picking over the charred remains of the Liberal Party and concluding that no phoenix could ever rise from that pile of ashes.

What we temporarily forgot, or at least minimized, was that the Conservatives were the party of the outs, of those who had failed every time since the First World War to demonstrate to Canadians a sense of compelling vision and competence that might have made the party the natural governing party of Canada. And we overlooked a lesson of recent history— that no party in Canada had won back-to-back majorities since 1949 and 1953, no matter how large its initial majority.

History should have cautioned us—and indeed the country—against expecting that this time, at last, things might be different. But the expectation was hard to resist. The Conservatives had won 70 per cent of the seats in all regions of the country, and the Liberal Party, as I wrote, seemed like a piece of crystal which, having fallen from a high perch, lay shattered in a multitude of pieces on the ground.

The Liberals have partly reconstructed themselves, although their internal incoherence is appallingly evident to those who take care to observe it. And there is such a demonstrable lack of enthusiasm for John Turner, combined with the disillusionment with the Mulroney Conservatives, that the New Democrats have soared to record heights in putative public esteem.

The core of the Conservatives' problem has been fear, the natural outgrowth of being unaccustomed to power. From fear arose the external desire to please and the internal uncertainty of conviction.

You could see the fear early on in attitudes toward the bureaucracy, the media and even, among the Prime Minister's entourage, toward ministers. You could sense the fear of public opinion which had so often turned against the Conservative Party. You could hear it in the vituperative attacks on those who dared criticize privately the people who had carried the party to its historic victory.

What the historic minority party needed to prove on gaining power in 1984, above all else, was competence, the vaguely defined idea that this crowd could be entrusted with the affairs of state. Yet the snafus that followed were so frequent, and the setbacks so constant, that the old, usually subliminal doubts about the Conservatives' basic competence were resurrected and magnified. Another extraordinary opportunity was missed to erase or modify those doubts.

Curiously, the Mulroney government was widely criticized for lacking an agenda when, in fact, it had one that included a tighter fiscal policy, better relations with the United States, national reconciliation and a somewhat greater reliance on the private sector. It has entered the second half of its mandate with four macro-policies that probably spell its only hope of salvation—a free-trade deal with Washington, a constitutional settlement with Quebec, social-policy reform and tax reform.

But its political weakness and the unpopularity of its principal spokesman will make it difficult to sell any, let alone all, of these policies to a country less interested in policies than in the government's attitudes and values. In the modern age, so heavily influenced by television, the credibility of the salesman affects the receptivity of those hearing the message. And the lack of consistent competence in the government of the historic minority party, coupled with doubts about the salesman's core attitudes and values, will make a resurrection one of the Herculean tasks of modern Canadian politics.

LIBERALS

The Style of John Turner *(February 8, 1990)*

Nothing better fitted John Turner's parliamentary leadership of the Liberal Party than his leaving of it.

Mr. Turner relinquished his duties as Opposition Leader in the Commons with grace, style and wit, and, more important, a sense of the occasion. At a time of linguistic tension in the country, concerned Canadians might properly look to Parliament for leadership. They found it this week in Mr. Turner, who, in contrast to Prime Minister Mulroney, put gamesmanship aside.

On Monday, in the long shadow of Sault Ste. Marie's gratuitous and wounding English-only resolution, Mr. Turner proposed a simple resolution reaffirming a commitment to bilingualism and linguistic tolerance.

It could have been called a motherhood resolution, except that for many Canadians bilingualism remains a source of fear and recriminations. Still, it might have been useful for Parliament to speak with one voice to those in the Soo and elsewhere who still do not appreciate the country's two official languages.

But the Prime Minister could not resist playing partisan games. Knowing that the Liberals and NDP are divided over Meech Lake, he rejected Mr. Turner's resolution, and linked bilingualism with the Meech Lake constitutional accord. The gesture was cheap, partisan and distinctly unhelpful in the current climate. It was also unfair to Mr. Turner, who suffered mightily within the Liberal Party for his pro-Meech stand.

Mr. Turner, by leading his party to two electoral defeats, will likely go down in history as a political failure. He is entitled to take such comfort as he can find from his political labours.

He insisted yesterday that he was "on the right side of history" on Meech Lake and free trade. Time will put those assertions into sharper focus, but my guess is that he will be seen (as I freely confess I did not fully appreciate at the time) to have been right about Meech, but wrong about free trade.

Mr. Turner saved his 1988 campaign with an impassioned attack on the free-trade deal. The campaign had begun in disarray. It deteriorated further when panic struck senior party members, who wondered privately about the desirability of his remaining as leader.

But he saved a measure of respect for himself, and dozens of seats for his party, with his performance in the television debate insisting that free trade meant the end of a sovereign Canada. It was sweet irony that a brief exchange on television—a medium that so frequently perplexed Mr. Turner, a child of the print medium's last days of supremacy in political reporting—provided the vehicle for his return to political respectability.

Free trade is a done deal for Canada. If the Liberals win the next election, they may wish to renegotiate certain aspects of the deal. But when that option inevitably fails, they will adapt themselves to its requirements. Only one of the leadership candidates, John Nunziata, wants to tear up the agreement, and he counts for next to nothing in the campaign.

Just as Pierre Trudeau was unable to turn over the Liberal Party to someone in his own image, so Mr. Turner may watch with dismay if the party opts for Jean Chrétien next June in Calgary. Here again irony, politics' constant companion, will reassert itself. It was the politics of nostalgia for a pre-Trudeau Liberal Party that gave Mr. Turner his victory in 1984, and it is the politics of nostalgia for the pre-Turner era that now animates Mr. Chrétien and his supporters.

Mr. Turner exemplified public decency, civic-mindedness, an abiding respect for Parliament and a deep concern for national unity throughout his years of leadership. He stood for these virtues to the end.

The Prospects of Sheila Copps *(March 3, 1990)*

VANCOUVER—Flashing that electric smile of hers, Sheila Copps proudly declared: "I think this demonstrates what a remarkable ability I have to unite the Liberal Party."

Even the other candidates couldn't help grinning over that one, since they had set up the line by all agreeing with what Ms. Copps had said. But it has been like that from the start of the leadership contest. Ms. Copps has surprised the other candidates, and plenty of other Liberals too, with her campaign. With an unerring eye for the clip, and her unbridled love of a good fight, she has thrust herself forward as the most intriguing of the leadership candidates.

John Crosbie had it half right. Leave the rest of the song aside: Ms. Copps is Tequila Sheila. Like tequila, she is best taken in short, sharp bursts. Prolonged exposure brings unhappy side effects.

Ms. Copps is the classic example of the opposition-party mentality at work, having spent her entire political career attacking federal and Ontario Tory governments. She is a relentless terrier of a critic, alert to every media opportunity, acutely sensitive to her adversaries' vulnerability and apparently impervious to the subtleties and trade-offs inherent in governing.

When she accused Mr. Crosbie's mouth of consistently running ahead of his brain, some of Ms. Copps's critics must surely have heard the sound of the pot calling the kettle black. She was not a founding member of the Liberal Rat Pack for nothing.

Watching her in the Commons and in the Liberal leadership race, it would be tempting, and not altogether inaccurate, to say that she can talk on a wide range of subjects, but not in depth and at length about very many of them.

And yet, there are qualities beyond tenacity and an eye for attention that flesh out her political character. Loyalty, for example. By temperament and intellect, she should not have been a close comrade of her former leader, John Turner. Indeed, she supported Jean Chrétien for the leadership in

1984. But she stood by Mr. Turner even in the darkest hours, winning admiration not only from him but from rank-and-file Liberals who understood that politics is ultimately a team game.

Then there is her support for the Meech Lake accord. She could have raised her political antennae and reckoned that opposing Meech Lake would help her in the leadership race. Some prominent women's groups dislike Meech Lake, as do a majority of English-speaking Liberals. But she stood by Mr. Turner's support for Meech Lake. Her defence of the accord in the leadership contest has been pointed and impressive.

Ms. Copps learned two languages, French and Italian—an intellectual accomplishment of note. Her French and feistiness impressed Quebeckers on her recent forays to that province. The prominent provincial Liberal organizers she attracted to her campaign may give her a few pockets of strength apart from the ones in and around her native Hamilton.

Ms. Copps regularly pitches Liberals by saying, "When I am Prime Minister. . . ." This is harmless conceit, brought on by the exigencies of pretense demanded of leadership candidates. She knows she cannot win, not because of her gender but because there are far too many doubts about her opposition-party mentality and, most critically, because on the ground, where it counts, she hasn't got the organizers.

But she has run a spirited, disciplined campaign, and one that has been fun for Liberals to watch. She is winning enough delegates here and there that, if Jean Chrétien cannot make it on the first ballot, every eye in the Calgary Saddledome will swing to Sheila Copps to see where she will throw her support.

Step Right Up, and See the Federal Liberal Party in Public Torment *(June 23, 1990)*

CALGARY—Seldom, if ever, has Canada seemed more like a small village than it did yesterday.

From St. John's to Quebec City to Ottawa to Winnipeg to Calgary, the news changed by the hour, rolling across the country, causing Canadians everywhere to wonder where their country was heading.

After three-and-a-half years of wrangling, two visions clashed and deadlock ensued.

In Calgary yesterday, Pierre Trudeau, resplendent and arresting as always, carried forward his campaign against Meech Lake. Calm down, kill Meech, he said.

Within his national party, Mr. Trudeau's legacy lives on, inspiring many of the supporters of Jean Chrétien. They, like Mr. Trudeau and Mr. Chrétien, refuse to believe that any sensible and lasting accommodation can be made between French-Canadian nationalism and federalism, the accommodation that lies at the heart of Meech Lake.

In St. John's, Liberal Premier Clyde Wells delivered an impassioned speech against Meech Lake. It was among the more cogent speeches against Meech Lake ever delivered, and it was clearly inspired by the vision of Canada articulated for so many years by Mr. Trudeau.

All provinces are equal, all Canadians are equal, and Meech Lake threatens both propositions, insisted Mr. Wells.

Yet here in Calgary another vision, or at least a different appreciation of contemporary realities, has made itself felt.

John Turner, the retiring Liberal leader, gave the speech of his life Thursday night. He spoke movingly on all subjects, but when he spoke in French about Meech Lake and the need to keep Canada together, he rose to levels he had seldom, if ever, achieved during six years as leader.

When his words rang through the Saddledome, the supporters of Sheila Copps and Paul Martin, pro-Meech candidates, roared their approval. Those in Jean Chrétien's camp sat mute. And high up in the stands, Pierre Trudeau sat impassively, listening to his successor offer a vision foreign to his own.

The agony of Meech Lake, a national psychodrama, has torn Canada apart, and the anger and hurt has ripped apart the Liberal Party, too. There is no way of disguising the divisions within this proud party. They are on public and painful display every hour of this convention.

Meech Lake is the more painful for Liberals since it strikes at the heart of the party's historical role as the nation's principal political bridge between English- and French-speaking Canadians.

It was this role, from the days of Sir Wilfrid Laurier, that set the Liberals up as the natural governing party of Canada. Now, before their very eyes, the Liberals are seeing that role slip away because Meech Lake has ripped them apart.

The bitterness this leadership campaign has revealed is compounded by memories of past personal betrayals. There is palpable distaste between Mr. Trudeau and Mr. Turner, between Mr. Turner and Mr. Chrétien and, now, between Mr. Chrétien and Sheila Copps and Paul Martin.

But the bitterness is not merely personal. It goes to the deeper level of political vision at a time when the future of Canada hangs by a thread.

These divisions are so deep that they sent Jean Chrétien to ground, refusing to state where he stands on whether to proceed with Meech Lake and the companion resolution. That abdication of leadership, for utterly tactical reasons, has merely envenomed an already tense situation.

Liberals, of course, are not the only formation wounded by the Meech Lake monster. It has reached out and hurt almost every politician forced to grapple with it.

But nowhere has the monster created more havoc than within the federal Liberal Party, havoc that remains on hourly display in Calgary, and havoc that will continue to do its work in the months, perhaps years, after Liberals return to their homes across a country that, because of this psychodrama, is about to be enormously changed.

The Message Is Loud and Clear, But Are the Liberals Listening? *(November 27, 1991)*

"The role of government is to represent the future to the present." So argued U.S. economist and writer Lester Thurow to the Liberals who assembled in Aylmer, Que., last weekend to discuss new policy ideas. Of all the startling messages in a conference loaded with them, this one carried the most punch for a party that has been driving via the rear-view mirror for seven years in opposition, and did the same for some years before that while still in power.

Indeed, it has been half a generation since the Liberal Party turned its back on the formula that made it Canada's governing party. In the mid-seventies, the Liberals began to forget about the liberalism of limits; that is, about governing within fiscal limits, designing social policy within those limits, and forging economic policy within the necessary and inescapable limits imposed by global competition.

As a result, the whole country has had to pay the price. In government from 1975 to 1984, the Liberals presided over the nightmare years of deficits: from a balanced budget in 1974 to an anticipated $36-billion deficit and a $200-billion debt ten years later.

Banished to opposition, they continued their escape from the liberalism of limits, succumbing to the apparently endemic clamour of opposition parties for more spending and support for every interest group that peeped. Rather than contributing, as the Democratic Party tried to do in the United States (with no electoral success, by the way), to a sensible debate on how to tackle the nation's fiscal crisis, Liberals in opposition consciously fled from that debate.

At the Aylmer gathering, when former Ontario deputy health minister Marvin Barkin put the federal deficit numbers on a screen to explain, in part, why Canada's health system is fraying at the edges, only the most obdurate Liberal could have failed to get the message: deficits necessarily impose limits.

When Ken Battle, formerly of the National Council on Welfare and an especially shrewd commentator on Canadian social policy, discussed the limits of what social policy can accomplish, how many Liberals were listening?

When Kenneth Curtis, a Canadian who is senior vice-president of the Deutschebank in Tokyo, talked about the challenges of Asia and how hard people there are prepared to work, he was speaking indirectly about the limits imposed on one country's self-indulgence.

And when Professor Thurow was asked if a small country in the global scheme of things such as Canada can compete without joining economic blocks, he replied: only with the greatest internal discipline. In other words, limits.

Speakers, then, hammered home the need to formulate policy within limits imposed by external pressures and internal constraints. No one thought Canada could hide, retreat into protectionism or slide back into the ways of the late 1970s. Were the Liberals listening?

The overriding problem at the conference wasn't with the quality of the speakers, for they were excellent. Nor did it lie with the audience, which was engaged and intellectually impressive. After all, these were Liberals who, in their private businesses, university careers or own intellectual work, know most of what the speakers were talking about.

Rather, the problem lay in the paucity of Liberal MPs and senators. Only a handful had been asked to attend, ostensibly to prevent them from dominating the discussion. (They do rather tend to speak more than they listen.)

Instead, the party should have made attendance mandatory for them. The MPs and senators should have been strapped into the front-row chairs, made to take notes and then sit for a three-hour examination on what they had heard.

After all, it was ominous and depressing to hear one MP, after the very first speaker, decry what she believed to be the requirement that a Japanese model be imposed on Canada, when no one had recommended any such thing. Later, spirits sagged further when a powerful senator from the Trudeau era dismissed what Professor Thurow had said as hogwash, or words to that effect.

As intellectual nourishment, the conference was absolutely first-class. In the corridors and at dinners, rank-and-file Liberals and invited guests talked animatedly about the liberalism of limits, about finding the right mix of fiscal reality and social progress.

Alas, those who needed the message most—the party's parliamentary representatives—were largely absent. That was sad enough. Sadder still, however, is the thought that, had they been there, they might not have learned a thing.

Voters Want Something More Than a Doughnut Hole to Get Their Teeth Into

(February 10, 1993)

When Jean Chrétien unveils more of the Liberal Party's policy alternatives tomorrow in a Toronto speech, he'll leave a big hole in the doughnut.

That hole will be his party's policy, or rather lack of policy, for replacing the Goods and Services Tax.

On Monday of this week, he and his advisers settled on a strategy for dealing with the GST. They may think the strategy clever; in fact, it's transparent and will haunt the party for months.

Instead of outlining an alternative to the tax, or promising to do so before the next election, Mr. Chrétien will say the party intends to study alternatives after the election, and will perhaps send the issue to an independent committee of experts.

Talk about dodging an issue. Mr. Chrétien is dreaming if he thinks a commitment to study something as large as the GST after the election will satisfy the inquisitive media or the thinking public.

His problem is of his own making. Some months ago, he changed his script on the GST. Instead of saying the Liberals would search for an alternative and leaving matters at that, he pledged in colourful language to replace the tax.

Ever since, he has been badgered to explain how he would do that. He kept stonewalling, insisting he could not adequately analyze the problem until he had studied the nation's fiscal books. That study could only come after the election.

The GST revenue figures are a matter of public knowledge. Roughly ten minutes' perusal of those accounts could instruct Mr. Chrétien on the GST's costs and revenues. To suggest that he could not craft an alternative to the GST because he could not see the government's books insulted the intelligence of the electorate.

The problem with electors these days is that they are tired of duplicity, convolutions and evasions. They want straight talk. Most of them also want to vote against the Conservatives.

The Liberals' evasion on the GST is troubling for a party ostensibly serious about preparing to govern. We're not talking about piddling revenues or a minor policy: the GST is a mighty revenue producer, and will be mightier still when the economy fully recovers.

Even more troubling, the Liberals' evasion sends a signal that, despite Mr. Chrétien's policy speeches, the party really isn't thinking hard about governing. It's thinking only about the election.

In a perverse way, dodging an issue such as the GST accomplishes the impossible: it puts the Liberals on the defensive instead of the Conservatives. Better still for the Tories, this Liberal failure allows the Conservatives to attack the Liberals at the heart of their overall weakness, the perceived lack of depth of Mr. Chrétien.

Without an alternative from the Liberals, the Tories' case grows stronger: that perhaps, just perhaps, there is no better alternative to the GST. Hate the tax. Rail against it. But unless a plausible alternative can be found, the tax is immutable.

The central flaw in the Liberals' strategy is their belief that the hole in the doughnut will go away. Instead, the media will properly keep pestering Mr. Chrétien about it; the Conservatives will attack him relentlessly about it. Every time he delivers his non-answer, he will reinforce the damaging perception that he's an old-style politician who won't talk straight to the Canadian public. That perception is especially debilitating for a politician who boasts about talking "straight from the heart."

What the Liberals should do is present an alternative, then watch the issue be submerged in the swamps of detailed debate about the merits of the alternative. Eyes will glaze over once the parties begin slinging numbers about the revenue-raising potential of different taxes.

The problem is, of course, that a lower tax rate would mean broadening the tax to cover items now exempted, notably food. And the principal reason the Tories opted for the GST in its present form was the sheer political fear of having to tax food.

So rather than detail an alternative that might lead to taxing food, the Liberals have opted for a strategy of stonewalling, a strategy that will bring them more grief than benefits in the months ahead.

NDP

Auld Acquaintance *(May 14, 1987)*

Cloud Nine Air departed Ottawa yesterday bound for Socialist Heaven, bearing aloft Prime Minister–in–waiting Ed Broadbent. When Cloud Nine arrived at Regina Manifesto International Airport, J.S. Woodsworth, Tommy Douglas and David Lewis rushed forward to greet the plane.

"We shall have peace in our time," shouted Ed, waving aloft the latest Angus Reid poll. "The victory of the middle class is at hand."

J.S. Woodsworth looked distinctly uncomfortable. "In my time, we paid more attention to souls than polls."

"Thirty-seven per cent of Canadian souls say they're going to vote for us, J.S.," shouted Ed. "They love me everywhere."

"Not on Bay Street, I hope," said David Lewis. "I presume you're still kicking the hell out of the Corporate Welfare Bums—General Motors, the banks and other leeches on the working class."

"David, General Motors has changed. They deserved that money for Ste-Thérèse. They put a billion bucks into expanding their plant in good old Oshawa. They're just a company trying to earn an honest buck."

"But the banks," cried Tommy Douglas. "Think how they squeezed the little people—the farmers, the fishermen and the toiling masses. Nationalize the banks, I say."

"Tommy, Tommy, times have changed. Why, just the other day I was chatting with Bill Mulholland at the Bank of Montreal. He's a swell guy. We're working together to stop Amoco from gobbling up Dome. Bill and I are going to stick it to the Yanks."

"Well, I'm glad to hear that," said J.S. Woodsworth. "We want no truck or trade with them. Thank God the movement still wants out of NATO and NORAD."

"Yes, well. Ah. Um. I suppose the movement does want that. However, these polls suggest perhaps we should give this some sober second thought."

"Speaking of sober second thoughts," said Tommy Douglas, "let's blast away at the Senate in the next campaign."

"Tommy, I'd like to do that, I really would. But this Meech Lake accord gives the premiers the right to present lists of potential senators. And Brother Pawley's phone hasn't stopped ringing since the news got out."

"You mean that New Democrats in Manitoba, my beloved native province, want into the Senate?" stormed J.S. Woodsworth.

"Not all of them, J.S. Just most of them."

"Well, if we can't bash the Senate," said David Lewis, "let's call for universal day care on a national basis. Or a guaranteed annual income."

"I'm afraid we can't do that any more, David. The Meech Lake accord probably makes those sorts of things passé, or at least very difficult."

"Well, I presume we thundered against this accord?"

"Not really, David. Times have changed. The polls show us doing awfully well in Quebec, and it was important to bring Quebec into the constitution, and we just had to compromise."

"Compromise?" cried J.S. Woodsworth. "Where would this movement have been if we had compromised? None of us got to Socialist Heaven by compromising. Compromises are for what we used to call the 'old line parties.'"

"Calm down, J.S. Politics, from what the polls tell me, is the art of compromise."

"But we weren't in politics. We were more than a party. We were a movement. Oh, how I remember linking arms and singing *Solidarity Forever* and *Keep the Red Flag Flying*. You still sing those immortal tunes, don't you?"

"I didn't see *The Big Chill*, J.S."

"But you're all still red-blooded socialists, aren't you?" asked Tommy Douglas.

"Well, times have changed. We're all Yuppies now."

"I hope," said Tommy Douglas, "that this acronym stands for Your Unity Propels Progressives In Erecting Socialism."

"Actually, Tommy, it stands for Your Usual Pragmatic Politicians In Electoral Struggle."

Mr. Broadbent's Choice   (*March 3, 1989*)

If, as the political cliché has it, a week is a long time in politics, then what about twenty years?

That's how long Ed Broadbent has laboured in public life—for that entire period as MP for Oshawa or Oshawa–Whitby, and since 1975 as leader of the New Democratic Party.

The personal rewards have been substantial—the intellectual stimulation; the contributions to national debates; the deepened understanding of the whole damnable complexity of Canada, an understanding that only a tiny fraction of Canadians attain; the sense of having stood for social-democratic principles he always valued; and the example he offered, in the face of public cynicism to the contrary, that politics can be a higher calling.

Politically, Mr. Broadbent has not achieved his objective. The NDP cannot yet break the Conservative–Liberal duopoly on power. The last campaign was his own and the NDP's greatest disappointment, in large measure because unrealistically high expectations had been created long before the election. The post-election letdown has been punctuated with sorrow, anger and bitterness.

After twenty years in politics and four campaigns as leader, Mr. Broadbent has earned the right to forsake the leadership. Tomorrow, two weeks shy of his fifty-third birthday, he will reveal his decision.

A compelling case can be made for him to remain. The disagreeable fact is that federal and provincial elections have left the party without even one obvious successor. None of those whose names leap to mind as leadership pretenders possesses the combination of factors that, *prima facie*, would enable him or her to slide easily into Mr. Broadbent's slippers.

A political leader seldom thinks that those waiting in the wings are quite up to snuff. That may well have been David Lewis's view when he watched an awkward, tweedy fellow named Broadbent assume the NDP leadership in 1975. Indeed, those who knew Mr. Broadbent early in his political career—and fate threw him and me briefly together sixteen years ago—could not have imagined what an impressive public figure he would become. So leaders can grow in their jobs. Perhaps a wild rose is ready to bloom among the pretenders.

A dozen other reasons can be summoned to argue for Mr. Broadbent's continued tenure, and these have been sincerely and urgently pressed on him from many quarters in the NDP. He has experience, popularity, a capacity in French and political wisdom, a combination that remains in short supply in any party. No wonder so many New Democrats are askance at the prospect of dispensing with it.

And yet, upon reflection, there is one overriding reason why Mr. Broadbent should take his leave—the personal, human side of politics. If he stays to fight another election, he will be fifty-seven or fifty-eight years old. If he then decided to leave, it would be more awkward to launch a new career and to refresh himself. He owes it to himself—and the party owes it to him—to think of less taxing but still stimulating ways in which he could contribute to his country and party.

Mr. Broadbent is a man of catholic interests and discriminating preferences. These have inevitably been curtailed by the demands of politics, and especially by the rigours of leadership. After twenty years in politics, he deserves a chance to let those interests and preferences take him in other directions.

His talents will not long be idle outside politics. Teaching, foreign service, writing—these and other avenues will lie open to him.

His departure would undoubtedly dismay many New Democrats, who will think of their party first. If they think of Mr. Broadbent, however, they will understand if he leaves now: a dignified man who did not check his principles at the door on entering politics.

The NDP Victory in Ontario Is Evidence that Politics Has Become a Vast Bazaar Filled with Haggling Voters Looking for Values in the Political Market *(September 10, 1990)*

A wise politician never says never, and if the wisdom of that advice is not yet universally appreciated, perhaps the Ontario election will contribute to its application as a general rule of politics and political reporting.

Consider the nevers demolished Thursday night. That Ontario would never elect a socialist government, or one that even looked remotely like one. That Ontario would never elect a premier from Toronto, given the envy of that city elsewhere in the province. That great swaths of rural and small-town Ontario would never vote NDP. That a party could never lose twenty points in a six-week campaign.

By demolishing so many nevers, Bob Rae and the New Democrats have changed the face of Canadian politics. As long as the NDP stood third, or a weak second, in Ontario politics, it would be considered a third party for pan-Canadian purposes, a party whose enduring strength was limited to intermittent successes in three western provinces. By cracking Ontario, the NDP has taken a giant step toward national competitiveness, provided the Ontario experiment with the party does not turn to ash.

Sober New Democrats will concede that theirs was a classic protest victory. But against what and whom? Superficially, of course, against Premier David Peterson and the governing Liberals. But at a deeper level, the NDP victory represented the ascendancy of largely non-ideological forces that are battering traditional party loyalties in many parts of Canada.

Foremost of these is the cardinal importance of ethical integrity in an age of mighty cynicism about governance. In the sweep of Canadian political scandals, the Patti Starr affair was small beer. So were the ministerial resignations that beset the Peterson government. But as politicians everywhere are learning to their sorrow—witness Prime Minister Brian Mulroney from 1984 to 1986 and even Premier John Buchanan in Nova Scotia these days—the electorate will no longer tolerate even the perception of scandal, let alone the genuine article. The cynicism about politicians is like a bed of coals: one strong breath and a flame erupts, singeing those it touches.

But integrity involves more than the avoidance of scandal. Integrity, politically speaking, increasingly means a discernible set of core values which the leader incarnates and communicates by words and policies. It matters less what those core values are than that the leader has them.

Television has much to do with this state of affairs. There is much that television cannot effectively do with modern politics, because government is extraordinarily complex, full of shadings and trade-offs and limits to action, all of which are anathema to a medium that craves visual excitements, black-and-white confrontations, rapid pace and, above all, personalities.

But television is ubiquitous. It follows leaders everywhere in public and over long periods of time, and from that exposure a merciless and uncannily accurate picture emerges of the persona of the leader. After a while under the lights—in the legislature, in scrums, in interviews, in photo opportunities, even in unguarded moments captured on film—a politician becomes eerily transparent. And that transparency captures the essence of the politician, and in particular, his or her core values.

It could be seen in governing, and in the election campaign, that David Peterson seemed bereft of any particular set of values. That he was personally honest, socially affable, earnest when required and intent upon competence were all duly noted, and found fundamentally wanting. There was no issue, save one, that seemed to summon passion from him, or require the injection of his convictions into public policy. And that one issue—support for the Meech Lake accord, in which he deeply and honourably believed— placed him on the wrong side of the issue and in cahoots with a process that not only disgusted so many citizens but did not even have the redeeming grace of succeeding in its own appointed objectives.

The calling of the election fatally confirmed, as things turned out, that he did not seek a mandate for reasons of conviction but rather of expediency. And expediency, which has never been removed from political calculations, was compounded by a campaign so poorly conceived and lamentably executed that it merely confirmed the widespread and latent cynicism toward politicians seen to be fighting for power in its own right rather than the right to use it for some compelling purpose.

It used to be assumed that the politics of Ontario was the politics of management. It still is, to the extent any incompetent government will be swiftly exposed and subsequently punished. But a variety of factors make mere managerial competence an insufficient yardstick of political success.

Managerial government is about trade-offs and acknowledgement of limits. But we now live in the age of interest group ascendancy, and interest groups, by definition, seldom recognize limits, at least in their public pronouncements and political actions. Theirs is zero-sum politics, magnified by easy accessibility to the media, especially television, which thrives on the confrontations and indictments these groups provide.

The rise of interest groups means that people increasingly participate in politics through occupational, ethnic, linguistic or single-issue associations, which are seen as more "representative," effective and persistent vehicles for achieving results than political parties with all their compromises.

Interest groups, television, an increasingly diversified population, the cynicism about parties: these are among the factors tearing people from traditional political moorings. Three times in six years, the Ontario electorate changed political horses. In Ottawa, the federal Tories yo-yo from assumed defeat to victory to the lowest polling standing on record.

Politics is now like a vast Turkish bazaar through which the electorate passes, haggling with the political vendors, assuming the vendors are in it for themselves, threatening to go elsewhere if the price is not right, and demonstrating that customer loyalty means next to nothing. In this bazaar, a political vendor who at least temporarily seems to believe in his product—somebody who has core values and ethical integrity—stands a fair chance of making a sale. But soon after the sale is made, the shopping begins again.

The NDP has its core vote of about 20 per cent in Ontario, customers who always shop at the same stall. That the NDP received 17 per cent above its core vote—and won a majority—does not mean, indeed it would be politically fatal for the NDP to assume it means, these one-time shoppers will be around next time. Plenty of these new NDP shoppers simply didn't like the goods from their most recent vendor, the Liberals, and remembered something vaguely disquieting about their old ones, the Conservatives.

In a curious way, the Ontario NDP benefited, as the federal Conservatives did in the 1988 election, because it was a group that believed in something, that was willing to tie its leader to a set of ideas that therefore made the leader and the party committed to using power for some public purpose rather than as an end in itself. Free trade saved Brian Mulroney's political career, because it seemed consistent with his political outlook, galvanized powerful interest groups to his side, and made it seem, however implausibly to his critics, that he had an idea on a major issue where he wanted to take the country. There was nothing so riveting as free trade in the Ontario election, but in an election where the Liberals seemed to stand for everything and therefore fundamentally for nothing, the New Democrats, who ran the most conventional of NDP campaigns, suddenly appeared to have a leader with core values, rigid ethics and a sense of political purpose.

Paradoxically for a party that claims deeper ideological moorings than the old-line parties, the NDP victory was not the triumph of ideology. The election was too much of a protest vote for that interpretation to be remotely plausible. But the party's win did demonstrate further the emerging trend in Canadian politics: that politics is about values and attitudes, and the policies that flow from them. Canadian politics is no longer about brokerage or management, but about parties seizing on ideas, anchored by values incarnated by the leader, and demonstrating one election at a time to wary, often cynical voters, that the party believes in what it is saying.

When the Unions Turn Their Back on the NDP, That's Opportunity (August 4, 1993)

Ontario Premier Bob Rae doesn't get much of a break from anybody these days. That's rather too bad, because he deserves better press than he's been getting.

The public-sector union leaders are all over him, of course, for the euphemistically entitled "social contract" that cut their members' wages. Lifelong New Democrats eagerly tell inquiring reporters why Mr. Rae has betrayed the party.

In Ottawa, former NDP finance critic Steven Langdon publishes a letter denouncing his old friend at Queen's Park. Federal NDP Leader Audrey McLaughlin mumbles and coughs and averts her eyes when Mr. Rae's name is mentioned. Her comments about him are, well, diplomatic, as if his government were responsible for the federal NDP's woes.

The business press in Toronto hounds him relentlessly. The bullhorns for business keep firing away. They locked onto a line of attack on Day One of the NDP government and, despite obvious changes in the government's direction, they're still locked on. They have been consistent, if not fair.

Speaking of consistency, over on the far Left, scattered critics in the universities who purport to be the last of the NDP's "true believers" lament Mr. Rae's abandonment of principle, failing to understand—to no one's surprise who has read them over the years—what happened in the real world; namely, that the Ontario electorate did not vote for socialism or anything like it almost three years ago. It voted against a Liberal government, and Mr. Rae happened to be around as the best alternative.

The "social contract" negotiations have been messy, chaotic and less successful than the government pretends, but they are nevertheless an Ontario reflection of a nation-wide trend. In every single Canadian province— Ontario simply being the last—governments have looked at the size and cost of their public service, matched that against actual and anticipated revenues, and concluded that the cost of the public service was too large.

Those who lambaste or bemoan Mr. Rae's performance must remember how politically difficult it has been to claw back money and break collective agreements for a party committed to generic links with the trade-union movement.

From his erstwhile friends in that movement, Mr. Rae has received what all politicians receive from outraged interest groups: insults and threats. These, however, are more hilarious than serious, since the threats to work actively against the NDP in the next election might help the Liberals and Conservatives.

Anyone who believes that a Liberal or Conservative government would be more to the liking of the trade-union leaders now threatening Mr. Rae is as out of touch with reality as most of these ladies and gentlemen are daily portraying themselves to be.

Although the short-term relationship between the political wing of the New Democratic Party and the trade-union leaders has gone sour, this souring might be exceptionally beneficial for the NDP.

For years—no, for decades—it has been obvious that the generic links between the party and the trade-union movement consign the NDP to almost perpetual opposition. The union leaders provide money and rhetoric, but seldom a majority of their members to support the party on election day.

The NDP did not win the last election because of trade-union votes; it won because for the first time ever hundreds of thousands of other Ontarians gave the party a one-time vote as a protest against David Peterson's Liberals, not because they endorsed the NDP policies or program.

What those one-time voters have since seen is the public-sector unions howling and complaining about their rights and wages, at a time when the province's economy is flat on its back, taxes have shot up, and the deficit remains huge. For the NDP to be tightly associated with these unions in the next election—and beyond—would be political suicide. Indeed, one of the biggest mistakes the NDP made was kowtowing to these groups shortly after the election.

From crisis comes opportunity, and the opportunity before the NDP is a weakening of its relationship with the public-sector unions that will cause short-term grief but provide long-term political benefits.

REFORM

The Two-Nations Paradox at the Heart of Mr. Manning's Reform Party *(April 9, 1991)*

SASKATOON—Preston Manning believes he can see clearly many elements of the Canadian condition, but paradox is obviously not among them.

The Reform Party, which Mr. Manning founded and now leads, has a profound paradox at its very core. How that paradox plays itself out will largely determine whether the party remains a second-tier party or completely remakes the Canadian political system outside Quebec.

The paradox is unwittingly revealed in almost every speech the leader makes. In his powerful address to the party's successful convention in Saskatoon, Mr. Manning asserted: "Reformers therefore say, 'Old Canada'— the Canada defined as an equal partnership between two founding races, languages and cultures, the English and the French—is dying."

A few moments later, he hammered home the same point, the cornerstone of his indictment of contemporary Canadian politics: "In considering the foundations on which to build New Canada, there will be those—the Mulroneys, the Chrétiens, the McLaughlins, the politicians of the old order—who will insist that we must continue to consider French–English relations as the cornerstone of Canada's future constitutional development.

"And I say to you that no more damnable advice could be given to the Canadian people at this point in time than that."

So Canada is not, and never has been, composed of two races, two peoples, two founding peoples, two nations, two major groups: just One Canada of many peoples where linguistic matters ought to have been purely local affairs. It's a message of explosive political potential outside Quebec, where an increasing number of citizens resent what they see as Quebec's excessive influence on Canadian life.

And yet, when Mr. Manning begins to explain how the future constitutional evolution of Canada should unfold, the paradox looms, then overwhelms the rest of his message.

For he proposes that Canada—the New Canada, as he calls it—get its constitutional act together, then sit down with the New Quebec and decide whether an accommodation can be reached to keep Canada united. The Great Canadian Constitutional Negotiation between duly elected negotiators for Quebec and Canada would follow the holding of constituent assemblies, perhaps a Quebec referendum and elections in Quebec and Canada.

Seldom, if ever, has a political leader articulated more forcefully, if inadvertently, the two-nations theory of Canada, the very theory Mr. Manning so urgently rejects. He is acknowledging by his constitutional position that there are two major groups or peoples or political entities or nations or races (the words are mine, not his), one in Quebec and one in the rest of Canada.

Similarly, his party will not organize, recruit candidates, raise money or try to influence opinion in Quebec, for any success in these endeavours might hinder the Reformers in speaking for the New Canada. In other words, a party that tries to represent Canadians everywhere—to appeal simultaneously inside and outside Quebec—cannot adequately represent only Canada outside Quebec. Two nations, in other words.

Paradoxically, if Canadians really do start thinking of themselves as two nations, or peoples, and if those two nations or peoples cannot get along with each other, each will probably turn to parties and individuals who speak only for that nation or that people.

This is precisely Mr. Manning's bet. He is counting on Canadians thinking of themselves as two nations or peoples or groups, so that his Reform Party can become the vehicle for English-speaking Canadians to articulate their vision of themselves and to defend their interests, all the while denouncing the two-nations theory of Canada.

If Canadians do approach a constitutional reconciliation by 1992—because English-speaking and French-speaking Canadians decide they do want to remain together by intermingling and co-operating—Mr. Manning's party, especially in Ontario, will be seen as a great danger to Canadian unity. But if Canadians feel their country is deconstructing, and the two nations are ready to go their own way, the Reform Party could turn from a Western Canadian flame into a raging political grass fire outside Quebec.

What Mr. Manning wants for New Canada is so antithetical to anything remotely acceptable to the New Quebec—and vice versa—that without ever stating it directly, he is positioning himself to be a major player in, or perhaps the leader of, the Canadian delegation for the secession of Quebec from Canada, or the divorce of the two nations or peoples that he denies even exist.

Reformer Preston Manning Infuses His Politics with the Religious Spirit *(April 10, 1991)*

SASKATOON—With just a few minutes left in the Reform Party convention, leader Preston Manning was still at the microphone—he seemed to have been there for much of the conference—and he asked all riding executive members to stand.

About one-quarter of the delegates rose, awaiting his words. "I charge you this day in the presence of the delegates to this assembly," he intoned, "to go out and find the very best candidates you can discover to carry the Reform Party's banner in the next federal election."

Mr. Manning did not ask them. He did not encourage or instruct or suggest. He charged them.

In secular society, to be charged is to have run afoul of the law. In economic society, to be charged is to be asked to pay. In conventional political discourse, to be charged is to be accused of failing to deliver. But in the church, to be charged is to be given a mission, to have hands laid on, to be infused with a higher calling, and to stand before one's peers—as at a person's communion or a minister's indoctrination—to accept the charge.

No other Canadian political leader would dream of using "charge" in this manner, infusing politics with religious language or framing a political statement in the trappings of a religious ceremony. Other leaders would find it too corny and awkward, for most of them have accepted the conventional assumption that religion and politics belong in separate spheres of public life.

But Mr. Manning springs from the political soil of southern Alberta, which gave the province Bible Bill Aberhart and Mr. Manning's own father, Ernest. These were Social Credit premiers for whom the calling of fundamentalist religion and the precepts of the Protestant churches blended, not just easily but urgently, with the politician's task of assisting others to achieve a better life.

Mr. Manning does not carry this blending too far, certainly not as far as Messrs. Aberhart and Manning Sr., but that he does it at all marks the Reform Party leader off from all other politicians in Canada. The cadences of his oratory, the religiously inspired phraseology, the frequent references to Abraham Lincoln, whose own oratory was so influenced by the Bible: these all bear witness to the blending of religion and politics.

So, too, does the sense of mission. In the formative days of the Co-operative Commonwealth Federation on the Prairies, this blending of religion and politics created a deep sense of mission. These days, however, the New Democratic Party is almost embarrassed by the ministers in its midst, an embarrassment never felt in the early days when so many men of the cloth preached the social gospel from the pulpit and the political platform.

Just as the eradication of sin and the curbing of desire inspires religious missionaries, so missionaries of the political variety think of party politics practised by the old-line parties as venal, unprincipled and corrupt, sacrificing the people's will to private interests and sullied compromises. Reformers today, like some CCFers of old, are therefore charged by their leaders to pull down the political temples and let justice and freedom, the earthly manifestations of His goodness, prevail.

Social Credit, the CCF, the Progressives, the United Farmers, the Non-Partisans, the No-Party League, the Comrades of Equity, the Direct Legislation League: all these prairie-based protests began as movements, thought of themselves as movements even after entering electoral politics, and as political movements remained uncomfortable with the inevitable constraints of party politics.

Not so the Reform Party. Although the leader's language is missionary, as is the fervour of the delegates, Reformers began as party members, accepted the trapping of party and now take their charge from the leader to organize, recruit and otherwise comport themselves as partisans. When Mr. Manning and those around him say they have learned from the failures and tribulations of previous protest movements, they mean, among other things, the refusal of those movements to prepare adequately for electoral combat.

This explains the attention paid at the convention to the party's constitution, the recruitment of delegates, and finance. Because the party has so many refugees from other parties who are accustomed to electoral politics, the Reform Party is not starting from scratch. Furthermore, the refugees have now been suitably charged by their new leader.

Behind the Man of Ideas Stand the Men of Anger and Grievance *(January 30, 1992)*

CALGARY—Preston Manning soaked up politics at his father's knee. All those years that Ernest Manning was premier of Alberta, his son watched, listened and then waited for his own big chance.

There were times, as he recounts in his recently published autobiography, when the younger Manning was invited to involve himself in the Conservative Party. But he was a child of a prairie protest movement and the Conservative Party was not for him. It was too traditional. It was also too variegated for him to lead.

Reading Mr. Manning's autobiography, a picture of a very determined young man develops. What has now emerged as the Reform Party began taking shape in his mind years before it inched its way onto the political stage. Indeed, all his consulting contracts, the books he read, the travels he undertook, seemed part of the conscious self-education.

Mr. Manning recounts that at one point in his life he read Will and Ariel Durant's *History of Civilization*. The Durants wrote a kind of common man's overview of world history, and their books, sold through mail-order clubs, adorned hundreds of thousands of bookshelves. They were books to be seen, not read, but Mr. Manning, being nothing if not disciplined, ploughed through all twelve volumes.

So, too, with other areas of interest. At another point, he set about reading the history of Western Canadian populism. At yet another, he immersed himself in the pre–Civil War period of the United States. Then he studied the standard works of Canadian history, and from them formed his own conclusions about the inherently unstable nature of the federation.

Anyone who listens to Mr. Manning, or converses with him privately, quickly understands that he is the best-read of the party leaders. Now, this may not be saying much, but it indicates that he is comfortable with ideas. He has formed a certain world view, anchored in his religious beliefs, the relationship of those beliefs to the secular world, and the experience of his father's Social Credit administration.

In many respects, the Reform Party is the national expression of the late stages of Alberta's Social Credit regime. Frugality in government, attentiveness to people, suspicion of bureaucracy, wariness toward central Canada, distrust of established money, tradition in family structure, simplicity of ideas—these were among the hallmarks of Social Credit that are reflected today in the Reform Party and its leader.

There was, too, a strong sense in Social Credit that the country's institutions and conventions had been set by French- and English-speaking elites in Ontario and Quebec, and that they did not reflect the settlement pattern, life experience or economic needs of Western Canada. Thus, Mr. Manning places the Reform Party squarely in the protest tradition of the West, which began, he says, with Louis Riel and carried on through the Haultain administration of the Northwest Territory and the political movements of the Progressive Party, the CCF and Social Credit.

Only the CCF transcended its regional starting point, in large part because its founders always saw themselves as committed to internationalist goals and moral principles that could be applied anywhere under propitious circumstances, and with proper leadership.

In taking the Reform Party into central and Atlantic Canada, Mr. Manning must distance himself from some of its antecedents and even some of its founders, who believed passionately in a new party only for western interests. After all, it's fine to run against central Canada in Lethbridge or Saskatoon, and to believe as gospel the editorials of *Alberta Report* magazine; it's quite another to go fishing for votes with the same message in Brampton or Beaconsfield.

In private and public, Mr. Manning is mild-mannered, almost boyish, personally considerate and moderate of language. But those who follow him are often consumed with anger and grievances for which the Reform Party is a convenient vehicle. Mr. Manning, therefore, provides a respectable cover and compelling voice for those who have felt excluded or put upon by government.

With anger as one of English-speaking Canada's defining characteristics these days, Reform Party supporters have found a mild man to articulate their hurts. The traditional parties would be foolish to assume others may not follow.

PART 7 *Politicians*

PIERRE TRUDEAU

Stardust Memories *(June 15, 1985)*

Was it only a year ago, Pierre, that you did that little pirouette on stage and waved us all goodbye?

You weren't too gracious to John Turner, sending him off with that silly little wave, but then you never could hide your contempt.

Indeed, Pierre, when I reflect upon what has changed in a year, it is the absence of rancour bordering on hate. You stirred up quite a few passions in your time, my friend. You tried to impose a relentless logic on a country that defies logic. You made so many accumulated enemies—some gratuitously, some in a good cause—that you alienated whole regions of the country and large swaths of the electorate.

But this was your style; no, this was your character. And so striking was its impact that no trace of it remains.

Nothing remains, Pierre, because the country couldn't take any more confrontation. It had suffered too many bruises and endured too much change; it felt drained by too many of your infernal challenges.

You said it yourself, but as usual the media weren't paying sufficient attention. You told the Liberal delegates that you never feared appealing over the heads of the premiers, the multinationals, the business community—in so many words, the elites—directly to the people.

And so you did, especially through television and on the few issues you cared passionately about. In this, you were a unique Canadian prime minister. You spurned trying to knit consensus among the diverse elites of this quiltwork country and appealed instead directly to individuals. For you, the nineteenth-century liberal, nothing should stand between the citizen and the state. Man defined himself as an individual, not in terms of his group, his heritage, his region.

This was all clear, compelling, even exciting, but it was quite unlike what Canadians had come to expect from their political leaders. And it is a testament to the stubborn grip of tradition that your style left with you.

Now, Pierre, the older, enduring style of governing Canada has returned with Brian Mulroney, as it would have with John Turner.

Brian, like John, is a network guy, on the phone all the time to pals, acquaintances, even strangers, taking stock, reaching out, wheeling and dealing, trying to feel his way to solutions. He'll move all right, but only after seeing what the boys think along the networks, around the Cabinet table, in the caucus, in the provincial governments and, yes, even in the newspapers.

You hated doing that. How much more intellectually satisfying to study an issue to death, to talk it through with a few whom you considered your intellectual equals, to test it on your political aides, then to sell it, regardless of what the premiers, or the farmers, or the business community, or the caucus thought. By your forceful mind, your relentless determination and your fierce pride, you won your fair share of battles.

It would be smugly comforting to agree with your remaining intellectual admirers that there was a magnificence to this way of governing, that we were somehow not worthy of you. But too many Canadians recall not only the magnificence and the Constitution, but the patronage, the regional alienation, the broken promises, the $35-billion deficit and the policy zig-zags, and paraphrase the general: "C'était magnifique, mais ce n'était pas la guerre."

A year later, Pierre, your greatness still obscures your virtues.

The Trudeau Presence *(August 29, 1987)*

Like an aging rock star, Pierre Trudeau's voice remains intact, but his music has gone somewhat out of style.

He can still sell tickets, though. An hour before Himself arrived, the Railway Committee Room was bursting with the curious. Time warp held us transfixed when the tell-tale trail of cameramen and photographers, all pedalling backwards, preceded him into the room, and the stir of anticipation hushed everyone inside it.

The thought could not be banished: how many times, and in how many places, had we seen all this before? The years blurred. Those eyes. The shrugs. The arched eyebrows. The arguments by *reductio ad absurdum*. The arrogance. The passion. "But who will speak for Canada?" "A Prime Minister should not be head waiter for the premiers." "Canada's unity will not be fractured." "Fish swim." The Victoria Conference, Nov. 15, 1976, the referendum, the Paul Sauvé arena, patriation.

For two-and-a-half hours, history was refought but not reshaped. His vision will not die, not because he articulated it but because it has always reflected an element of the Canadian reality. But for now, as he must know, the other element—the province-building, decentralist one—is in the ascendancy, for reasons of political expediency and circumstances. The most important of these is a nation-wide reaction against the excesses, real or perceived, of his years running federal-provincial relations.

He always knew his audience, especially the one he could not see. Those in attendance Thursday night were props. Out there, in the hearts and minds of Canadians, that's where his audience was, as always. And those who listened could not have remained indifferent, for they had never been in the past. They despised or loved him; they respected or denigrated him. He represented what they would have liked to become, and what they would not have liked to be.

This was political theatre, at which he always excelled, but any good theatre requires a gripping script. He had one, the same one he had had for forty years, the lines pregnant with meaning, their impact almost entirely dependent on circumstances.

Within the Liberal Party, of course, his performance rendered everything more difficult. But then, he never was much of a party man. The party was a vehicle of convenience, not his life. He shook hands with the Liberal MPs Thursday night, then shook the party again.

The Meech Lake accord, the subject of current debates, is already history. It cannot be undone, or even substantially changed, for the politicians who consummated it are committed to their progeny. Federal-provincial deals cut in the dead of night withstand the light of day, because the intricacy of their compromises confounds subsequent reconsideration lest the whole deal fall apart. We shall only know the consequences of Meech Lake many years from now. Nothing he said could alter that stark political reality.

Nobody else seemed ready to articulate that vision of the country for which he, and so many others, fought. So he spoke, intemperately to be sure, arrogantly perhaps, provocatively, compellingly. He did not win; he cannot win. History heard his words; the present remains deaf.

Maybe he was the general fighting old wars, a prisoner of obsolete strategies. Probably, though, fashions will change, new crises will emerge, the balance of federalism will swing too sharply the other way, and he will be heard again, from some distant place.

Old Colleagues May Drift Away, But Mr. Trudeau Holds His Course *(September 23, 1992)*

Forty-two years ago, as he wrote this week, Pierre Trudeau contributed his first article to *Cité Libre*.

Ever the trenchant polemicist, he has returned to the superb pamphleteering style he displayed in that magazine, the style he finds most comfortable.

In *Maclean's* and *L'Actualité* this week, he excoriated the same demons of Quebec nationalism that incurred his wrath as an intellectual gadfly in the 1950s in Montreal.

The wheel has come full circle. Forty years ago, he was at the margin of political debate in Quebec. Now, eight years after leaving high office, he finds himself again at the margin in Quebec.

In the meantime, he served for sixteen years as Prime Minister and as a federal MP for nineteen years. He left an indelible legacy in Canada, mostly outside his own province.

Having railed quite brilliantly against the Meech Lake accord, he now has the Charlottetown accord in his sights, because both agreements attempted to accommodate, rather than confront, Quebec nationalists not already committed to secession.

Even among his erstwhile intellectual soulmates, precious few support the absolutism of his views. During Meech Lake, most of his former Cabinet colleagues from Quebec dissociated themselves from his attacks. Now, even Senator Michael Pitfield, a close Trudeau friend, has said he will grudgingly support the Charlottetown accord. Reportedly, former Trudeau Cabinet minister Marc Lalonde has said the same.

Mr. Trudeau has been left dispiritingly alone, deserted by almost all those who answered his call in Quebec through five general elections. He has returned, therefore, to the place he occupied in the Quebec political firmament four decades ago.

By virtue of his standing and his roots in Quebec, he can say things which, if uttered by any English-Canadian politician, would be dismissed at best as unsympathetic to Quebec, at worst as exceedingly hostile. It is part of his appeal, albeit one he would not wish, that his views can be so easily turned to advantage by those who are truly antagonistic toward Quebec.

Much like former British prime minister Margaret Thatcher, Mr. Trudeau has not opted for a silent retirement. The two seldom operated on the same wavelength as world leaders, but their characters were not dissimilar, and the depths of their convictions were identical. They simply cannot remain silent about issues they consider vital to the future of their countries.

They both sense, not without reason, that a subsequent crop of politicians is allowing their legacies to slip away. They decry the softness of their successors, their "wetness" (to use a Thatcherism), their willingness to make dangerous compromises and their failure to operate from first principles.

Both start, however, from fundamentally different premises. Lady Thatcher warns Britain against the perils of federalism represented by a more integrated European Community; Mr. Trudeau warns Quebec against leaving an integrated federalism. She does not believe multi-ethnic federations can long survive; he believes them to be humankind's best political response to diversity.

Mr. Trudeau's polemic skewers many nationalists where it hurts: in their ultimately craven refusal to believe fully in their own prescriptions. Not once in this generation have the firmest among them dared to present Quebeckers with the genuine alternatives: secession or federalism.

Instead, Quebec politics swings around various intermediate formulas: profitable federalism, cultural sovereignty, sovereignty-association, special status, asymmetrical federalism, a European-style common market, more decentralization, distinct society.

Mr. Trudeau was always the Cartesian, wanting to draw straight, logical lines from premises to conclusions. As such, he remained endlessly compelling as a public figure but, forty years ago as now, a marginal figure in the Quebec political culture, where ambiguity is prized over clarity—the classic reflex of a minority always looking for leverage against the majority.

Mr. Trudeau had a dream—a very noble dream—about the organization of Canadian society. It is a tragedy, but also a fact, that this dream wound up having more takers outside his own province than within.

At least he had a dream, however, which is more than can be said for those who now view Canada, as he once said, as a collection of shopping centres.

BRIAN MULRONEY

Travels with Brian   *(June 19, 1986)*

Date: September, 1985
Memo: To all staff
From: Prime Minister's Office

As you know, the boss will be travelling soon to New York. He will be staying at the Pierre Hotel for $1,200 a night. Fred Doucet will be accompanying the

Prime Minister. Fred is setting an example to us all by staying in a $600-a-night room. The Prime Minister wishes all PMO staff to note Fred's sacrifice.

The Prime Minister will also be taking twenty-nine suitcases on the trip. Each will be appropriately tagged with PMO markings. Here is a list of what each will contain:

Suitcase 1: Robert Coates's political corpse.

Suitcase 2: Mr. Mulroney's shirts.

Suitcase 3: Copies of *Where I Stand.*

Suitcase 4: Mr. Mulroney's suits.

Suitcase 5: The collected travel writings of Suzanne Blais-Grenier.(Mrs. Blais-Grenier has given us invaluable travel advice in planning the trip.)

Suitcase 6: Mrs. Mulroney's wardrobe.

Suitcase 7: Mrs. Mulroney's wardrobe.

Suitcase 8: Mrs. Mulroney's wardrobe.

Suitcase 9: Mrs. Mulroney's wardrobe.

Suitcase 10: Mrs. Mulroney's wardrobe.

Suitcase 11: Canned tuna.

Suitcase 12: Mr. Mulroney's ties.

Suitcase 13: Mr. Mulroney's socks.

Suitcase 14: Copies of the Prime Minister's speech.

Suitcase 15: Gifts for foreign dignitaries.

Suitcase 16: Moosehead beer. (See Suitcase 15.)

Suitcase 17: Mr. Mulroney's overcoats.

Suitcase 18: Mr. Mulroney's shoes.

Suitcase 19: Government of Canada travel posters.

Suitcase 20: PMO photographic equipment.

Suitcase 21: Mr. Mulroney's accessories.

Suitcase 22: Pictures of the Prime Minister.

Suitcase 23: Pictures of the Prime Minister.

Suitcase 24: Pictures of the Prime Minister.

Suitcase 25: Copies of the Progressive Conservative Party's election commitments. (This suitcase to be dumped into the East River so that it will not wash ashore in Canada.)

Suitcase 26: Empty, in case Mrs. Mulroney has time to shop.

Suitcase 27: See above.

Suitcase 28: See above.

Suitcase 29: See above.

The Prime Minister asks all staff to please note that this trip will cost only $62,225.10, or roughly $15,000 per day. He is disturbed by rumours that his forthcoming trip to Paris will cost $520,024.17, or about $70,000 per day; and that the budget for the Washington trip in March is $229,403.92, or about $75,000 per day. He does believe the $50,000 to be spent on the official dinner in Washington will be worth the extensive publicity this slap-bang affair will bring Canada.

As everyone in receipt of this memo knows, Mr. Mulroney campaigned on eliminating "waste and duplication" in government as a means of reducing the deficit. He expects everyone on staff to bear this in mind at all times.

To this end, no backup planes will be required for his flight to New York. Only one Canadian flag, one podium, one official seal of Canada and one complete technical support crew will be used. Backup equipment will not be taken. No Hercules will be used on this trip.

In planning these and other trips, please remember the boss's words from *Where I Stand*: "How can a government call on a nation to restrain itself and to be more realistic in its collective demands upon our economy when its own record is an unbroken string of fiscal excess? Canadians may be many things. Stupid we are not."

The Blarney Factor (*August 27, 1986*)

Travelling in Quebec last week, Prime Minister Brian Mulroney was asked about polls showing his party in the dumps in the province.

Now, a wise politician never comments on polls because they are often (1) unreliable, (2) misleading, (3) wrong and (4) changeable, month over month. But, if pressed, the wise politician mumbles a few platitudes which are quickly forgotten.

Mr. Mulroney, however, could not resist temptation. "I'm telling you today," he said, "that not only will we win the same number of seats we did last time in Quebec, we are going to improve on it." And so another marker went down against which Mr. Mulroney will be judged, a marker unnecessarily planted a long way from current reality.

The Prime Minister's prediction could easily be dismissed as the usual political guff if it were not symptomatic of his apparently incorrigible propensity to exaggerate, a propensity that drives some of his friends to distraction and lands his Conservative Party in the uncomfortable gap between promise and delivery.

Mulroney markers lie across the Canadian political landscape. The last Conservative campaign was built on promising the moon to every group and region. Since then, the Prime Minister has responded to most attacks by putting down additional markers. The trouble is that these markers establish expectations which any government would be lucky to achieve.

Not long ago, some of Mr. Mulroney's friends outside the government sent along comments about ways of improving his performance and image. Curb the exaggerations. Cut down the blarney. Those were two of the most urgent suggestions.

Other friends, inside the government and beyond, had made similar suggestions before. Occasionally the Prime Minister promises to reform. But his love of hyperbole and partisan political debate always gets the better of him.

You could see the problem watching Mr. Mulroney in his constituency. He'd talk quite sincerely for a few minutes about the problems of isolated communities or the need for tolerance and understanding. Then he'd switch gears into the usual political pattern, drag in John Turner, add a couple of boasts and generally puff things up. The performance was all so unnecessary, because the people of tiny, isolated villages do not come to hear political speeches.

Mr. Mulroney can contain himself when he tries. He didn't fall for any senseless Margaret Thatcher bashing after making an important contribution at the Commonwealth mini-summit. He didn't rise to the provocation of Alberta Premier Donald Getty's speech condemning the federal government for treating the West with the same disdain as the Liberals. But the containment effort apparently couldn't be sustained. He could not resist adding that his government had done more for the West than any previous federal government, which might surprise students of John Diefenbaker's record.

All politicians are forgiven political flights of rhetoric. The trouble with constant exaggeration is the perception of phoniness that accompanies each statement. If exaggeration becomes the norm, even modest statements look contrived.

Constant exaggeration can also create the sneaking impression that the politician really doesn't know what he wants to say or where to take the country. Or, it can make a politician seem to be hiding something. Unfairly or otherwise, these impressions about Mr. Mulroney are definitely around the country.

In the television age, where the image of the messenger rivals the importance of the message, Mr. Mulroney's exaggerations are hurting the party. The question is: can a politician in mid-term alter, not his tactics, but an important part of his character?

The Mulroney Image *(July 28, 1987)*

Wandering about the country these past two weeks and visiting three provinces has confirmed that the Conservatives' biggest problem remains Prime Minister Brian Mulroney.

Almost everywhere that you engage someone in conversation about federal affairs, the same theme keeps coming back—Brian, Brian, Brian. Of course, dyed-in-the-wool Tories give you a different answer, sometimes.

The leader as deadweight is a cruel and somewhat unfair reality. The Prime Minister put the Meech Lake agreement together, and, whatever doubts you may have about the agreement, the agreement was an intricate political achievement.

Or the national park on South Moresby. There's no doubt the package came together because of the personal intervention of Mr. Mulroney, who persuaded the Premier of British Columbia, against the wishes of his caucus, to change his principles for a bag of federal coin.

So, too, the conventional wisdom around Ottawa, shared by yours truly, was that the government had enjoyed three or four solid months before the parliamentary break. When things go wrong, everyone properly blames the Prime Minister. When things go right, logic dictates he should receive the credit.

And yet, out there in the country—so far as one could gather—the Prime Minister's image remains unrelievedly poor. You could feel it palpably in Newfoundland. Here's a prime minister who gave the Newfoundland government its Atlantic Accord over the offshore, and who has sanctioned bucketloads of federal spending for the province. Yet to hear voters talk, it was as if none of this had ever happened. They just felt uncomfortable about him at best, hostile at worst.

It was the same on the Prairies. Mr. Mulroney has competent ministers in the three Prairie provinces. His government has pumped lots of money into the grain industry. It is battling for free trade, a historic demand on the Prairies. It is pushing ahead with transportation deregulation, which speaks to the West's historic sense of injustice about transportation rates. And yet, Mr. Mulroney isn't cutting it on the Prairies.

Rightly or wrongly, there is a sense that the Prime Minister can't be trusted, or at least that he doesn't say what he means. That has been a problem for several years, and it doesn't seem to be on the mend, despite his efforts to reduce the bombast and to become less involved in the cut and thrust of Commons debates.

He knows that the sniff of scandal, or at least of insufficient attention to ethics, hangs around the government's neck. That's why the government is proceeding with what may be called a package of reform in government ethics. The lobbyist-registration bill, the election-expenses reforms and the forthcoming conflict-of-interest proposals are part of the package.

Whether these measures can reassure the country about the government's values and attitudes remains to be seen. Certainly, the suspicions are exceedingly deep. With the Sinclair Stevens inquiry report due this fall, the influence-peddling trial of a Quebec Tory MP pending, and the Attorney-General of

Quebec's decision forthcoming on whether to prosecute in the Oerlikon affair, there will be plenty to remind the country of its suspicions.

The Prime Minister was apparently in an upbeat frame of mind after the parliamentary session, seemingly convinced that his government had turned the corner. It's not the first time he has believed that. If the imperfect guide of many conversations scattered across the country is indicative, the corner still lies ahead. And the Prime Minister himself, more than any other factor, is preventing the government from turning that corner.

Mr. Mulroney's Farewell Tour of U.S. Ex-Presidents and Millionaires *(April 8, 1993)*

At Prime Minister Brian Mulroney's fifty-fourth birthday bash three Saturdays ago, guess who showed up?

None other than one of Mr. Mulroney's good friends, the Canadian expatriate Ross Johnson, up from his American lair, the *numero uno* Barbarian at the Gate.

If by your friends ye are known, then friendship with Ross Johnson is not to be recommended, according to the portrait of him drawn by the authors who chronicled his failed inside takeover of RJR–Nabisco. Still, he has been a friend of the Prime Minister—he was made an officer of the Order of Canada while Mr. Mulroney was Prime Minister—and apparently so remains.

Sprinkled among the Canadian guests that evening were assorted U.S. millionaires, up from Chicago or New York. Nothing unusual about that. Mr. Mulroney likes Americans, preferably rich and powerful ones, the kind for whom he once worked at Iron Ore and who owned the paper mill in his childhood town.

Mr. Mulroney came to office opposed to free trade but committed to good relations with the United States. The Americans, undoubtedly pleased at his election, then got more than they bargained for but all they could want, because Mr. Mulroney admired Americans as no other prime minister except, perhaps, Mackenzie King.(King worked for the Rockefellers, knew Franklin D. Roosevelt well, although Roosevelt patronized him, and generally presided over English-speaking Canada's shift from admiring all things British—an affection that still lingers among our dwindling band of monarchists—to things American.)

As part of his farewell lap, Mr. Mulroney is visiting former presidents this week—Ronald Reagan in Santa Barbara and George Bush in Houston—for public bouts of mutual affection and speech making.

And it is curious that these speeches, like previous ones at Stanford, Harvard and Chicago, should have been given before American audiences, for they represent Mr. Mulroney's most considered view of U.S.–Canada relations and of world affairs generally.

There is nothing wrong with speaking on world affairs in the United States, for that country is the only superpower and, by definition, must be involved in international issues. But that a Prime Minister of Canada should give most of his summary speeches on this subject there bespeaks a certain lack of confidence in the interest Canadians might have in these matters, a reflection perhaps of the enduring Canadian notion that inherent value comes only when recognized publicly by others, preferably Americans.

It was an extraordinary and telling gesture that former president George Bush chose to spend his last weekend at Camp David with Mr. Mulroney and his wife. Mr. Bush didn't ask his extended family for one last look around the presidential retreat, or even his closest aides. Instead, he asked Mr. Mulroney. You can't get cosier than that.

There were, to be sure, trade irritants between the two countries on Mr. Mulroney's watch. There always have been and always will be, given the intensity of trade between the two countries. And there were mild disagreements over this and that. But generally, Canadian foreign policy in the Mulroney era was characterized by a ready-aye-ready attitude toward U.S. initiatives and exceptional harmony in Canadian–U.S. affairs. His departure will represent the high-water mark of Canadian–U.S. harmony for the simple reason that the water cannot go higher. Plenty of Americans disagreed more frequently with U.S. foreign policy over the past nine years than did Mr. Mulroney.

It is better to talk to Americans than shout at them, a maxim usually forgotten by those Canadians whose reflexive anti-Americanism colours their view of foreign and domestic policies. That Mr. Mulroney talked extensively to them, and was accorded a hearing, did him credit.

He could not solve every bilateral problem, for many are beyond the control of any U.S. administration, given the divided nature of American government. That he was listened to was itself an accomplishment, given the self-absorption of American debate and the lack of attention paid to Canada in particular.

Still, Mr. Mulroney shrank excessively the margin of difference that Canadians prefer between their country and the United States. Difference for difference's sake is self-defeating and self-deluding, but the next prime minister, whoever that may be, will likely seek to restore some of the margin.

Perhaps, as a consequence, he or she will not do a kind of Mulroney farewell tour of former U.S. presidents and be given such a send-off by American millionaires. Canada could probably survive.

JEAN CHRÉTIEN

Soul of the Party *(February 28, 1986)*

Jean Chrétien was a man having an affair with his own popularity.

Like all affairs, Mr. Chrétien's began in temptation and ended in heartache. The ardour was waning, but sufficient flickers of passion remained to make painful the affair's inevitable conclusion.

Mr. Chrétien left politics believing his party had made a grievous error at the 1984 leadership convention, a belief confirmed, at least in his own mind, by the Liberals' lamentable electoral result.

His leadership defeat, a consequence of monumental miscalculations by the Liberal establishment, left his popularity intact but his options reduced. He could not make that popularity the servant of his ambition, because as the months wore on it became clear that his ambition had no place to go.

His popularity could sell books; it could not make him leader of a party whose whole history induced discipline, loyalty and even subservience in the ranks. His popularity could draw crowds—he remained to the end the Liberal speaker most in demand at party functions—but it could not precipitate revolt.

He bathed in his popularity. It warmed him and nursed his wounded pride. It was his popularity and his alone, a popularity he could offer to the party but would not place at the disposal of its leader.

The affair of the presidency of the Quebec wing of the party merely brought to a head the conflict between himself and John Turner that began in the hours following the leadership vote. That conflict could be resolved only in one of two ways—by another leadership fight, or by Mr. Chrétien's departure.

For many months, Mr. Chrétien pondered the possibility of another fight. His friends told him to keep a low profile and to wait on events, but his popularity beckoned him to the limelight. He sold books, he travelled, he attended fundraisers, he campaigned in provincial elections; in short, he continued the affair with his own popularity until too many eyebrows were raised, too many jealousies were aroused and too many friends began expressing their dismay.

His popularity never extended to the nationalists, the intellectuals and the new bourgeoisie of his native province. They mocked his colloquial French, cringed at his broken English, snickered at his down-home manners and, most of all, detested his unvarnished love of Canada.

In English Canada, where nationalism is muted and often ambivalent,

Mr. Chrétien gave people something to cheer about, namely themselves. He made them laugh. He tugged at their hearts. In a world of smooth talkers, he spoke the rough language of his true convictions.

He leaves a vacant constituency, St. Maurice, in which the first true Liberal–Tory test of this Parliament will be played out. He leaves a leader who can now relax a bit. He leaves politics, probably forever, because when the time comes to replace Mr. Turner, the Liberal Party will have other francophone alternatives to Mr. Chrétien.

Most of all, he leaves a party searching now for a bit of its soul. Between Mr. Turner's dry incantations and the shrill squawkings of the Liberal backbenches, no one now speaks for humour in Liberal discourse, for patriotism, for generosity of spirit.

Jean Chrétien earned his popularity. In the end, it was all he had left, a personal testament of a kind denied to all but a few in public life. He served his party and his country well for twenty-three years, and it was immensely sad to see his career sputter in petty recrimination and unrequited ambition.

He deserved a better fate, or at least a more graceful end. His popularity, indispensable to him, threatening to others, did him in.

Enter Mr. Chrétien, Carrying the Political Baggage of Years Past (December 18, 1990)

QUEBEC—Jean Chrétien arrived in Quebec yesterday like a truck with a string of tin cans attached to the fender.

Mr. Chrétien spent the better part of twenty-five years in politics, and some of his past deeds and statements are not easily forgotten or forgiven in his native province.

Thus, it was probably inevitable that when the federal Liberal leader sat down before the members of Quebec's commission on its constitutional future, the past would figure as prominently as Mr. Chrétien's thoughts about the future.

Sure enough, within seconds of the start of questioning by commission members, the tin cans started clanging. Bear in mind that Quebec is a small society, not in the spiritual sense but in the sense that all the elites have known each other, and often fought with each other, for decades. The memories in Quebec are profoundly collective, and Mr. Chrétien is definitely part of them.

The referendum campaign of 1980: why did Mr. Chrétien promise that if Quebeckers voted no, Ottawa would favour major changes, and then deliver the 1981-82 package that left Quebec weaker?

The patriation exercise of 1981-82: why did Mr. Chrétien accept it over the objections of Quebec? When Mr. Chrétien replied that Quebec's refusal to accept the 1981-82 changes was "traumatizing for me," most people in the room and the galleries laughed.

Meech Lake: why did Mr. Chrétien, working with Newfoundland Premier Clyde Wells, sabotage the deal? After all, as one intervener noted, we wouldn't be here assembled in commission if Meech Lake had passed.

Mr. Chrétien, who has lived with some of these tin cans for a long time, had all the answers, some more satisfactory than others.

Predictably enough, the strong *indépendentistes* took after Mr. Chrétien, starting with Parti Québécois Leader Jacques Parizeau. Labour leaders, too, stuck their knives in, but they too are hard-line *indépendentistes*.

Given their source, these questions scarcely counted; Mr. Chrétien has been the *bête noire* of these people for a very long time. Rather, it was the questions from the so-called soft federalists that hurt.

Repeatedly, these representatives asked: how can we believe your sincerity in wanting to bring major changes to federalism with the track record you have? Put another way, what credibility do you expect to have, given the events of the past decade?

Mr. Chrétien, undoubtedly conscious of those tin cans, went to great but probably insufficient lengths to demonstrate his flexibility. He talked about a Senate of regions, major changes in the division of powers between Ottawa and the provinces, and an amending formula that would give Quebec a veto. He insisted, in various tortuous answers, that he really had been in favour of Quebec's five original Meech Lake demands.

To this, Quebec Intergovernmental Affairs Minister Gil Rémillard replied: we could have heard these suggestions two decades ago.

Mr. Chrétien joked, upon taking his place, that he had arrived in the lion's den—a play on the title of his memoirs in French. Clearly he was in unfriendly territory, since the Bélanger–Campeau commission's drift is exceedingly hostile to his vision of Quebec in Canada.

At one point, he tried to pin one on labour leader Gérald Larose by arguing that Quebec's two thousand bourgeois would gain from independence, but the workers would lose. How is it, Mr. Larose replied, that all polls show that the workers overwhelmingly support sovereignty, while the bourgeois hesitate?

Mr. Chrétien, true to himself, gave nothing away. He was combative, colourful, often windy, and, like a trained politician, turned questions he did not like to his advantage. His audience, after all, did not sit in the room, but rather sat in the living rooms across Quebec where the commission's hearings are being televised live.

He stressed the enormous difficulties in disentangling Quebec from Canada, and in that he was undoubtedly correct. It was a useful message to deliver, since the prevailing view at the commission has been that sovereignty would be almost as simple as crossing the street.

Did Mr. Chrétien help himself? Perhaps, if only because his standing in Quebec is so low he can only go up. His long brief did touch on many issues and, as such, made a worthwhile contribution to the debate.

But those tin cans still rattled. And in a society where collective memories run so deep, they'll keep rattling for as long as Jean Chrétien remains in public life.

Chrétien's Shrewd TV Persona Means He Hardly Appears at All *(March 28, 1995)*

After so many years of prime ministers dominating the public limelight, Canadians now have one who appears only intermittently.

The last few weeks offered further testimony of how Prime Minister Jean Chrétien delegates responsibility in his government, and manages his own public appearances.

In both the fish squabble with Spain and the rail strike, departmental ministers carried almost the entire load of public explanation. Occasionally, Mr. Chrétien chipped in with a comment. But for the most part, he worked on the files out of public view. He was very much in charge of overall strategy, talking to European leaders in the fish dispute, for example. But that was hardly apparent on a daily basis in what was reported in the media.

Think back to the government's biggest political challenge: the budget. Mr. Chrétien gave several interviews in English and French, and a speech to a partisan crowd, defending the budget. For the rest, the Prime Minister counted on Finance Minister Paul Martin to travel the country, delivering speeches and giving interviews.

What a contrast Mr. Chrétien's relatively low profile provides with that of prime ministers Pierre Trudeau and Brian Mulroney. Mr. Trudeau was so endlessly fascinating, bestrode his Cabinet so utterly and became so closely identified with his government's major priorities that he seldom escaped extensive media coverage. The government's initiatives were invariably perceived as his personal initiatives.

Mr. Mulroney, despite his reputation to the contrary, often tried to lower his profile and allow ministers to carry the ball, or sometimes the can. Remember how Mr. Mulroney allowed Joe Clark, then constitutional affairs minister, to lead the federal government's campaign leading up to the ultimate stage of the Charlottetown accord.

But Mr. Mulroney enjoyed the limelight to a fault and often felt himself the government's best communicator. He liked to mix things up in the Commons, often could not resist partisan attacks, and wound up being personally identified with many of his government's initiatives. His persona, like that of Mr. Trudeau, coloured almost every government initiative. The opposition parties, sensing his unpopularity, tagged him personally with every controversial decision. So they called it the "Mulroney budget," or the "Mulroney trade deal," or the "Mulroney constitutional deal."

The Trudeau and Mulroney governments were also invariably in the face of Canadians, demanding that they change, suggesting that they were somehow inadequate or at fault in how they thought about issues. These governments pursued policies from patriation of the Constitution to the National Energy Program, from Meech Lake to the Charlottetown accord, from free trade to the Goods and Services Tax that infuriated large chunks of the Canadian electorate.

Along comes Mr. Chrétien, repeating that "Canada is No. 1," ducking away unerringly from political trouble, preparing public opinion through the most widely leaked budget in history, delegating public explanations to his ministers and carefully selecting his own public interventions.

There's an extraordinary shrewdness, whether intuitive or intellectual, to this approach of limiting prime-ministerial interventions, because television cruelly overexposes those who appear regularly. Television—and to a lesser extent the rest of the media—also excessively dramatize and personalize most stories.

By picking his spots to intervene, Mr. Chrétien carefully avoids finding government initiatives tagged to his persona, so they do not become the "Chrétien" this or that. He also maximizes his own interventions by limiting them, just as U.S. President Franklin Roosevelt's "fireside chats" were so successful because he delivered them only occasionally.

Limited interventions also keep the Prime Minister associated in the public's mind with what he considers important, rather than being associated with all sorts of secondary and tertiary issues.

It takes a certain discipline and a quiet rather than an overbearing confidence for a leader not to intervene publicly. It also takes a shrewd sense of when and how to intervene, a sense honed perhaps over the years of watching his predecessors.

LUCIEN BOUCHARD

Man of the Hour   *(February 4, 1988)*

Lucien Bouchard, where are you?

The Prime Minister needs you. The Conservative Party needs you. Leave Paris forthwith and return to Canada. Your days as Ambassador to France are numbered, if not over.

The firing of Supply and Services Minister Michel Côté makes your jump into politics imperative. Your Hamlet-like period of indecision about your political future must end.

The Conservatives in Quebec, splattered by allegations and scandal, desperately need a white knight. And who better than Lucien Bouchard, whose reputation is unsullied, whose stint in Paris has been carried off with intelligence and panache, and whose personal relations with the Prime Minister are superb?

The list of Quebec Conservative ministers and MPs in trouble is distressingly long. Michel Côté—fired for failing to report a loan. Marcel Masse—under a cloud for election spending. Roch LaSalle—the king of old-style patronage. Suzanne Blais-Grenier—extravagant over-spending on a European trip. André Bissonnette—charged in connection with the Oerlikon affair. Michel Gravel, MP—charged with fifty-one counts of influence-peddling and breach of trust. Clément Côté, MP—under investigation for allegedly putting members of his personal family on the payroll. Maurice Tremblay, MP—fined $500 for assaulting his riding association president.

But the list is also misleading, because in the Conservative sweep of 1984 a number of progressive, highly intelligent MPs appeared from Quebec. They are the party's future in that province, provided the party has a future after all the travails of the last three-and-a-half years.

What these MPs need is someone around whom they can rally, someone they can hold up to the Quebec electorate while saying with pride, "Follow us with him." Lucien Bouchard is that man.

Some commentators, yours truly in the lead, debunked Mr. Bouchard's appointment three years ago as typical patronage. He proved us completely wrong. He mastered the vagaries of the French government, paved the way for the summits of French-speaking countries and put a sock in the mouths of all the diplomats at External Affairs who thought him too green to take on the French.

Brian Mulroney has invited Mr. Bouchard to run in the next election. Now that invitation becomes urgent, because the Côté affair, coming on top of everything else, calls into question the morality and ethical conduct of the government, and particularly of the Conservative Party in Quebec. Maybe it shouldn't raise those questions, but it will in the real world of politics.

What are columnists for if not to produce aimless suggestions, so here is one. Mr. Mulroney is awfully chummy with "mon cher Robert" Bourassa, Premier of Quebec, in whose hands Senate appointments largely lie as a result of the Meech Lake constitutional accord.

Why not ask "mon cher Robert" to put Lucien's name forward for the Senate right away? That way the Prime Minister can bring Mr. Bouchard immediately into the Cabinet. Mr. Bouchard would stay there only until the next election, when he would run for the Conservatives. After that, "mon cher Robert" could appoint any Liberal worthy he wanted. Maybe Mr. Mulroney would even throw in a nuclear-powered submarine as a cherry on the cake.

Michel Côté's star began falling two years ago. Mr. Mulroney took jobs away from him, then demoted him in the Cabinet. His fizzle as a minister was quite spectacular, even before he forgot about/neglected/covered up a personal loan he ought to have declared. Stung by so many previous scandals, large or small, Mr. Mulroney gave him a speedy chop.

Embarrassed again, Mr. Mulroney needs help. Lucien, where are you?

On the Front Lines   (*April 1, 1988*)

He of whom much, perhaps too much, is expected surfaced in Ottawa yesterday insisting quite properly in fact, if incorrectly in perception, that he is no saviour for the Conservative Party in Quebec.

Still, Lucien Bouchard returns from his job as Ambassador to France with enormous hopes reposing on his shoulders. Never having been elected dog-catcher, he suddenly finds himself not only Secretary of State, but a member of the Cabinet's crucial priorities and planning committee.

Some people spend a lifetime in politics without coming close to where Mr. Bouchard has landed. Such are his talents, friendship with the Prime Minister and political history that, given the plight of the Conservatives in Quebec and elsewhere, they needed him now.

The deal was therefore fixed that he would return to Canada as a Cabinet minister last week when Brian Mulroney, his Chief of Staff Bernard Roy and Mr. Bouchard all gathered in Quebec for the twenty-fifth reunion of the Laval University law class of 1963. Mr. Bouchard could have entered the Cabinet via the Senate, but he opted for the risky business of a by-election in a yet-to-be-announced riding.

Prime Minister Pierre Trudeau found out how risky this business could be when he tapped Pierre Juneau for the Cabinet, then sent him to the

Montreal riding of Hochelaga to get a Commons seat. The electors thought otherwise and wrecked Mr. Juneau's political career.

The Quebec Conservatives, splattered unfairly by scandal and innuendos, desperately needed someone of unimpeachable integrity. They also wanted someone of solid nationalist credentials—Mr. Bouchard voted "yes" in the referendum on sovereignty-association—to appeal to Péquistes who formed an indispensable component of the Conservative coalition in 1984.

Mr. Bouchard's arrival—temporary or otherwise, depending on the whims of the electorate—has filled one gap. John Crosbie's shift from Transport to International Trade has plugged another.

After the Easter break, the decks of the Commons will be cleared for the free-trade legislation. Pat Carney, formerly the trade minister and now shifted to the Treasury Board, has some evident talents, but a command of the House is not among them.

Mr. Crosbie, by contrast, is the Conservatives' best verbal brawler, and he is about to enter the brawl of his federal political life. By way of historical curiosity, a Newfoundlander who in 1944 wanted his country to form an economic union with the United States now gets to push through the Commons bills creating free trade with the United States. Who says politics doesn't run in long cycles?

Gerry St. Germain's appointment to the Cabinet as Minister of State for Transport gives British Columbia four Cabinet voices, a fair reflection of that province's political muscle. After all, B.C. gets four new seats under redistribution, and things have not been going well for the Conservatives on the west coast. Premier William Vander Zalm is in full howl against Ottawa, and the federal New Democrats bid fair to rack up major gains unless the Tories turn matters around.

Mr. St. Germain's nomination can't suddenly change the province's political climate, but it won't hurt. He has been a solid chairman of the Conservative caucus and deserved the promotion.

Still, the Conservatives cannot win a majority without a healthy slice of Quebec in the next election. With the Bouchards now in senior positions—Lucien as Secretary of State and Benoît as Minister of Transport—the Conservatives have created their Quebec ministerial team for the fight.

It will be a tough, even merciless struggle in Quebec next time, and the Tories need all hands on board. Hence the arrival of Lucien Bouchard.

After the Triumph *(June 22, 1988)*

Now comes the hard part for Secretary of State Lucien Bouchard—learning about the whole damnable complexity of Canada.

That Mr. Bouchard knows Quebec is self-evident; that he understands the rest of Canada remains unclear. But as Secretary of State, with responsibilities for citizenship, official languages, the federal role in post-secondary education and royal visits (future headline: "Quebec Nationalist Greets Queen Mom"), Mr. Bouchard will confront the delights and frustrations of the Canadian mosaic, of which Quebec is only one part, albeit a crucial one.

Mr. Bouchard can begin his education almost immediately, courtesy of a convincing by-election triumph in Lac-Saint-Jean, a triumph that set off the deepest possible sighs of relief in Conservative circles across Canada.

To have lost Lac-Saint-Jean, when everything pointed to an easy victory, would have been utterly humiliating. That he won comfortably at least allows Conservatives to imagine better times ahead.

Bear in mind what it took to win Lac-Saint-Jean. First, the Tories polled a number of Quebec ridings before settling on Lac-Saint-Jean. They would have preferred that Mr. Bouchard run elsewhere, since they already have a powerful minister, Benoît Bouchard, in the Saguenay region. But the party polls showed Lac-Saint-Jean to be the safest available seat, and the Conservatives were not about to try anything heroic with the former ambassador to France.

The government unloaded bucketfuls of federal cash on the riding, and threw in promises of additional munificence. This was politics of the old style, and it apparently worked.

The Prime Minister spent parts of three days there, an extraordinary commitment of time. And just for good measure, Mr. Bouchard picked up the coded endorsement of Quebec Liberal Premier Robert Bourassa, who as a consequence calmly added yet another IOU to an already impressive collection. Liberals, who had scrambled to find a candidate to run against Mr. Bourassa and finally fielded a dud, immediately began sputtering about Mr. Bourassa's alleged perfidy. He kept his counsel, knowing full well that federal Liberals these days are almost as beholden to him as are federal Conservatives.

The rest of Canada will soon discover in Mr. Bouchard a man of discernment, refined intelligence and great subtlety. In a Cabinet of pragmatic or plebeian minds, Mr. Bouchard's will stand out as one at ease in the world of ideas. He also possesses considerable personal charm.

Mr. Bouchard has also demonstrated a capacity to learn and adapt. Without any diplomatic experience, he learned the ropes quickly as Ambassador to France, even impressing Canada's career diplomats, who frequently delight in mocking political appointments.

In politics, his constant touchstone has been fidelity to Quebec nationalism, a fidelity that makes him a perfect fit for the Saguenay region. That fidelity once made him a Péquiste; it now finds him as a Conservative.

Marrying that fidelity to the Canadian reality, and in particular to his responsibilities to run a federal department, will be his greatest challenge. And that he should be there, at the Prime Minister's right hand, brings the Conservative Party's history full circle in this century, for it was the marriage of Sir Robert Borden's English-speaking Conservatives with Quebec nationalists which helped the Conservatives win in 1911.

Mr. Bouchard's victory now enables the Conservatives to use him to lure other Quebeckers of quality and reputation into the electoral fray. And if they choose the correct ridings, support them with federal cash and experienced organizers, confront weak Liberals, and keep Premier Bourassa on side, who knows how far the Conservatives can go in Quebec?

Lucien Bouchard Assumes His Role as a Political Saint-in-the-Making (June 15, 1990)

The political beatification of Lucien Bouchard continues apace in Quebec.

There he was the other night on Pierre Nadeau's interview program, slapping various Nadeau offerings around the field like an accomplished spray hitter. Beside Mr. Nadeau sat a singer— we're talking here about soft public-affairs programming—who chimed in with several adoring questions, which Mr. Bouchard promptly whacked far beyond the centrefield fence.

Having served up those puffballs, the singer then sat beside a *chanteuse*, and the two of them cooed for a minute or two about the wonders of Mr. Bouchard before getting on with the business of song.

Finding this all a bit much for public-affairs programming, I switched to *Le Point*, Radio-Canada's equivalent of *The Journal*, only to find—you guessed it—none other than Mr. Bouchard. Madeleine Poulin, the show's intelligent and luminous co-host, tried a couple of high hard ones which Mr. Bouchard ignored, preferring to display his power on questions of the batting-practice variety.

As if this weren't enough, I had just read Mr. Bouchard's first column in *Le Devoir*. The column itself was utterly predictable—but then, who am I to throw stones on that score?—but no less remarkable for that. You have to scratch your head and think hard about another serious paper willing to give a weekly soapbox to a sitting MP. It would be as strange as *The Globe and Mail* hiring Michael Wilson or Herb Gray to write a weekly column.

Anyway, Mr. Bouchard now has his *Le Devoir* soapbox, where he joins another fervent *indépendentiste*, Daniel Latouche, as columnist and the new editor, Lise Bissonnette, herself a strong Quebec nationalist. Only a dispiritingly small band of Quebeckers read *Le Devoir* any more, but with a polit-ical saint-in-the-making and the intelligent and articulate Ms. Bissonnette in the paper, things may start looking up.

Through the pages of *Le Devoir*, his easy access to television and his repeated speechifying, Mr. Bouchard is setting himself up for big things in Quebec politics. He might be considered a possible leader of the Parti Québécois, except that Jacques Parizeau occupies that post and is not ready to step aside. Mr. Bouchard doesn't carry a PQ membership card, but that's just a convenience that furthers his self-positioning as a man above politics.

Like Charles de Gaulle, Mr. Bouchard is waiting for the call. Just when and how it will come remains unclear, but there can be no doubt he expects it. He stresses repeatedly that Quebec, post-Meech, needs *une concertation nationale*, a national coming-together, in a grand, glad movement above and beyond partisanship. Not for him, at least not now, the sullying of hands in the dirt of politics. Just a clarion call for national pride, solidarity and vision with himself as Pied Piper.

Nobody has yet pressed him to explain, and he has not yet satisfactorily explained, why he argued in the days after his departure from Ottawa that he favoured both Meech Lake and sovereignty-association. These are not intellectually compatible positions, but that kind of spitter of a question wasn't thrown his way on television the other night.

Mr. Bouchard was Brian Mulroney's political creature. The Prime Minister made him what he is by appointing him Ambassador to France, political minister for Quebec and environment minister. With an astute sense of timing, Mr. Bouchard left at the moment designed to deliver max-imum damage to Mr. Mulroney and maximum advantage to himself. He is Mr. Mulroney's Brutus.

Mr. Bouchard has a message perfectly suited to Quebeckers who now feel that Meech Lake, having provoked such a negative reaction in parts of English Canada, isn't much of a prize. He bids them to share his pain, pre-fabricated though it may be, and through this mutual sharing achieve a higher sense of purpose that is the calling of all saints-in-waiting.

A Reading from the Book of Saint Lucien in the Gospel of Secession *(November 3, 1995)*

And Saint Lucien spread forth his arms and cried: Lord, the People of Quebec, beseech me no further. Come unto me no more, for I am heavy laden.

With his wife he begat two children, and verily he said unto her that he would leave his burdens and give no more sermons from the mount once the flock had reached the Promised Land. He would sit instead amid the olive groves of the law.

But the Almighty works in mysterious ways. Lo, the waters opened before him and the path grew firm, and driving the oxen and asses of the Premier's Office, he bid the people follow. And they followeth, crying "Lucien, Lucien."

And he said unto them: they who hath humiliated me, and thee, they with whom we were once joined at the hip, I will smite them mightily. I will cause thunderbolts to fall upon them. The skies will rain fiery words. Thine enemies will become mine. With girded loins and rhetorical swords, I will place the fear of the Almighty into them that their land be blasted and come asunder at the power of my word and the anger of our soul.

Saint Lucien had wandered for years searching for the Promised Land. False gods had tempted him, and he had succumbed to sin. The federalist Satan had delivered him unto the top of the mountain and said all that lay below could be his if he would forsake the anger in his soul.

He had been summoned to an oasis in the desert called Meech Lake, from whose waters he would refresh himself. Yet the water had been poisoned by his people's foes, and he pronounced it no good. He had taken himself toward Damascus in a strange place called Canada, when a blinding light appeared and the skies opened and the People's Voice cried: "Lucien, Lucien, thou know not what thou doest." And he fled, and it was good.

Beware false gods, Saint Lucien warned the flock, for they offer the temptations of the flesh. And he thrust out his arm and bid them behold a golden calf strangely called Constitution, around which men in blue suits were dancing. Let not your souls be tempted, as mine was. Swear not to false prophets. Come instead unto me, all ye who are heavily laden, and I will refresh you and we will walk to the Promised Land together.

Yet they, the enemies of the People, pressed a crown of thorns upon his brow and heaped further humiliations upon his soul. They who would deny the People the Promised Land spat upon him. They mocked him and caused sticks to be piled upon his People's back. The People groaned under the burdens heaped upon them, but he uplifted them. Go forth and multiply, he cried through his pain, so that we can replenish our stock lest we lose the faith of our ancestors. Fear not, for I am with thee and thou art with me.

Yea, as they neared the shores of the Promised Land, the waters closed and the city on the hill was lost from view. Ethnics and money, cried a leader as the waters devoured him.

But Saint Lucien cried, glancing back at the Sodom and Gomorrah on the Rideau, we shall never return there.

Yet he did not turn into a pillar of salt, but a halo grew around his head.

Then Saint Lucien espied the Tower of Babel, and cried: look what the men in blue suits have created, tongues that cannot comprehend each other in their great cities. We shalt not follow them; nay, we shall scorn them; that is except their silver and gold that we shall welcome. And their passports.

And we shall build a Tabernacle, he promised them, upon the St. Lawrence, a place of great wonder and majesty that will be thine own. And if she with whom I begat those children will allow it, I shall take myself thither and become thy Servant, ever more praising thee and saying: *gens du pays*.

KIM CAMPBELL

Kim Campbell's Progress *(February 27, 1990)*

If you have a spare dime and are looking for a bet, place 10 cents on Kim Campbell to lead the Conservative Party some day.

Named Justice Minister last week after only fifteen months in federal politics, Ms. Campbell has suddenly become the Tory to watch in Ottawa. Not since a fellow named Pierre Trudeau burst on to the federal scene in 1965 has a newcomer been catapulted so fast into the justice portfolio, traditionally a senior portfolio in the federal Cabinet.

Ms. Campbell, a refugee from British Columbia's Social Credit government, should never have made it to Ottawa. She got a late start in the 1988 campaign in Vancouver Centre, a riding that should have been won by the national president of the New Democratic Party, Johanna den Hertog. But Ms. Campbell campaigned like a demon in one of Canada's classic swing ridings, the Liberal candidate siphoned off anti–free-trade votes from the NDP, and Ms. den Hertog's campaign seemed to sputter. On election night, Ms. Campbell was on her way to Ottawa with a plurality of 269 votes.

Vancouver Centre is one of Canada's heartbeat ridings. If you represent Vancouver Centre, by definition you're in touch with many of the most important issues of the day. You also half kill yourself flying back and forth from Ottawa, trying to do ministerial work in the national capital, political work in B.C. and constituency work in a swing riding.

Ms. Campbell is bright and feisty, aggressive in debate but sensitive to other points of view. She has received a sound and diversified academic training in Soviet studies and law. Her French is passable, and with some additional work she can bring it up to acceptable fluency for national leadership purposes.

Defending Tories in B.C. these days is akin to rolling boulders up the Rockies, but Ms. Campbell has not shied from the challenge. Her robust defence of free trade in the last campaign impressed Conservatives. Her pleas for the Meech Lake constitutional accord have not gone unnoticed by Quebec caucus colleagues.

As Justice Minister, she now has the abortion hot potato on her plate. She is a pro-choice advocate; indeed, she split with Premier William Vander Zalm on that very issue. But as a team player, with an eye on the big chance, she will defend to the limit the government's compromise abortion legislation.

So, sure, she has hurdles galore to overcome before being considered for her party's top job: a fickle constituency in a province gone sour on the government, a demanding portfolio with its fair share of potholes, a steep learning curve in grasping the damnable complexity of the whole country, and the challenge of improving her French.

But Canada is crying out for a bilingual leader from Western Canada. The English-speaking parts of Canada are awash with people who wonder whether someone from outside Quebec will ever again lead a national party. When Brian Mulroney leaves—and depending on the circumstances of national unity at that time—rank-and-file Tories will be searching the landscape for candidates from provinces other than Quebec. Western Tories, in particular, would love one of their own at the top.

Efficient French will be mandatory, and that requirement will exclude most of the English-speaking ministers in the present Cabinet. Marry Ms. Campbell's linguistic abilities, talents, determination and political savvy, and the magic mix might be found.

Her gender won't hurt, either. All else being equal, parties these days want to give the most serious consideration to women for high posts.

Whatever the future holds, Kim Campbell has come a long way in a short time. Watch her closely in the years ahead.

Ripples of Sexism Still Make Waves in Political Waters *(June 11, 1993)*

When Flora MacDonald endorsed Kim Campbell last night, it brought to mind what is now called the Flora Syndrome.

In 1976, Ms. MacDonald was running for the Conservative leadership, the first time a woman had done so. She had friends galore in the party (and enemies, too, among the Diefenbakerites), contacts across the country and commitments from hundreds of delegates.

Or so she believed. But on the first ballot, Ms. MacDonald finished sixth with only 214 votes, representing only 9 per cent of those cast. She was crushed emotionally and, of course, politically. And in the aftermath of that result grew up the notion of the Flora Syndrome: promises given but not delivered to leadership candidates, and especially to a woman.

In 1976, the Conservative Party was not ready to elect a woman as leader. On Sunday, the country will know whether the party has sufficiently changed to choose a woman.

Ms. Campbell's gender has not been the factor in 1993 that Ms. MacDonald's was in 1976, at least not in a negative sense. Still, there are reverberations of sexism that occasionally ripple public waters.

The other day, MP Terry Clifford announced his defection from the Campbell camp to that of Jean Charest, explaining that Ms. Campbell had been twice divorced and therefore did not incarnate "family values."

Perhaps this comment reflected only one man's view, and a not very enlightened one at that, but would it have occurred to anyone even to raise the issue had the candidate been a man?

After all, Canada has elected three bachelors as prime minister: R.B. Bennett, Mackenzie King and Pierre Trudeau. The last married and separated while in office, yet won re-election after the separation. If my memory is correct, Mr. Trudeau even won some sympathy for remaining stoic during the public carryings-on of his wife, Margaret, during the 1979 campaign.

Similarly, there is this subtle undercurrent to the campaign against Ms. Campbell suggesting that she is not quite stable. Whether she is or not, the fact that it is being whispered suggests a double standard, since some of the most prominent male politicians have been demonstrably unstable in private without mention ever being made of it.

When Mr. Mulroney, for example, was running for the leadership in 1976 and again in 1983, it was widely known among friends that he drank and smoked quite a bit. (He quit both cold turkey, by the way.) Ontario Premier John Robarts was a notorious lover of good scotch; indeed drinking among the boys was part of the political ethos not that many years ago.

More than a third of Canadian marriages end in divorce these days, and women by the way usually wind up the biggest losers from the crackups. Keeping a marriage together with the demands of a political life is never easy, especially if the MP spends hours each week commuting from Western Canada. Even Bill and Hillary Clinton admitted that theirs had been a rocky marriage at times.

The other day, Lysiane Gagnon wrote a column in *The Globe and Mail* about the media and Kim Campbell. It was, as is often the case with Ms. Gagnon, the shrewdest piece of writing around, streets ahead of most of the predictable stuff about the campaign. Ms. Gagnon felt there had been a bias against Kim Campbell, a subtle bias perhaps but a measurable one.

Take, for example, the argument that Ms. Campbell is ambitious. This is considered somehow suspicious, and yet Brian Mulroney was consumed by ambition to be prime minister without anyone finding this strange. Excessive perhaps, but not strange. Without ambition, people don't usually succeed.

I suspect Kim Campbell got to where she is on her own talents, driven by ambition to be sure, not whining about victimization, and with some of her faults on public display.

Her gender helped propel Ms. Campbell to public prominence because a lot of Tories felt the time had come to elect a woman as leader. Now the question is whether she is the right woman, but that question itself hints at a double standard, since no one asks whether a male candidate is the right man.

She May Be Super Kim, But She Has a Long Way to Go in Quebec (June 15, 1993)

The Conservative leadership race demonstrated yet again that paradox and irony are central to politics, as they often are to life.

Before the Conservative contest officially began—perhaps even before Brian Mulroney decided to resign—many influential Conservatives had decided that Kim Campbell was the one and only candidate.

This burst of support, reflected in the early media coverage, created a set of expectations for Ms. Campbell that almost proved her undoing.

The support drove prominent Conservatives who wanted to run from the race, including Cabinet ministers Barbara McDougall, Michael Wilson, Bernard Valcourt and Perrin Beatty. They were quite simply scared off by the apparently unassailable lead Ms. Campbell attained before even declaring her candidacy.

The same sort of thing happened in the U.S. campaign. President George Bush was considered so politically invincible after Operation Desert Storm that the majority of Democratic heavyweights were scared off running, leaving the field open to Bill Clinton.

As for Jean Charest, he was considered a sacrificial regional lamb, the "Quebec candidate" running for next time. And nobody gave the other three candidates, including Jim Edwards of Alberta, a ghost of a chance.

When the other candidates refused to run, a first-ballot victory of staggering proportions seemed inevitable. The race was not between Kim

Campbell and Jean Charest, but between Kim Campbell and the surreal expectations that had been created for her.

She was Super Kim, able to leap tall political obstacles at a single bound, the largest being the visceral unpopularity the majority of Canadians felt for Mr. Mulroney and the Conservative Party.

If the other candidates had run, no one would have assumed a first-ballot victory by her. Instead of a coronation, the party and the media would have expected a pitched battle.

Her French, much creakier than unilingual anglophone journalists kept reporting, would have been more frequently (and favourably) compared to that of Perrin Beatty, Michael Wilson and the others, rather than exclusively to that of the effortlessly bilingual Mr. Charest. She would have been compared, in short, to other candidates rather than the expectations.

The overwhelming impression of early strength, therefore, wound up being a severe liability in changing the race into one she could never win. Once she began to lose the contest with her expectations—a race, let it be said, she lost more decisively than was necessary—Jean Charest was given an opening that he brilliantly exploited.

Starting yesterday, the expectations game will change for Ms. Campbell. Her own performance has lowered expectations. They will remain high, for she will soon be Prime Minister of Canada, but not surreal.

Similarly, she will increasingly be judged in relation to other party leaders, especially Jean Chrétien (and, in Quebec, Lucien Bouchard).

Ms. Campbell's No. 1 problem is now Quebec, and if she doesn't understand that political fact then she is probably doomed. The only deeply hurt feelings during and after the convention were among Quebec Conservatives, many of whom believe the party blew its re-election chances by spurning Mr. Charest.

The Campbell campaign performance disappointed plenty of Quebeckers outside the Conservative Party, as did her creaky French. Against Mr. Charest, she looked inferior as a campaigner in English and not even in the same league in French.

She should, of course, make Mr. Charest the deputy prime minister, a role he earned in the campaign, and construct a Cabinet with Quebeckers in three of the top six portfolios.

Although Ms. Campbell does not like to admit error or acknowledge weaknesses, she should simply state that the campaign revealed the inadequacy of her French. Instead of holidaying this summer, she should spend as much time as she can in Jonquière or Trois Pistoles, drumming the language into her head.

Successful Canadian prime ministers, francophone or anglophone, have practised bridge-building between Quebec and the rest of the country. As an anglophone leader who defeated a francophone candidate, if she doesn't build as many bridges as she can, Super Kim will fast become like Superman himself—a figure with a past rather than a future.

JEAN CHAREST

Can Someone Whose Life Has Been in Politics Make a Good Political Leader?

(April 21, 1993)

The liveliest moment, which isn't saying much, in last week's Conservative leadership debate came when Jean Charest defended politicians and, by implication, himself.

Part of the cynicism surrounding politicians, he asserted, stemmed from their defensiveness. They should be proud to be parliamentarians, defend Parliament and carry on in their honourable work.

His sentiments are admirable, for political service can be an honourable calling. The more that unbridled cynicism is directed toward those who enter public life, the less probable it is that people of quality will take the risk.

That said, Mr. Charest's enthusiasm for the political life was a trifle revealing. He is, and has been for all but three years of his adult life, a politician. He practised law briefly in Sherbrooke after being called to the bar, but did not practise long enough to establish a career in law. A few months after his twenty-sixth birthday, he entered the House of Commons. Now thirty-five, he seeks to become party leader and prime minister.

His youth will be held against him by some, perhaps many, who believe a country's leader should have experienced and suffered more. But the more serious question is whether a political lifer is the best political leader.

Like Perrin Beatty and Joe Clark, two other Conservative ministers, Mr. Charest essentially knows little beyond a life in politics. He has developed into such a popular MP in Sherbrooke, his home town, that he bids fair to keep getting re-elected.

A life spent in politics produces certain undeniable benefits. Political lifers receive an instruction in the complexities of Canada far beyond the experience of most people who work in the private sector. The good politicians see matters in the round, appreciate trade-offs and tackle a wide range of difficult issues.

They also get to sit atop large bureaucracies, although they do not run them. The running of departments is essentially left to deputy ministers, and politicians must usually worry more about bureaucracies running them than the other way around.

The drawbacks to a life in politics, however, are many. For starters, serious Cabinet ministers—and Mr. Charest is certainly one of these—find their schedules so crowded and their time so circumscribed that each day they eat into their intellectual capital.

As time goes on, they run the risk of shifting according to the political winds rather than acting on reflection, because they have not had time to reflect.

Moreover, if they have not pursued a career before entering politics, they lack points of reference—extensive reading or private-sector experience or trade-union leadership or whatever—to guide them in tough situations.

Political lifers risk becoming political animals for whom the hunt for votes overwhelms all other considerations. They are surrounded by fellow vote-hunters, smothered by the adulation of staff, buoyed by the roar of the crowd.

After a while, the questions arise: In what do these lifers really believe? How would they react in a crisis? On what issues will they not compromise? What are their values beyond making a favourable impression? Can they be relied upon to do what they believe is right, as opposed to what is popular?

Throughout his years of leadership, Brian Mulroney was plagued by an inability to answer these questions. He opposed free trade with the United States during the Tory leadership campaign, then endorsed it. He opposed getting too close to Quebec nationalists, then made an implicit alliance with them. If he would change his position on such important issues, why would he not shift and spin and manoeuvre on any others?

Mr. Mulroney fell somewhere between politician as lifer and someone who brought extensive outside experience to politics. He had run Iron Ore of Canada and practised law in Montreal, but everyone who knew him from his university days assumed he was a politician at heart.

The ideal political person is one who accumulates experience and wisdom outside politics, brings those attributes to public service for a portion of his or her life, then tries something again after politics.

Those who stay too long or know little outside politics are least able to escape its dangerous enticements.

Charest's Age and Gender May Not Matter, But His Quebec Roots Do

(June 8, 1998)

Some of his friends urged him as a former prime minister not to endorse anyone, but Joe Clark unbuttoned the worst-kept secret in federal politics yesterday and endorsed Jean Charest for Conservative leader.

Mr. Clark's public support was carefully timed to launch the final week of Mr. Charest's leadership campaign. Mr. Clark will bring along his delegates from Yellowhead riding, and perhaps others who have been Clark loyalists inside the Conservative Party.

Without mentioning Kim Campbell by name, Mr. Clark underlined the biggest knock against her: "An effective prime minister requires . . . the kind of temperament that can stay calm in crisis and draw different forces together."

The inference was clear: Kim Campbell is somehow not quite stable enough to be prime minister and her sometimes-abrasive personality will divide more than it unites.

Mr. Clark then inferentially attempted to deal with the two biggest concerns about Mr. Charest: his age and Quebec roots. "Some people worry about his age. The real issue is maturity, and in the Cabinet as in the campaign, he [Mr. Charest] has demonstrated consistent maturity and good judgment."

Mr. Charest presumably displayed both in Mr. Clark's eyes when he supported the former leader in his 1983 leadership struggle with Brian Mulroney.

Mr. Clark tried to deflect concerns about the country getting yet another leader from Quebec by stressing Mr. Charest's national vision. Seldom, Mr. Clark asserted, had he met a Quebec minister with a larger vision of all of Canada.

The question raised by a Charest victory, to be followed by an election campaign against the Liberals led by Jean Chrétien, is what message this combination of circumstances would send to the rest of Canada.

With two brief exceptions, Canada has been governed by prime ministers from Quebec for a quarter of a century. Millions of Canadians have known nothing but prime ministers from Quebec.

A Chrétien–Charest campaign would produce a winner from Quebec who, with a majority government, would remain in office until 1997 or 1998. That would make three decades of prime ministers from Quebec, with the brief exceptions of Mr. Clark himself and John Turner.

Imagine the reaction in Quebec if all prime ministers for thirty years had been from Ontario. Quebeckers might believe that perhaps the political deck was stacked against them.

Quebeckers have dominated federal party leadership for a variety of reasons. The province presented strong candidates. They were bilingual in an era when capacity in two languages counted. And they were deemed superior to their adversaries in combating secessionists in Quebec. Indeed, Mr. Clark said yesterday he believed Mr. Charest would do better against the Bloc Québécois than Ms. Campbell would.

The secessionist threat in Quebec, therefore, hobbles candidates from outside the province, who are deemed less capable of dealing with it. But at some point Quebeckers' virtual monopoly on the top spot must end or else resentments in the rest of Canada will understandably boil over.

If all that is keeping Quebec in Canada is a Quebecker at 24 Sussex Drive, then the national-unity game is over anyway, since eventually someone other than a Quebecker will live there for more than a few months. The longer a Quebecker monopolizes 24 Sussex Drive, the harder it will be to sell Quebec's case in the rest of Canada.

Mr. Charest, to his credit and that of his Quebec organizers, stunned the Campbell forces in Quebec. Ms. Campbell had the big-name organizers and the well-known ministers, but they were out-manoeuvred by the Charest team.

La Presse has reported, and the Campbell camp accepts, that Mr. Charest won a clear majority of Quebec delegates. The notion that a majority of Quebec delegates would understand that it was the "turn" of someone from outside the province proved to be false. That argument impressed some high-profile Quebec Tories; it obviously left plenty of rank-and-filers cold.

The leading candidates complain that their policy pronouncements are being obscured in debates over gender and region. Sorry, but their prescriptions are not wildly different. This race is about who can win the country— and region, if not gender, counts in that contest.

JOE CLARK

Everyone Loves a Winner—Except Canadians. We Prefer Persistence

(October 8, 1991)

With due apologies to Margaret Atwood, the resurrection of Joe Clark to the good graces of the Canadian people has much to do with survival.

Ms. Atwood noted, in her survey of Canadian literature entitled *Survival,* that many characters in Canadian fiction have been anti-heroes, people who persevere against climate, distance, environment and other forms of adversity. They don't flourish; they survive.

Deep in the Canadian character lurks a distaste for easy success—indeed, for almost any kind of success. We pride ourselves on not celebrating success as Americans do. We do allow ourselves the luxury of emotion when faced with personal success. Terry Fox, battling against adversity, is our idea of a hero.

Ms. Atwood's insights into Canadian literature translate into one way of interpreting Canadian politics. Once in a generation, Canadians are prepared to admire and give their affection to a politician, or a group of politicians. But that affection seldom endures.

Ask Pierre Trudeau. In 1969, Canadians opened their hearts to him, and the phenomenon was called Trudeaumania. It lasted maybe eighteen months before the bloom faded from the rose, and Canadians returned to their apparently more comfortable attitude of churlishness.

The same thing happened to John Diefenbaker, who galvanized the country in 1957-58, sweeping out the Liberals en route to what was then the largest majority in Canadian political history. By 1960, the Diefenbaker craze was over, although it took another three years to eject him from office and four more to dislodge him from the Conservative Party leadership.

Throughout his sixteen years in office, Mr. Trudeau was kicked, villified and battered. Canadians came within an eyelash of defeating him in 1972, then finally sent him packing in 1979. Or so they thought. But Joe Clark's bungling as prime minister gave Mr. Trudeau another chance.

Now, Canadians are delighted to denigrate and despise Prime Minister Brian Mulroney, whose level of villification eclipses even that heaped on Mr. Trudeau during his darkest moments.

Mr. Trudeau roused a kaleidoscope of emotions in the Canadian public. One perception, held by critics and admirers alike, was tenacity. Even his opponents conceded he was one tough cookie. He counter-punched. He attacked. He scorned his critics.

A gladiator's heart is a mandatory requirement for survival in Canadian politics, and Mr. Trudeau had one. He demonstrated, like him or not, the ability, indeed the willingness, to suffer whatever abuse was directed his way and to carry on. Just after his departure, a journalist asked him what had been his most significant accomplishment. "I survived," he replied.

Which brings us to Mr. Clark. Since his brief days as prime minister, arguably no Canadian has suffered more public abuse. There was profound humiliation, too, in losing the Tory leadership after a prolonged fight led by people within his own party, including Brian Mulroney.

And yet, in those awful moments of personal torment, Mr. Clark carried himself with dignity. He was defeated, humiliated. But he remained a gladiator, determined to carry on, if necessary to suffer more, like someone caught in a heavy storm who presses on against the wind and snow and cold.

Something in that perseverance resonates in the Canadian spirit, a kind of stubbornness that has unenviable qualities but also can be ennobling. Now that Mr. Clark carries the national-unity file in public almost by himself— the Prime Minister's unpopularity having removed him from public association with it—his dogged persistence and political survival offer modest hope that, perhaps from a long period of self-inflicted adversity, the country too can survive.

It is almost as though Canadians made Mr. Clark suffer as an expiation for his sins—the physical awkwardness, naiveté and inexperience that undid his performance as prime minister and turned much of the country against him. Adversity has taught him much, and it shows.

Now that those alleged sins have been expiated, he has been forgiven and, in an age of overwhelming distaste for Mr. Mulroney and deep distrust for politicians everywhere, Mr. Clark has emerged as a figure of dignity for having survived. In the curious way of the Canadian world, he has come to symbolize for Canadians a part of themselves.

Decency, Dignity, Charity and Loyalty— the Legacy of a Political Survivor

(February 23, 1993)

Joe Clark could have crawled out of an English-Canadian novel.

English-Canadian fiction, we are told by Margaret Atwood and others, depicts the struggle for survival. Prominent in the novels are anti-heroes who slog through the driving snow, struggle against formidable geography, battle with loneliness, persevere amid adversity.

Joe Clark was the political anti-hero of our time, more respected for having survived than for having succeeded. His electoral and constitutional defeats far outweighed his triumphs, but in a country profoundly suspicious of success, his lack of it secured his reputation.

Canadians have elevated the denigration of politicians to an art form unknown in other Western countries. Indeed, such denigration has become a unifying characteristic of contemporary Canada.

Only if a political person has suffered and survived repeated denigrations will Canadians begin to accord him or her respect, and no one suffered more humiliating denigrations than Joe Clark. But having survived them, he drew Canadians together in their respect for him.

A nation of victims insists upon claiming victims, and it claimed Joe Clark. By virtue of becoming a victim, he won a respect that would never have been accorded had he succeeded.

Pierre Trudeau personified Canadians' aspirations; Joe Clark personified themselves. In the long struggle between the two men, which began with Mr. Clark's leadership victory in 1976 and ended with the defeat of the Charlottetown accord, Mr. Trudeau won most of the important battles.

Mr. Trudeau attempted to shape society according to his ideas; Mr. Clark tried to shape his ideas according to society.

The deductive Mr. Trudeau bettered the inductive Mr. Clark in part because in their years of political combat, Canada had changed so profoundly that the fissures of society could no longer be bridged by deal-making, brokering, accommodation and compromise.

If it were true, as Mr. Clark believed, that Canada was a "community of communities," then it ought to have been possible for a community of interests to be located. And yet, perhaps tragically, whenever Mr. Clark attempted to discover that community through laborious negotiation, it eluded him.

Mr. Clark lived a Canadian myth, that if Canadians only talked long enough among themselves, or if they only got to know each other better, such a community of interests might be found. His pursuit of it—as between Ontario and Alberta over energy, or between Western Canada and central Canada on a range of issues, or between Quebec and the rest of Canada on constitutional issues—led him into unsustainable compromises or dead-end streets, but also won a lasting measure of respect for his doggedness and sincerity.

Mr. Clark both transcended his roots and was captured by them. He learned creaky French, unlike almost all the other English-speaking politicians of his generation. He absorbed far more about the damnable complexity of Canada than any of the other young western Tories of the early 1970s. Among his most eloquent speeches were those to young people in Alberta about the majesty and potential of Canada.

Yet he carried his anti-establishment roots from small-town Alberta in his view of the media, the financial establishment, Toronto and to a lesser extent Montreal. As a quite competent external affairs minister, Mr. Clark often seemed more comfortable dealing with Third World countries than with Europeans.

He was old before his time, in manner, dress and demeanour, but he was too young to be prime minister. It showed in the decisions he made and the tragedies that befell his government. Now, as he leaves, he would better understand the discipline of power. Timing in politics, however, is everything; for Joe Clark, the timing was always a trifle off.

He did not change the course of Canada, as Pierre Trudeau did and as Brian Mulroney is doing. Mr. Clark's legacy is himself, rather than a body of ideas or a string of accomplishments. That legacy is one of decency in adversity, dignity in distress, charity in pain, loyalty in service, patriotism in everything.

Paying Tribute to Gordon Fairweather, One of the Last Red Tories *(May 4, 1993)*

For those with a taste for endangered species, Ottawa was the place to be Friday night.

In a room in the Parliament buildings, several hundred people gathered to salute one of Canada's few remaining Red Tories, Gordon Fairweather, long-time New Brunswick MP and recently retired chairman of the Immigration and Refugee Appeal Board.

Judges, lawyers, former associates and staff members, civil servants and former NDP leader Ed Broadbent came to salute Mr. Fairweather. So did the dwindling band of Red Tories.

Former Conservative leader Robert Stanfield delivered a customarily witty and thoughtful speech. Former Cabinet minister Flora MacDonald, a veteran of many campaigns with Mr. Fairweather, circulated through the hall.

Red Tories such as Mr. Fairweather were never the most numerous breed of Canadian Conservatives. They often looked out of place in the party, like a pair of brown brogues at a fancy-dress ball.

They could be a trifle difficult to pin down. Tories with a heart. Conservatives with a social conscience. Progressive conservatives.

Red Tories often embodied somewhat contradictory political emotions. They also drove their more meat-eating Conservative colleagues to distraction with their concerns.

Like Mr. Fairweather, the Red Tories were eminently decent, civilized, educated people. A disproportionate number were Maritimers, perhaps because in that region politics was not too ideological. Similarly, it was hard to be an anti-government zealot in a region with so much economic hardship.

Mr. Fairweather came from the Saint John River valley, upstream a bit from Saint John. He arrived in Ottawa when John Diefenbaker led the Conservative Party, having served as New Brunswick's attorney-general, and became a voice of moderation on the Tory benches.

His riding was Fundy–Royal, hardly a hotbed of progressive thinking in Loyalist New Brunswick. Around Ottawa, anyone with a passing acquaintance with anglophone New Brunswick marvelled at how Mr. Fairweather got elected time after time.

He stood against capital punishment and for bilingualism. He was open to social reform. He had a courtly bearing, interested himself in such matters as immigration and human rights, and generally seemed ill-suited to Fundy–Royal. When he left, the riding reverted to form and elected a mainstream but undistinguished Conservative.

Mr. Fairweather was Edmund Burke's model politician: he owed the electors of Fundy–Royal his best judgment. And although he adopted unpopular positions, they stuck with him.

When Pierre Trudeau's government created the Canadian Human Rights Commission, Gordon Fairweather became its first chairman.

The appointment testified to Mr. Fairweather's long advocacy of such a commission and his standing with all political parties. Since then, the commission and its counterparts in the provinces have been advocates for various minority concerns.

Indeed, the existence of these commissions and the Charter of Rights and Freedoms has spawned an ever-increasing number of codes of behaviour and judicial decisions in the human-rights field.

After moving from the federal commission, Mr. Fairweather ran the country's refugee system and guided it through tumultuous years of backlogs and adjustments to the Supreme Court's 1985 Singh decision, which overturned the entire operation. (The court ruled that anyone physically in Canada was entitled to Charter protections.)

Always an advocate of a generous refugee policy, he did warn that abuses of the policy could sour public opinion on the admission of refugees and, more broadly, of immigrants.

Just about everyone who ever met Gordon Fairweather liked him. More than that, they respected him for his integrity, compassion and quiet wit. He was a big man who never got too big for his britches.

Under Brian Mulroney's leadership, Red Tories became an increasingly rare breed. They were kinder, gentler Tories, if you like, and Gordon Fairweather was one of them.

Eugene Forsey Was a Fine Man with a Sharp Mind, and a Sharp Pen to Boot

(February 21, 1991)

Senator Eugene Forsey was a jewel of a man: firm principles, sharp edges, brilliant refractions.

Eleven years ago he reached seventy-five, the mandatory retirement age for senators. But the title "senator" stuck with him to the end, which came yesterday in Victoria, partly because he personified what senators were supposed to be but seldom were: independent of mind, steeped in their country's history, witty and wise.

Eugene Forsey lived, as he said with typical modesty in his memoirs, a "life on the fringe." British parliamentary democracy, English literature, social justice and Canadian political history were the causes of his life, and he sent his fertile mind, infectious enthusiasm and mastery of the language into any fray to support those causes.

Causes extend beyond partisanship; so, in the pursuit of these causes, Senator Forsey knew no fixed political boundaries. He admired Conservative Prime Minister Arthur Meighen's love of Parliament and command of English. In pursuit of social justice, he was "present at the creation" of the Co-operative Commonwealth Federation (the precursor of the New Democratic Party). And, to the astonishment of friends, he accepted a Liberal appointment to the Senate because he supported Prime Minister Pierre Trudeau's quest for a strong central government to combat Quebec separatism. True to form, he later gave up his Liberal affiliation.

His memoirs recount how, in the age before television and radio, he read and read and read, often aloud to adults. And they read to him: Macaulay, Thackeray, Dickens, Galsworthy, names utterly foreign to the Nintendo generation.

How Eugene Forsey could write. His pen was as sharp as his mind. His prose was clean and cutting, sprinkled with literary allusions, turns of phrase, puns, quotations (he once clobbered me in an exchange of correspondence with an extensive quote from Goethe, in German); in short, the whole panoply of literary tools. Like all gifted writers, he wore his craftsmanship lightly.

Early on, at Ottawa Collegiate, he was marked for intellectual distinction: straight honours in high school, McGill in a breeze, a Rhodes scholarship to Oxford. He then put that intellectual training to use at the Canadian Labour Congress and at McGill. Not many of the labour movement's battles from the 1930s to the 1950s did Eugene Forsey miss.

He could be a fast friend or a formidable foe. As a boy, he listened to debates in the House of Commons, and always appreciated or denigrated politicians according to their respect for the institution of Parliament and their vision of Canada. Atop his list of political devils stood Prime Minister Mackenzie King.

King spoke badly and wrote worse. His slipperiness drove Mr. Forsey to distraction. His political treachery in the King–Byng crisis of 1926 impelled Mr. Forsey to write his masterpiece on the royal power of dissolution. To the end, Eugene Forsey could scarcely find a soft word for King.

Quebec nationalists, puffed-up businessmen, careless academics, sloppy journalists—they all felt the sting of Eugene Forsey's pen. True, he could be inflexible, even pedantic; and, as the years went on, he became more of an intellectual counter-puncher than a creative thinker.

Perhaps that was because so many people were drifting away from the standards he considered essential. Quebec nationalists and their appeaser friends in the rest of Canada (like me, he thought) supported the dangerous Meech Lake accord. Journalists (again, like me) were tearing away at the Senate, an institution that did much good in his eyes and little harm. But he was always fun to argue with, for he loved an argument second only to his family.

He also loved this newspaper. He read *The Globe and Mail* thoroughly and critically. The private letters he sent *Globe* writers correcting syntax or debating assertions are all to be treasured; the public ones form an unmatched body of letters to the editor.

According to the friend at whose house he died yesterday, Eugene Forsey sensed that the end was perhaps near when, at breakfast on Tuesday, he was too tired to read *The Globe and Mail.* Later, his host said yesterday, Senator Forsey felt well enough to read the whole paper, and mentioned several letters he needed to write to the editor.

Alas, we shall not read them. Canada lost a jewel when Eugene Forsey died. This newspaper lost a friend.

The Lougheed Imprint *(June 27, 1985)*

With Alberta Premier Peter Lougheed's resignation, the last and most effective of the provincial barons is gone.

New barons will inevitably emerge over time. But for now, the federal-provincial stage is denuded of the impressive spokesmen for provincial interests who clashed repeatedly with Prime Minister Pierre Trudeau.

The changing cast of characters began with Allan Blakeney's defeat, a defeat that robbed Saskatchewan of a spokesman whose national sweep extended far beyond his province. Then came the resignations of William Davis of Ontario, René Lévesque of Quebec and now Mr. Lougheed.

Of all these, Mr. Lougheed left the greatest imprint on the country. Mr. Davis, in contrast to his successors, pursued a Little Ontario policy that left his province defending its own interests rather than playing honest broker between Ottawa and other provinces. In this Ontario-first role, the province was more isolated and less effective in federal-provincial relations than at any time since the Second World War.

Premier Lévesque's vision died with the referendum defeat of 1980, a defeat which deprived the Parti Québécois of its *raison d'être* and enabled Mr. Trudeau to win the subsequent patriation struggle. And Mr. Blakeney's downfall obscured the tenacious and successful fights he waged to give his province a greater say over resource development.

But Mr. Lougheed, through relentless determination and a mastery of his briefs, changed both Canada and the role of Alberta in the country.

Oil and natural gas, of course, gave Mr. Lougheed the lever he required to assert Alberta's interest and those generally of Western Canada. In the battle for jurisdiction and revenues, Mr. Lougheed fought tirelessly for greater provincial control.

Sometimes he went too far. His obstinacy in negotiating a new energy pricing deal seriously wounded the Conservative government of Prime Minister Joe Clark. (Federal Justice Minister John Crosbie used to call Mr. Lougheed the "Ayatollah.")

His insistence that what was good for Alberta was good for Canada earned him justified suspicions in other parts of the country, especially Ontario. His own profound suspicions about the Ottawa bureaucracy, about the Central Canadian Establishment, about even the federal Conservative Party precluded a national vision that might have made him, given his impressive talents, one of the commanding national politicians of our time.

No one can gainsay his political success. He completely transformed Alberta politics, sweeping away the entrenched Social Credit regime and replacing it with the country's most solidly entrenched political party.

So, too, no one can deny his impact on national affairs. He put Alberta on the map as it had never been before. He presided over the diversification of his province's economy. He made Alberta a province whose importance in federal-provincial relations eclipsed its population, a process that began before the OPEC crisis placed a premium on Alberta's oil and natural gas.

Mr. Lougheed leaves with a national energy policy he could almost have written himself. The Constitution's amending formula is close to the one he sought. The West's Cabinet contingent is more powerful than at any time since the Diefenbaker government. And he leaves a party utterly dominant in the province.

Not since John Robarts played such key roles in the national debate about Quebec's role in Canada and in the federal-provincial negotiations for health insurance and pensions has a provincial premier been more influential on the national stage. Mr. Lougheed's successor will have a tough act to follow.

Don Jamieson   *(November 22, 1986)*

EDMONTON—They'll bury a great patriot in the stony soil of a tiny Newfoundland hamlet today, hard by the sea at the top of Placentia Bay, which, amid all the glitter and clutter of an extraordinary life, he always considered home.

Swift Current never strayed far from Don Jamieson's mind in life, and it will shelter his body in death—a clutch of houses where the road he got the government to finance begins its long descent down the rocky finger of the Burin Peninsula.

To Swift Current he retired when his term ended as High Commissioner to London, the last stop in a career of broadcasting, politics and diplomacy that made him one of Newfoundland's most famous sons. There, he was living quietly with his wife, Barbara, reading the British and Canadian papers, writing his memoirs and extending to occasional visitors that exceptional hospitality which was among his trademarks.

Late last June, when I arrived from St. John's, he plunked himself down at 6 p.m. and began his favourite pastime, talking. Eight hours, countless cigarettes and a lobster dinner later, he seemed perplexed that his visitor, nearly thirty years his junior, was flagging.

For eight hours, he reminisced about the passion of the 1949 referendum, the pioneering days of broadcasting in Newfoundland, Joey Smallwood, Pierre Trudeau, the Liberal Party, his years in London, famous world figures he had known, flashes from a panoramic life that began in the humblest of circumstances and ended in financial security and a worldwide network of friends.

Don Jamieson knew how to create and to seize opportunities. A strong anti-Confederate, he joined the Newfoundland team negotiating the terms of union as an adviser to John Crosbie's father, Chesley, whom Mr. Jamieson idolized almost as a son would. He had never been west of Halifax before arriving in Ottawa for those negotiations, during which he filed radio and newspaper reports back to Newfoundland, thus launching what became his enormously successful career in broadcasting.

When Jack Pickersgill left the federal scene, Mr. Jamieson took over as Newfoundland's watchdog in Ottawa. He represented the vast Burin–Burgeo constituency in southern Newfoundland, visiting voters in roadless outports by boat, helicopter and seaplane.

With his mellifluous voice and endless repertoire of anecdotes, he easily eclipsed all other Cabinet ministers in the art of oratory. Honed on the television screens of Newfoundland, his gifts of public discourse soon become known to all Canadians.

Don Jamieson lived a life of passion for, and commitment to, Newfoundland. His was not the only vision for that distinctive province whose presence so enriches the nation. But even his foes could never gainsay his abiding affection for a place whose joys he shared and whose setbacks he endured.

Wherever he lived, he took with him his collection of Newfoundland art, his Newfoundland books, his Newfoundland memories. It never occurred to him, as it might have to others, to retire anywhere but in Newfoundland.

Don Jamieson left all who were privileged to know him with a deeper appreciation of the place he loved so well. He served his causes, his province and his country with distinction and an uncommon joy.

I can see him in my mind's eye, when the moment came, beside the stern hills and grey waters, with the fishing boats of Swift Current bobbing at their moorings, and I am sure that he was at peace.

Good Night, Barbara, and Adieu, Roger Lemelin *(March 27, 1992)*

Cancer claimed Roger Lemelin last week, and yesterday the disease took Barbara Frum, leaving each of Canada's two solitudes poorer for their passing.

Outside Quebec, Mr. Lemelin's death got barely a couple of paragraphs on the inside pages of newspapers. But in the province, as befitted his stature, the death of the creator of La Famille Plouffe made front-page news, accompanied by testimonials and analyses of his enormous contribution to Quebec letters, journalism and broadcasting.

Mr. Lemelin, an author much beloved by readers of French, was editor of *La Presse* newspaper from 1972 to 1981, but his reputation with the general public probably rested on the televised portrayal from 1953 to 1959 of his novel about the fictional Quebec family, les Plouffes.

Despite his many other talents, especially as a writer, it was television that carried Mr. Lemelin's fame to a mass audience in Quebec. But, of course, television's power in the 1950s was a pale shadow of its reach today.

Barbara Frum, of course, was well known as a longtime host of CBC Radio's *As It Happens*. But she moved into the national limelight as TV co-host, and subsequently only host, of *The Journal*.

Marshall McLuhan, who was often difficult to decipher, once observed in a moment of clarity that modern North America was the first civilization that went inside for community. Inside their homes, North Americans put themselves in touch with each other at first by radio, then massively by television.

Television became—dare a print journalist admit it—the principal way people learned about their society and the world around them. Surveys today illustrate that in the news business, people rely more on television than newspapers, trust the accuracy and balance of TV reporting more than what they find in newspapers, and watch in vast numbers. Whether this trend bodes well or ill for an informed citizenry is incidental to the fact that the trend exists and is becoming more evident with every passing year.

In this country, anyone who travels outside the major urban centres is immediately struck by the omnipresence of television. Indeed, the more isolated the area, the greater the dependence upon it.

Into this world of television-as-national-community slipped Barbara Frum, and it was a testament to her talents and durability that she lasted so long as an invited guest in the living rooms of the nation.

Television's craving for personalities, and the sometimes peculiar criteria for selecting them, often means spitting out those personalities when ratings fall, audiences get mad, or the stars simply get old. For women, in particular, this can be literally a career-threatening challenge, since there is a bushel of evidence that a woman's youth and looks count with TV network executives concerned about ratings.

Barbara Frum happily fell victim neither to this implicit sexism nor to television's propensity to search for fresh faces. Of course, there were people who sometimes disliked her interviews, or detected this or that bias in her work or approach which they themselves did not share. She was satirized, parodied, and as recently as a few weeks ago in a French-language newspaper, viciously attacked. Such is the inevitable fate of being so firmly in the focus of the public's eye.

She cared passionately about the CBC, not just because she worked there, but out of a widespread sense that, without it, the country would be a much poorer place. The periodic criticisms of her were a backhanded compliment, because people cared enough about the institution for which she worked to get themselves fired up.

Just as it would have been inconceivable for private television in Quebec to try something like *La Famille Plouffe*, it's hard to imagine private TV in the rest of Canada putting on something akin to *The Journal.* Barbara Frum knew that, and so did millions of Canadians.

Her longevity, her sense of being a member of an extended family, and what I might call her trustworthiness, are equalled in this country only by Bernard Derome, Radio-Canada's superb anchorman.

Maybe her epitaph should be the words used by thousands of persons she interviewed: "Good night, Barbara." You only say those words often, after all, to a member of the family.

He Led His Time *(February 25, 1986)*

Fifty-six years ago, a young Baptist minister began his pastoral work in Weyburn, Saskatchewan.

Two years later, Rev. Thomas (Tommy) Clement Douglas took his first tentative steps toward political involvement, steps which later took him to the highest office in his province and led Canada to become a more tolerant, equitable society.

Few Canadians in this century have left such a mark on their country as T.C. Douglas, who died yesterday. For forty-three years—twenty-six in the House of Commons; seventeen in Saskatchewan politics—T.C. Douglas fought for social democracy with passion, eloquence and self-deprecating wit.

Tommy Douglas took issues more seriously than he did himself. He was a marvellous *raconteur* with felicitous turns of phrase and an ever-present twinkle in his eye. As Liberal Leader John Turner said in a fitting tribute, Tommy Douglas had a "Christian commitment" to widen opportunity and to combat injustice.

At the University of Chicago, he won the gold medal for debating, dramatics and oratory, skills he deployed throughout his life on innumerable public platforms from the back of a haywagon to the floor of the House of Commons. In my own time around Ottawa, he stands among the two or three best Commons performers.

Everywhere we turn in contemporary Canada, we see issues and accomplishments that bear the stamp of Tommy Douglas. The arrogant doctors of Ontario are hurling themselves recklessly against his legacy, publicly funded medicine. The federal government is trying to chip away at the cost of other social programs for which he fought so hard.

Other aspects of contemporary society we take for granted he supported before they became politically fashionable—rural electrification, the right to strike for public employees, a bill of rights.

As Premier of Saskatchewan from 1944 to 1961, Mr. Douglas led North

America's first social-democratic government. He suffered the most withering abuse within his own province, including from striking doctors, and from those throughout Canada and the United States who saw communism lurking behind the social-democratic label.

The lot of a socialist in North America has always been that of an iconoclast. Tommy Douglas never shied away from that often difficult role. Indeed, his finest moment in federal politics came Oct. 16, 1970.

On that day, Prime Minister Pierre Trudeau told the Commons that the War Measures Act had been imposed. Temperatures were at a boiling point in Quebec and in the House of Commons. Liberals and Tories supported the Act; Mr. Douglas led his New Democrats in majestic opposition.

His speech was continuously interrupted by Liberal and Tory catcalls. But he persevered above the din and argued: "We are not prepared to use the preservation of law and order as a smokescreen to destroy the liberties and the freedom of the people of Canada." He ended his speech with these telling words: "The Canadian people will look on this as a black Friday for civil liberties in Canada." It has taken sixteen years, but a federal government has now committed itself to replacing the War Measures Act with something less Draconian.

The New Jerusalem toward which Mr. Douglas believed Canada was slowly marching is still over the horizon. But Canada has come a long way from the dusty thirties when Tommy Douglas began his political career amid the destitute families of Saskatchewan. The heresies of Tommy Douglas's early days are now part of the warp and woof of contemporary Canada.

NDP leader Ed Broadbent deserves the last word about one of his predecessors: "He was a great man, a truly rare individual who changed the course of history."

PART 8 *Issues*

EDUCATION

No Time to Waste in Restoring Common Sense to Our Education System *(May 15, 1991)*

"There can be no meaningful pursuit of educational outcomes, no effective remediation to keep students from accumulating crippling deficits of knowledge and skills, and no real accountability within our system of education, until clearly defined learning objectives are established for every stage of the process."

—George Radwanski, 1987

OUTCOMES. Accountability. Defined learning objectives. George Radwanski was slightly ahead of his time. In 1987, the former editor of *The Toronto Star* was asked by Ontario Premier David Peterson's Liberal government to examine the province's dropout rate. Mr. Radwanski produced a report so full of common sense and pedagogical wisdom that, predictably, it was slain by that well-known but deadly and deadening trio: interest groups defending their entitlements, bureaucracies defending their empires, and politicians defending their butts.

Mr. Radwanski was trying to reverse the disastrous course on which Ontario (and many other provinces) embarked in the mid-1960s when the province's Hall–Dennis report was all the rage. Regrettably, his assault on the lack of accountability and standards was shelved by ministers, patronized by civil servants and abhorred by teachers. Somewhere at Queen's Park it gathers dust; in the lives of parents and other concerned Canadians, its ideas simmer.

Hall–Dennis, named for the last names of its co-authors, emerged in the 1960s, and its prescriptions soon spread far beyond Ontario. Flower-power was everywhere in conflict with established authorities. "Systems"—political, economic, educational—were all under attack. People had to discover themselves, be liberated, express themselves.

Hall–Dennis argued that students should discover themselves, not through discipline, but through choice. Out went province-wide examinations, core curriculums, the idea that the acquisition of knowledge can be—and should be—regularly tested and compared. As Mr. Radwanski noted, Hall–Dennis suggested that "the acquisition of specific knowledge should be subordinated to more abstract goals of individual self-fulfillment and self-esteem."

Coincidentally, the Hall–Dennis era coincided with an explosion of the educational system and the burgeoning of powerful teachers' unions. Bureacracies and teachers' unions, each protecting entitlements and prerogatives, proceeded to re-make the educational system according to the new theories.

Indeed, the Hall–Dennis ideas that prevailed in the 1960s are still finding new outlets. The Sullivan Royal Commission into education in British Columbia made recommendations embraced by the government and implemented by the province's school boards.

Exams, tests and other objective measurements were out. If students didn't learn something, they still moved on, an approach reflected in this statement: "Students will not be required to repeat a whole unit of work or set of units because some portion of a unit has not been completed."

If a student struggles, "then different learning resources and teaching approaches are usually indicated, not a repeat of the same material and activities that were unsuccessfully attempted previously."

The whole B.C. education system has now been organized along the Sullivan model. It's one huge mistake. It's also curious, but perhaps revealing, that a system where exams and province-wide measurements of output are seriously frowned upon should be leading the charge for some kind of national testing.

A national testing program has been proposed by the usually ineffective Council of Ministers of Education, an interprovincial body. No sooner did the idea emerge than Ontario dropped out, saying the test would not reflect Ontario's ethnic diversity. That decision, again, showed the reluctance to measure output and standardize more curriculum.

In Ontario, fourteen of the thirty credits required to graduate from high school are optional ones. That means students can graduate from high school having taken only two math courses, two science courses, one Canadian history course (Grade 10) and one Canadian geography course (Grade 9).

Twenty-five years after Hall–Dennis, analysts such as Mr. Radwanski, the trustees and administrators he interviewed, parents everywhere, the population in general, and, belatedly, governments are examining the results of the Hall–Dennis era and finding them wanting.

A long-overdue debate is brewing over this country's education system. For once, turning back the clock would be a significant advance.

Maybe Retelling the Old Tale Will Help, But It Needs a New Chapter *(October 30, 1991)*

For those who waded through some or all of Michael Porter's 855-page book, *The Competitive Advantage of Nations*, the Harvard professor's recent diagnosis of the Canadian economy was no surprise.

His assessment of what ails Canada, based on the model he used for investigating ten other economies around the world, is not necessarily wrong—just predictable and, as such, probably not worth the money paid to him by the Business Council on National Issues and the federal government.

A whole series of independent studies of what's wrong with the Canadian economy had presaged Professor Porter's findings, including the Macdonald royal commission, studies by the Economic Council of Canada, the De Grandpré report, analyses by the Conference Board and the C.D. Howe Institute, and a string of studies on Canada's unemployment and training programs.

The Canadian economy still relies too heavily on the export of unfinished or semi-finished raw materials. The country's productivity—its real Achilles' heel—is low by world standards (second lowest among the Group of Seven leading industrialized countries); its governments too anxious to prop up declining industries; its unit-wage costs, especially in manufacturing, eclipsing those in the United States; its education system extremely expensive but insufficiently results-oriented.

Unable to change the country's political culture by internal means, the present government turned to free trade with the United States to administer shock treatment to the economy. And the political results have been completely foreseeable: a retreat in many quarters from the demands of that agreement and, by extension, from the entire world challenge of global competition.

Perhaps one more re-telling of these old tales will succeed where others failed in inducing a change of mentality in individual Canadians and their associations. But there is also something missing from Professor Porter's analysis, the kind of bottom-up view of what makes an economy competitive.

What he says, like others before him, is essentially correct but incomplete. Productivity and competitiveness depend, yes, on well-managed, outward-looking corporations, better labour–management relations, more sensible government policies, and a society-wide commitment to better performance. But the economy's health is also determined by what kind of drag is exerted on it by those with difficulty competing, either individually or collectively.

The poor, as they used to say in Britain, will always be with us. But the larger their numbers, the greater the unused potential of the economy.

Canada's much-vaunted social programs in the past decade have merely served to prevent the distribution of income in Canada from widening. Without the programs, the social cleavages would have been even larger. Put another way, the most affluent fifth of the population has roughly the same proportion of national income as it did a decade ago, and the least affluent fifth the same proportion too.

The more young women who are socialized out of science and engineering, the smaller the pool of brainpower available to fill our chronic shortfall in those areas. The more single women on welfare with children in their care, the more vicious the circle of deprivation in which they find themselves and the greater the drain on society's resources. The more aboriginal people who live in squalor, the more of society's resources are diverted.

Hungry children often make poor students. Poor students, for whatever reason, make for high dropout rates. High dropout rates mean more people who cannot catch up with the competitive pressures of the global economy.

As Robert Reich and other American writers are demonstrating, in the emerging services economy—and 70 per cent of Canadians are now employed in the service sector—the gaps are widening between those with skills and those without. It's the same message conveyed by the Economic Council of Canada's report *Good Jobs, Bad Jobs*.

And yet, Canada has the industrial world's most perverse system of labour support. It spends most of its money in this area on such passive support as unemployment insurance, and its private sector has a lamentable record of training.

In other countries, such as Sweden, the formula is reversed: very little passive support for programs such as unemployment insurance, but a big commitment to training by public and private sectors. They recognize that competitiveness and productivity mean what Professor Porter means, but also that an economy does not run well with so much poverty, illiteracy, income inequality and poor education standards.

Under-Investment, Fighting, Not Enough Skills—That's What to Blame

(January 9, 1992)

For obvious reasons, the bleeding of Canadian manufacturing jobs makes headlines for newspapers, unemployment for workers and managers, and grist for ideological mills.

Free trade, to those who originally opposed it, is the culprit. The high dollar, high interest rates, fiscal restraint, the GST—all are advanced to explain the agony of central Canada's manufacturing industries.

But perhaps more telling is this sentence from a recent report of the Canadian Labour Market and Productivity Centre: "Over the cyclically neutral peak-to-peak 1981-89 period, Canada had the slowest rate of output-per-hour growth in manufacturing among the G7, less than one-half the [Group of Seven industrial countries'] average."

The Centre, which brings together labour and business, continues: "This poor productivity performance has been a key factor in the deterioration of the cost competitiveness of Canadian goods in the American market."

Unhappily, from 1985 to 1990, Canada's hourly output from manufacturing barely budged, whereas it rose by about 4 per cent a year in Japan and Britain, 3 per cent in the United States and France, 2.5 per cent in Italy and 2 per cent in Germany. Right there is the key to explaining why Canada has competitive problems in manufacturing. The country has been losing ground every year to its major trading partners.

What about the economy as a whole? To this, the Centre replies: "Canada's aggregate productivity has also been very weak in the 1980s relative to [that of] other countries. Over the 1979-89 period Canada had the lowest rate of growth of total factor productivity in the G7 [tied with the United States]."

And yet, according to the World Economic Forum's comparative ranking of productivity, Canada ranked seventh, fourth and fifth in the past three years. How to explain the difference?

The answer, in part, is that Canada has been living on its resources and drawing on its capital through large deficits and borrowings. Those resources remain valuable, but they count for less in the competitive scheme of things, because comparative advantage (as the Japanese and Koreans have shown) depends less and less on natural resources.

Instead, a trained workforce has never counted for more. Investment in plant and equipment counts, too. In both areas, Canada slumps badly.

According to figures published by the productivity centre, public-sector investments, often a spur to growth, have fallen as a percentage of gross national product. Machinery and equipment investment has been the lowest in the G7. The country's research-and-development effort remains poor.

Just boosting R&D, while useful and even important, provides an insufficient assurance of productivity gains. As Richard French, a senior executive with Bell Canada said recently, tying R&D to products, marketing and new management techniques is the answer. "While Japan and Germany have achieved a strong relationship between the intensity of R&D in their economies and growth in productivity, other countries such as Canada have not."

What about training and education? Here Canada stands the record of successful economies on its head. The Canadian private sector spends less per capita on training than other private sectors. The public sector's spending is about at the average for industrial countries, but it is misdirected.

Canada spends 75 per cent of its labour-market programs on income maintenance, largely through unemployment insurance. Traditionally socialist countries such as Sweden laugh at that priority. In Sweden, only 30 per cent of public funds in this area go for income maintenance; in Germany 50 per cent.

Similarly, the Centre's report reminds us that our hugely expensive public-education system leaves plenty to be desired. High-school graduates have actually declined from 73 per cent to 66 per cent of 18-year-olds in the last half of the 1980s. Nearly seven million people between 16 and 69 years of age "do not have the reading skill levels to meet most everyday reading requirements." Enrolment in university science and mathematics programs has declined.

The basics of the Canadian economy are wrong. Plant and capital investment is too low. Labour and management fight too much. Governments are far too heavily indebted. Skill levels are declining; dropout rates are increasing. Government programs encourage income maintenance rather than training. The school system does not teach enough of the basics.

No wonder productivity remains stagnant. When productivity is stagnant, economies lose ground.

Swedish or German Accent Needed to Reform the Unemployment Program

(December 7, 1992)

In bad economic times, about one of every six tax dollars Ottawa spends goes to unemployment insurance. In good times, about one of every ten goes to UI.

The sums are enormous: $20-billion this year out of total federal spending on programs of nearly $120-billion.

Ottawa will spend slightly more on UI this year than on senior-citizens benefits. UI will cost twice as much as defence, $4-billion more than the operation of the entire federal bureaucracy, and more than twice what Ottawa sends to the provinces for post-secondary education and health combined.

Nowhere else in the federal budget is so much money spent on one program. It's little wonder a cost-cutting government would be drawn to trimming spending.

In a previous budget, Finance Minister Donald Mazankowski tightened the criteria for receiving UI in traditionally low-unemployment areas. Last week he froze UI benefits through 1994-95 and ended benefits for people who voluntarily leave their jobs. These measures, he said, will save $850-million in 1993-94 and $1.6-billion in 1994-95.

Simultaneously, the government will use an additional $300-million from UI for retraining. That will bring the total amount of UI money for retraining to about $3.5-billion—roughly 15 per cent of the $20-billion spent on UI.

Turn the figures upside down. About 85 per cent of UI money goes to recipients for what economists call "passive income maintenance." People get their cheques, demonstrate that they are looking for work in order to receive more cheques, and receive them.

An intellectual revolution, coupled with fierce political will, is required to reorient UI from this essentially passive system to one that prepares the workforce for flexibility, adaptation and the challenges of what Mr. Mazankowski calls "massive restructuring."

Sadly, the Tories are not well-positioned to make the changes. Conservatives, with their hard right-wingers, are suspect when they talk about UI. People think they have a "hidden agenda" not to reform the system but to gut it.

Just as Republican President Richard Nixon opened American doors to China in defiance of his party's traditional hostility to communism, so it will probably take a Liberal government in Ottawa to reform UI.

Reform means turning Canada's unemployment scheme into something approximating the Swedish or German models. In those countries, a minority of government money spent on labour markets goes for passive income maintenance; the majority goes to training.

Liberals in Ottawa seem only dimly aware of the challenge ahead. In their comments on the Mazankowski economic statement, they opted for the easy political points about freezing UI benefits.

In Atlantic Canada, where Liberals rule in three provinces, premiers understand the perversity of UI. Frank McKenna of New Brunswick, Joe Ghiz of Prince Edward Island and Clyde Wells of Newfoundland have seen the result of the existing system, and they don't like it.

They understand that their provinces will never go anywhere economically without a radically altered use of the billions spent there for UI. Mr. McKenna has embraced experimental programs to get people off welfare and into training, and he's trying to reform his education system to get young people better trained in the basics. Newfoundland produced the best, and most damning, indictment of the existing UI system in a study done under the aegis of Doug House of Memorial University.

Because there is a patchwork of federal and provincial programs for training, and because Ottawa is uniquely responsible for UI, reforming the UI system will require extensive federal-provincial negotiations. Labour and management must also be involved.

In their first term, the Tories proposed using $800-million of UI money for training. A political storm broke over these modest proposals, led by the Liberals in the Commons and Senate. A commission into UI reform under Quebecker Claude Forget split apart, with two minority reports spoiling the entire exercise.

After the next federal election, the new government's highest priority must be to tackle this $20-billion program again and reform it profoundly, so that Canadian labour-market policy actually prepares people for restructuring instead of poking politically at the margins of the problem.

Never Mind Input Variables—What Canada Needs Is a Rebellion *(December 16, 1992)*

Here's a frightening paradox. Canadian teachers are better-educated and better-paid than ever before. Student–teacher ratios have declined by about one-third since the 1960s. By world standards, Canada spends handsomely on primary and secondary education.

And yet, a million Canadians will emerge illiterate from the Canadian school system in this decade. The high-school dropout rate reaches 30 per cent in some provinces. Students score badly in mathematics and sciences on international tests. From 1966 to 1991, average test scores on a range of skills at Grade 4 and Grade 8 levels actually declined.

How is it that Canada can spend so much on education, be blessed with such well-educated teachers, and yet produce meagre results that cripple too many students and place Canada at a competitive disadvantage with other countries?

The day the Economic Council of Canada was axed by the Mulroney government, a draft report was completed on education and training in Canada. That report, which was at last released this week, expands on (and thereby deepens the depression about) themes first developed in the council's April 1992 report, *A Lot to Learn.*

A lot to unlearn is really what Canada needs, notably the errors of wrongheaded educational theorists and their friends in education bureaucracies. A generation of students has now passed through the system they designed. The task for the next generation will be to unlearn the bad habits of the previous one.

More spending is not the answer, as demonstrated by the council's statistics. Canada already spends the highest percentage of its gross domestic product on education among the G7 countries. Teachers' salaries and administration costs have risen faster than the inflation rate since 1961.

Teaching continues to be a highly desirable profession, although a recent study for the Canadian Teachers Federation found that many complain of excessive stress and insufficient respect. But teachers colleges are overflowing; the average teacher's income in Canada in 1990 (for a nine-month teaching year) was about $47,000; and their pension funds are among the largest in the country.

As the council notes, however, there are few rewards for the best teachers. Teachers are now unionized, and apart from raises for seniority, few incentives exist to sort out good ones from bad.

Curiously, although the school system recognizes students of different abilities and slots them accordingly, the same sorting process does not affect teachers. When the council recommends stratifying teachers into instructors, career teachers and lead teachers—as a way of rewarding effort—you can just imagine the response of the teachers' unions.

Levelling among teachers, of course, is just one part of a general levelling of standards that came with the abolition of systematic testing and province-wide exams, less emphasis on core curriculum and the switch to "child-centred learning." These were the "reforms" of the 1960s that have had such disastrous consequences for the country.

In Ontario, it appears that nothing has been learned, since the Ministry of Education is ploughing ahead with de-streaming in Grade 9, against the wishes of the province's teachers.

Canada needs an intellectual rebellion against many of the "reforms" of the past quarter-century. What the council calls "input variables"—student–teacher ratios, teacher education, teacher experience, teachers' salary, expenditures per pupil—do bear on the education system. But the council surveyed hundreds of studies about what produces proficiency in education and discovered these factors to be of marginal relevance.

"There is no convincing evidence that the input variables . . . have a substantial and consistent influence on student achievement . . . ," the council found.

More consequential is the structure of the curriculum, the standards expected of students, the feedback they receive through test results, parental guidance (students from two-parent families tend to outperform those with one parent) and a generalized respect for learning and achievement in society. These have all been eroded by changed family patterns, and the practical application of wrong-headed theories rejected everywhere but in North America.

It was the height of arrogance for Canadians and Americans to believe we had answers that had eluded Europeans and Asians. A generation of experience demonstrates that they have the answers, and we have the questions.

IMMIGRATION

Immigration Policy Has Been Out of Sync with the Economy for Twenty Years

(October 25, 1994)

With some honourable exceptions, we in the media tend to report immigration by peering down the wrong end of the telescope.

We are quick to jump on sad tales of immigrants fighting to be reunited with loved ones. Or we play up tales of criminals who have escaped deportation.

Ministers of immigration must quickly respond to these media stories. And the public, not surprisingly, focuses on these scattered stories of pathos and drama.

For example, the current Minister of Citizenship and Immigration, Sergio Marchi, responded with a "get-tough" policy on deportation of criminals after several violent incidents in Toronto made headlines. Reform Leader Preston Manning, at the party's just-completed convention, tried to make hay from this deportation problem.

Meanwhile, every day immigration policy writ large changes the face and nature of contemporary Canada. What really counts in immigration policy is how many immigrants Canada needs, or should accept, and what kind of immigrants (and refugees) are admitted.

Canada, after all, is one of only three countries in the world that accept large numbers of immigrants—the United States and Australia being the other two.

The laws of supply and demand therefore run heavily in Canada's favour. The demand for entry into Canada is large; the supply of places is small relative to that demand, because the absorptive capacity of Canadian society is not without limits—budgetary, social and economic.

With the arithmetic of supply and demand running heavily in Canada's favour, it's curious, or perverse, that for many years Canada's immigration policy has tilted in favour of those classes of immigrants over whom we have the least control for admittance (families) and away from those over whom the country has the most control (independents).

On November 1, Mr. Marchi will announce new immigration levels for the forthcoming years and unveil changes in the administration of immigration policy, notably the categories of immigrants. Both the levels and the categories need overhaul. Here's hoping the minister gets the policy right.

Levels have been rising steadily since the low point of 84,302 in 1985. Since then, the levels have been 99,219 in 1986, 152,098 in 1987, 161,929 in 1988, 192,001 in 1989, 241,230 in 1990, 230,781 in 1991, 252,842 in 1992, 254,321 in 1993. Government policy, which may soon change, forecast levels of 250,000 in the next few years.

These levels were perverse, since immigration is supposed to rise in good economic times and fall in recession. That didn't happen in 1990 to 1992, nor in the previous recessions of 1973 to 1975 and 1980 to 1982. Immigration has been out of sync with the economy for two decades.

The effect of high levels during the 1990-92 period was especially perverse in Ontario, the arrival point for 52 per cent of immigrants and 60 per cent of refugees, where the 1990-92 recession wiped out 300,000 jobs and increased unemployment and welfare case loads by 400,000 and 300,000, respectively. Metropolitan Toronto, clobbered by the recession, took 71,956 immigrants in 1993, or 20 per cent of the national total, and 7,101 refugees, or 29 per cent of the national total.

More perverse still was the mismatch of resources. The immigration department's budget was being cut and the number of employees reduced at the very moment when immigration levels rose. Snafus and morale problems were a perfectly normal response to this mismatch.

But the mismatch went further. While immigration levels rose, federal funding to provinces declined. Ottawa set the targets—the highest targets since the period just before the First World War—then dumped on the provinces (except Quebec, which enjoys a particularly lucrative deal with Ottawa) the additional costs of absorbing the immigrants through settlement programs, language training and welfare. (Federal transfers for welfare were capped at increases of 5 per cent for Ontario, British Columbia and Alberta.)

Mismatches of resources and the highest levels in seventy-five years, for which no compelling reasons were given, soured public opinion on immigration. So did the categories of immigrants, which defied the advantages of supply and demand.

Immigration Policy Needs to Balance Families, Refugees and Independents

(October 26, 1994)

Canada's yearly immigration levels have nearly doubled in this decade without Conservative and Liberal governments fully explaining the need for such an increase.

From 1990 to 1993, immigration averaged 244,793 a year, compared to 125,982 in the eighties, 144,491 in the seventies and 136,903 in the sixties.

While overall levels jumped, so did the share of immigrants admitted under the family-class category, the one over which the government has the least discretion. From 1991 to 1993, family-class entrants grew by about 25,000, whereas independent immigrants, the category over which governments have the most discretion, grew by only about 1,800. Investors and entrepreneurs increased by another 15,000.

This year, the same tilt is at work. The two classes over which the country has the least discretion—families and refugees—will outnumber the independent immigrants, over which Canada has the most discretion, by 138,300 to 110,700. And those numbers understate the tilt, because among the independents are 35,200 who are assisted relatives counted as independents.

Debate swirls in the public, as it did in Citizenship and Immigration Minister Sergio Marchi's national consultations on immigration, about the relative merits of the family-class and independent immigrants. Of particular concern were the 43,000 parents and grandparents admitted each year under the family-reunification category, since few of these are likely to enter the workforce.

Emerging data, here and abroad, suggest independent immigrants do economically better than other classes, and faster. They also subsequently bring family members with high academic achievement or skill levels.

Preliminary data from the Department of Citizenship and Immigration show that compared to average earnings for the general population of $434.60 a week, independent immigrants earn $481.34, entrepreneurial immigrants $502, assisted relatives $420.33 and other family-class immigrants $405.

A study from 1980 to 1988 showed a widening gap throughout the period between earnings of independents and family-class immigrants. An Australian study revealed exactly the same trends.

The shift toward family class has increased the pressures on language training. A study by Derrick Thomas, a federal civil servant, showed that before the expansion of the family and refugee classes in 1978, only a third of new arrivals spoke neither French nor English, compared to about half now. Other studies clearly show a link between language acquisition and educational knowledge before arrival in Canada.

One of Mr. Marchi's working groups charged with defining social and economic objectives for immigration concluded that a shift from family to independents was required. That group suggested a two-tier approach. Tier 1 would include humanitarian immigration consisting of refugees and persons in similar circumstances. Tier 2 would be economic and family immigration, with a "need to balance family immigration against the intake of immigrants chosen for their skills and entrepreneurial abilities."

Immigration can bring benefits, especially to a country such as Canada which has the luxury of choosing among so many who wish to immigrate here. Canada could, if it so desired, find a better balance in the nineties between utilitarian and humanitarian immigration objectives.

For immigration to work better for Canada, policy needs to find a better balance between those objectives by moving closer to the average levels of the past three decades and increasing the number of immigrants whose skills rather than family affiliation count toward admission.

Policy, which must remain blind to race, ethnicity or religion, especially needs to fit Canada's straitened fiscal circumstances and a changing economy with its requirement for higher skills.

In this fashion, Canada would create a sensible and balanced immigration policy supported, as it should be, by the general public, as opposed to the unbalanced one now largely favoured by certain interest groups and immigration lawyers.

Canada Has a Chance to Get Its Immigration Policy Right This Time

(October 28, 1994)

Much of what the Liberal Party said about immigration in its pre-election red book, whose pronouncements have assumed biblical proportions in official Ottawa, was careful and bland, allowing the party to move in almost any direction.

The party's one specific pledge was to achieve immigration levels of about 1 per cent of the national population. That would require increasing existing levels of immigration, which are now running at about 250,000 a year.

Like so much else in the red book, that promise was half politics, half wish. It was certainly not grounded in reality, since the government does not have the resources to pay the costs of higher immigration, nor do the provinces. So when Citizenship and Immigration Minister Sergio Marchi announces new immigration targets next week, he will set them somewhat below existing ones, although probably higher than the average of the eighties—about 126,000 per year.

Mr. Marchi has been learning that the world in government looks quite different from the world in opposition. Therefore he must deal with real problems, such as the breakdown of sponsorship for immigrants. These breakdowns wind up costing the federal government about $700-million a year.

Mr. Marchi is also discovering that family-class immigration, which in opposition he wanted to increase, is less economically advantageous than independent-class immigration. He's been told that by his department, by the Department of Finance, by outside experts he consulted, and by international experience. Watch for him to take note of this accumulating evidence in his statement next week.

The minister will likely also tighten up supervision of entrepreneurial immigrants, a highly desirable change. The previous government introduced this new class of immigrants who could enter Canada by agreeing to invest large chunks of cash in Canada.

That program has had too many scams and suffered from insufficient monitoring. It also smacks of people buying their way into Canada, and in that sense is as offensive as those who enter the country illegally or who claim refugee status when they are in fact economic migrants.

On the refugee front, my sense is that Mr. Marchi has already created future problems for himself by appointing to the Immigration and Refugee Board so many refugee advocates. Canada already accepts a far higher percentage of refugee claims than any other country, a percentage that has grown since the Liberals took office.

Mr. Marchi's political position deserves some sympathy, since the Liberal Party's coalition has always included many so-called ethnic groups. Every seat the party won in British Columbia, and many in Ontario, feature large concentrations of people who have arrived in Canada in recent decades. Indeed, one of the Liberal Party's enduring contributions to Canada has been its ability to welcome new arrivals to its political ranks.

The minister has therefore been under some political pressure from within Liberal ranks to keep immigration levels high. He also feels the heat from those who want to maintain high numbers of family-class immigrants, because people who want to bring family members to Canada are already here and, in many cases, can vote. And like any minister of immigration, he is hectored constantly by advocacy groups and immigration lawyers with considerable exposure in the media.

Mr. Marchi has a chance to get policy right next week. Sound policy would mean: lowering immigration levels to what governments can afford, say something between 150,000 and 180,000 (still higher than in the Trudeau years); shifting the balance from family class to independents; eliminating, or at least monitoring more closely, the entrepreneurial class; forcing sponsors to post bonds or otherwise ensure financing of those they bring to Canada; maintaining a generous attitude toward refugees and insisting that Canada's policy remain non-discriminatory toward any racial, ethnic or religious group.

In Response to Low Fish Stocks (*May 7, 1990*)

If Professor Leslie Harris of Memorial University is correct, then the Mulroney government's assistance package for the Atlantic fishing industry is probably based on a false premise.

Professor Harris and his team of experts analyzed the state of the northern cod stock and found that even the current reduced levels of permitted fishing were too high. To conserve and rebuild the stocks, which provide the economic mainstay for dozens of Newfoundland and Nova Scotia communities, Professor Harris recommended reductions this year to the 197,000-tonne allowable catch, with a much lower catch next year.

That crucial recommendation was thrown overboard in the $426-million, five-year plan outlined yesterday by the government. Perhaps the government simply does not trust the scientific analysis of Professor Harris and his team. After all, a Department of Fisheries and Oceans scientist recently testified in a court case that the stocks were in better shape than Professor Harris had suggested.

More probably, the government could not face the fiscal implications and social hardship of reducing the catch. As it is, the government has found $426-million from its contingency fund for the next five years to supplement the $158-million already announced.

A smaller catch would have meant forking over even more money, and would have thrown more people out of work in the outports of Newfoundland and the towns and villages of Nova Scotia.

But the underlying issue of the Atlantic fishery is the state of the stock. There can be no long-term economic security for people in the fishing industry if the stocks are not rebuilt. A catch of 197,000 tonnes this year does not contribute, and probably hurts, the essential task of rebuilding. Indeed, the 197,000-tonne figure exceeded by 7,000 tonnes the recommended quota from the Fisheries Department because International Trade Minister John Crosbie tried, unsuccessfully as things turned out, to keep open a plant in his riding.

Wisely, the government has allocated large sums for retraining fishermen and re-equipping plants to handle under-utilized species. Some of this shifting away from cod is already underway; more must still be done.

And wisely, too, the government has resisted the siren song of "community-based quotas," which would inevitably pit community against community and make less efficient an industry that must compete on international markets, given the small size of the Canadian one.

Critics will undoubtedly scream about the "paltry" additional sum of $426-million spread over five years, roughly $90-million a year, and compare it to the $500-million for this year recently offered the western grain farmers. They'll point out that Prime Minister Brian Mulroney promised a package for the fishery as generous as the one offered the farmers. It isn't as generous, but then almost no government subsidy can possibly compete on a per capita amount with the money pitchforked in recent years into the grain sector.

About 35,000 people work in the Atlantic Canadian fishing industry, but there are probably full-time jobs for only half this number. That so many are employed has everything to do with unemployment insurance, which has enabled workers to share part-time work in the fish plants while collecting UI the rest of the year.

The European Community fishermen have contributed to the problem of depleted stocks by over-fishing outside the 200-mile zone. So have Canadians through inadequate scientific management and sloppy fishing practices, including false reporting of catches.

But the crux of a long-term solution remains rebuilding the stocks. Yesterday's announcement didn't help.

Cutting Royal Ties Would Be Canada's Crowning Achievement *(June 10, 1992)*

Eleven years ago, on a lovely London morning, two young people got married in St. Paul's Cathedral.

They were long on looks and pedigree but a bit short on brainpower. Still, all Britain watched agog. From my seat in the cathedral, it was truly a special day, full of British pageantry, the voice of soprano Kiri Te Kanawa, medals clinking against chests, a bit of the ages on display, a future king and queen beginning their lives together.

Lady Diana, for reasons now apparent, was kept far from the media, apart from obligatory photo opportunities. And Charles, well, he did sound a trifle barmy whenever he opened his mouth, but then no one expected the royals to say anything important, especially the young ones.

These memories flooded back when reading tales from London about the latest episode in the Charles and Diana soap opera, which follows hard on the heels of the equally enthralling tale of the younger prince and his equally forgettable wife, whose faces graced the cover of *Maclean's* magazine and so enthralled the editors of *Chatelaine* on their last "royal" visit to Canada.

Reading this stuff from London made me wonder: why do Canadians, in the middle of yet another bout of constitutional angst, put up with the monarchy? The Queen is nice enough, but compared to the queens of Spain and the Netherlands, she is no conversation stopper.

As for the brood, well, most of them are split up or should be, and not one of them would merit a dinner invitation from anyone looking for interesting, let alone important, conversation.

So what, say you? And you are right, since royalty never did depend upon intellect. They are there for ceremony, and it must be hellishly difficult to remember that any original thought, let alone personal opinion, will land them in controversy.

But there is, or ought to be, a sense of dignity about royalty. Lord knows, apart from the Queen herself, how little of that precious commodity is about these days.

Far beyond the peccadillos of the current crop of royals, the question arises of what do they do for Canada apart from providing grist for *Chatelaine*? This country long ago severed its umbilical cord with the United Kingdom, although close relations thankfully remain.

The Statute of Westminster sanctioned Canadian freedom in foreign affairs; the patriation of the British North American Act snapped the vestigial link with the British Parliament. Only the Crown remains, and one wonders why.

In Quebec, of course, nobody cares about the monarchy, but people have the good taste not to rub their indifference into the face of the rest of the country.

Outside the province, the monarchy has slipped far beyond the Charter, the anthem, flag and multiculturalism as very important national symbols. According to one poll, the monarchy outside Quebec ranks about on a par with bilingualism as an important national institution. And yet bilingualism is deemed divisive and unpopular, whereas the monarchy is considered a unifying and important symbol.

It certainly does not unite Canadians, since so many remain indifferent to it. The institution does animate a dwindling number of souls who would presumably take great umbrage at any attempt to snip the link and create an indigenous head of state. That umbrage presumably paralyzes politicians.

Royalists insist that monarchy ennobles public life, but the argument lies in tatters these days. They further insist that it places the state above government, a helpful arrangement, but one which could be otherwise be enshrined by indigenous means. They also insist it keeps traditions alive, but these are of an era through which Canada long ago passed.

Anyway, these ruminations are merely idle chatter, since changing the monarchy in Canada would require unanimous consent of the federal government and the provinces, and we know how they can barely agree that today is Wednesday. None of them has breathed a word about the monarchy in the interminable constitutional talks that continued droning on in Ottawa yesterday.

So, although the country might, in this time of angst and searching for national symbols, hold a useful debate and maybe even a vote on the monarchy, all is silent. The monarchy will remain. The soap operas across the Atlantic will presumably continue. *Chatelaine* will not lack for cover stories.

Thanks to Our Amending Formula, the Monarchy Is Safe in Canada *(March 18, 1996)*

The news that the Duke and Duchess of York, otherwise known as Prince Andrew and Sarah Ferguson, otherwise known as Andy and Fergie, are divorcing keeps the royal pattern alive.

First there was Princess Anne, who split from her husband and remarried. Then there was Prince Charles and Diana, whose soap opera will soon culminate in divorce. And now Andy and Fergie. No wonder the youngest of the royal offspring, Prince Edward, must be wondering if marriage is such a good idea.

The escapades of the British royals have nonetheless served a useful purpose for those of us in faraway Canada, highlighting just how unmajestic (the Queen excepted) the family has become. Next week, when the slightly wonky Prince Charles graces our shores, Canadians can ask themselves again whether they really want this chap as head of state. Apart from unregenerate monarchists who get misty-eyed at the mere mention of the institution, the answer from huge numbers of Canadians will be no.

Just ask yourself the straight-up question: do you want Charles as head of state, his picture on the currency, his persona the one to which we swear allegiance, his character the one we admire, his institution one that makes us proud and more Canadian?

No sane person would elect Charles dogcatcher. He's there, well, because he's there, and he's there because, well, the monarchy's there, and increasingly the monarchy's there, well, because it's always been there. The institution, which had great resonance when Canada was more obviously linked to Britain, scarcely creates a ripple of interest for a majority of Canadians, apart from the comic relief offered by the family members. The whole institution, lacking relevance, has degenerated into fodder for tabloid magazines.

The monarchy's redeeming virtue is the separation of head of state from head of government, so that one person and at least one institution stands above the fractiousness of politics and the pluralism of society. Curiously, the institution of monarchy in Canada has been used for political purposes, witness to which are the variety of lieutenants-governor and even governors-general who got their jobs in no small measure because of their past service to the party in power. Not all got there this way, but some certainly did, including a sampling of those now serving.

It would help if the institution of head of state actually derived from the society it serves, but in modern, bilingual, multicultural, North American Canada, the monarchy in the persons of the British Royal Family can hardly be seen as an emanation of the Canadian society it purportedly serves. Put another way, there is almost nothing apart from nostalgia and the thunderous proclamations of loyalty from ardent monarchists that would link the Royal Family to contemporary Canada. And there is certainly nothing in the upbringing, conduct or demeanour of the Queen's offspring that suggests this situation will change.

Monarchists and anti-monarchists can have their sport next week when the Prince does his walkabout, and they can flail away for years to come. Happily for the monarchists, Canada's constitutional amending formula will make it unlikely in the extreme that the insitution will vanish. Changing the monarchy would require unanimous consent from the federal Parliament and all provinces, and since they can barely agree on the day of the week, let alone on constitutional amendments, the monarchy is safe thanks to the amending formula.

There could, of course, be referenda in each province and across the country to change the Constitution, but we know how uncertain these can be. If only one provincial electorate voted to uphold the monarchy, it would remain.

Some day, the monarchy will die a death from public disdain, but not likely any time soon. The Australians and New Zealanders, who at least have been debating the future of the monarchy, will likely move out from under the monarchy before Canada, although neither of our Australasian friends now seems in a hurry. The previous Australian government wanted a referendum on getting rid of the monarchy, but the government fell in recent elections.

There are non-political ways of choosing a Canadian head of state, including selection by members of the Order of Canada. We're not going to see them used soon. So hail to the Prince, for now.

The Trouble with Trying to Compensate Groups for Historical Wrongs *(June 14, 1990)*

Prime Minister Mackenzie King once remarked that "if some countries have too much history, we have too much geography." Geography Canada still has in abundance, maybe even surplus; but as for the dearth of history, I wonder.

Canada is staggering through the final days of the Meech Lake trauma, in which history—or, rather, an acute sense of historical grievance—ran through the debate. In Newfoundland, where Meech Lake's fate now rests, every school child knows about the Churchill Falls hydro-electric deal in which Quebec, after the early years of the agreement, fleeced Newfoundland unmercifully.

In Manitoba, memories of the CF-18 maintenance contract that went to Montreal instead of Winnipeg colour contemporary attitudes toward Quebec. Nor has time dulled memories of the angry debate not so many years ago about French-language rights in Manitoba.

With the Meech Lake debate still fresh in our minds, it's worth reflecting on the use and abuse of history—especially the obligations of today's generations in regard to mistakes of the past—in connection with the Pandora's box opened by the government's 1988 decision to offer financial redress to Japanese Canadians interned during the Second World War.

When the Mulroney government made its decision in September 1988, Minister of State Gerry Weiner insisted that the treatment of Japanese Canadians was "unique and unparalleled." In this space, a certain columnist opined that Mr. Weiner was "dreaming in technicolour if he thinks the compensation package for Japanese Canadians doesn't set a precedent."

Predictably enough, it did. The Ukrainian Canadian Committee hit Ottawa this week asking for redress for internment of Ukrainian Canadians during the First World War. It followed on the heels of organizations representing Italian Canadians and Chinese Canadians who seek similar kinds of redress for historical injustices.

The government originally thought it might have to pay redress to about 12,000 Japanese Canadians. By the end of May, however, payments had been made to 16,350, with roughly another thousand cases pending.

The Ukrainian Canadian Committee might have been satisfied with a statement of apology, some historical plaques and possibly the financing of university chairs in Ukrainian studies. But once the government agreed to give financial compensation to Japanese Canadians, the Ukrainian-Canadian organization, like those representing Italian Canadians and Chinese Canadians, demanded money too.

Where does this end? Do we compensate Acadians who were expelled? The Irish who were badly treated when they arrived? Those interned during the War Measures Act of 1970? Native Canadians who signed iniquitous treaties? Do we compensate Canada's Jewish population for the grievous injustice done to their community when Canada turned its back on Jews seeking admittance to the country before and during the Second World War?

History has many, often contradictory, lessons to teach us. It is essential to remember those that cast Canada in a dark light, so that they won't be repeated.

But there comes a point at which, in a linguistically and ethnically divided country, the search for restitution for past wrongs not only creates precedents that lead we know not where, but also risks piling up more divisions in a country already quite divided.

The search for war criminals in Canada pitted ethnic groups against each other. The redress for Japanese Canadians irritated other groups, including some veterans. And redress given to one group has obviously emboldened others to seek similar treatment, forcing today's generation to pay for policies and attitudes of generations past.

Having said yes to Japanese Canadians, the government cannot make a credible case for saying no to another group. A mixture of noble sentiments and crass multicultural politics produced the previous decision, and that same mixture beckons the government again. For better or worse, the country will be forced quite literally to pay for its history for many years to come.

Looking Back in Anger: The Pitfalls of Interpreting History *(November 20, 1992)*

A few years ago, a University of British Columbia professor published a book suggesting that Caligula was an unfairly maligned Roman emperor—he was not nearly as bloodthirsty and demented as we had been led to believe.

That debates about Caligula could be fired up nearly two millennia after his assassination in AD 41 illustrates that historical revisionism, or at least different historical perspectives, know no statute of limitation.

Just this year, various groups commemorated the 500th anniversary of Columbus's "discovery" of North America. Columbus certainly believed he was doing God's work; he is now viewed in some quarters as having done the devil's.

Which brings us to the senselessly vituperative debate over the CBC documentary *The Valour and the Horror*, which alleged various sins of omission and commission by those charged with executing military strategy in the Second World War.

Courtesy of the veterans' lobby and certain sympathetic senators with time on their hands (a redundant description, I admit), the producers of the documentary and CBC brass were hauled before a Senate committee.

A more fruitless exercise can scarcely be imagined. Neither the senators nor the producers are trained historians, and even if they were, practitioners of this craft do not always agree, as anyone acquainted with historical writing can attest. The whole point of scholarship is to test and re-test assertions of fact and analysis made by previous generations.

Douglas Wilson, writing in *The Atlantic* about the treatment of Thomas Jefferson, warns against the perils of "presentism," a pitfall into which the producers of *The Valour and the Horror* may have fallen. "'Presentism,'" he writes, "is the term that historians use for applying contemporary or otherwise inappropriate standards to the past."

Clearly, the producers were determined to make their point about incompetent senior military personnel, and they did so through a variety of cinematic devices. Their variations on themes of "war as hell" and the incompetence of generals were as old as military commentary itself. Even the genius Hannibal led his troops to defeat.

Prominent historians believe the producers garbled some material and misrepresented or ignored other parts of the historical record. My own instinct is to trust these historians' competence over that of the producers, but so what?

The historians have had their say in a variety of forms, and now a somewhat debunking historical revisionism comes along. What should have been passed off as one soon-forgotten TV series has been elevated, courtesy of the blundering of the Senate and the anger of the veterans' lobby, into front-page material.

The CBC, quite properly, investigated the programs after receiving complaints. For this the network is being lambasted. Imagine the furore if the publicly funded corporation had told the complainants to get lost, or had conducted a cosy little internal review.

The CBC is owned by the taxpayers, is ultimately responsible to them and therefore must take criticisms seriously. That does not mean, however, that it turns itself into a pretzel to please every lobby group or letter-writer.

The CBC ombudsman filed his report, which was immediately and predictably attacked by the producers as biased, unprofessional and high-handed. The report does not read that way to me, but nothing short of unvarnished praise would have satisfied the producers.

A CBC review was preferable to an investigation by the Senate, which failed to remember that in a democracy the authorities should keep their noses out of the media. A free press is better assured by alert citizens, competition of ideas and legal frameworks than by self-appointed political watchdogs.

There is so much resoundingly dreadful programming on television every night that to isolate one controversial series for Court of Star Chamber treatment by senators who answer only to themselves simply heaps more disgrace on that absurd institution. And the premise that one "true" historical record can emerge displays a misunderstanding of historical inquiry.

Some historical analyses are more credible than others, especially if the perils of "presentism" are avoided. But the battle for that credibility should not take place in the Canadian Senate.

Let's Say It's Cold in Winnipeg, So Lindros Won't Put on His Skates

(December 19, 1991)

QUEBEC CITY—Assume for the purposes of what follows that Eric Lindros had been drafted by the Winnipeg Jets and had said: "Look, it's nothing against Winnipeg, I just don't want to play there."

Asked why not, Mr. Lindros shrugged and said something about the cold winters, the small market and just not feeling very comfortable in The Peg. "I've got nothing against Winnipeg, I just don't want to play there."

Now, how do you think the citizens of Winnipeg would feel about a potential megastar from southern Ontario thumbing his nose at them? Imagine their reaction, too, had Mr. Lindros, a star on Canada's Olympic team, declined an opportunity to play an exhibition game with the national team in Manitoba. Don't you think Manitobans would be a trifle annoyed?

Now shift to Quebec, where *l'affaire Lindros* is worth a few Meech Lakes in conveying to Quebeckers how they are regarded by the rest of us.

I know, I know. It isn't fair, you say. Eric Lindros doesn't represent the rest of Canada. Just a lot of it. Or so it seems in Quebec, and especially, of course, in Quebec City, where he has loudly and unequivocally announced he will not play for Les Nordiques.

Last autumn, during the Canada Cup, the fans at Le Colisée in Quebec City displayed remarkable class by only booing Mr. Lindros at times. But then Quebeckers, and especially Quebec hockey fans, are like that: classy. They know something Mr. Lindros does not yet understand—that the game is bigger than any one player, no matter how large the size of his swelled head. It's a lesson that dough-head of an National Hockey League president John Zeigler hasn't yet grasped.

Anyway, people in Quebec City have quickly put two and two together and made a perfectly logical connection. Since Eric Lindros is supposedly a member of the Canadian Olympic team but refuses to play in Quebec City, he shouldn't be an ambassador for Canada in the Olympics.

"We assume that Olympic athletes are proud to represent Canada—all of Canada," says Charles DeBlois, Conservative MP for Beauport–

Montmorency–Orléans. "But the perception here is that Mr. Lindros does not respect Quebec, our language and our culture, and he has nothing but contempt for the Québécois people."

Now Mr. Lindros would presumably reply, if his mother okayed it, that he loves Quebec, or at least has nothing against the place. He just doesn't want to play there. He can make zillions more playing elsewhere, and he doesn't have to put up with those funny words on the street signs. It's a free country, he would reply. Indeed, but not a very happy one, for a variety of reasons, including *l'affaire Lindros*.

The shame of the whole thing is that Mr. Lindros, had he displayed a different attitude, would have found the streets painted with gold in Quebec City, one of Canada's truly agreeable cities.

Quebeckers naturally love their French-Canadian stars, but they appreciate others too. Just ask Bob Gainey, Ken Dryden, Dickie Moore, Gump Worsley, Kurt Muller, Joe Sakic, Ron Tugnutt, Rusty Staub, Gary Carter and any number of English-speaking Canadian or American athletes who have made some or all of their careers in Quebec.

If Mr. Lindros had played to his potential with Les Nordiques, and expanded his brain by learning a tiny bit of French, they might have named a street after him in Quebec City. He'd have been a somebody, which he won't be playing in New York, where a hockey player walking down Fifth Avenue worries more about being mugged than about being recognized.

It's easy in the rest of Canada to say Quebeckers are over-reacting. But hockey in Quebec City, with its long winters, is a kind of secular religion. And there is always a temptation in the entire province to turn issues into a them-against-us morality play, which in this instance puts Mr. Lindros in the role of English-speaking devil.

No wonder that callers to the hot-line shows in Quebec City are burning with indignation over *l'affaire Lindros*. If the tables had been turned, however, and Mr. Lindros had snubbed the Jets, there's not much doubt that the lights would be dancing on the switchboard of Peter Warren's hot-line radio show in Winnipeg.

Remembering Those Who Fought on the Battlefields of Two World Wars *(November 13, 1990)*

Every year on Remembrance Day, we high-school students crowded into the auditorium for a service that was supposed to be, well, memorable. The band played, the teachers sat on the stage, the students took their assigned places, a teacher read the honour roll and a few students sniggered.

I thought about those ceremonies, and how little they apparently meant to too many of us, the first time I walked through the Canadian war cemetery at Beny-Sur-Mer in Normandy. Row after row of gravestones sliced through the Norman countryside, each with a maple leaf chiselled into the stone.

I was twenty-three at the time, my whole adult life before me. I'd read plenty of books about the war and seen my full share of war films and documentaries. I was supposed to have been trained in something called international relations. Yet looking at those gravestones, I realized that in fact I knew nothing.

Many who had died were younger than me. The names became a blur, but they came from every corner of Canada, French-speaking and English-speaking, and a lot of them were 18, 19, 20, 21, 22 years old. I tried to see myself in their shoes, and to imagine what those fields looked like all those many years ago, with men dying and guns roaring. I couldn't.

The same feelings came over me in 1982 on the ferry from England to Dieppe. I was standing at the front of the boat with a handful of bemedalled veterans of the Dieppe raid, watching the cliffs loom up on the horizon. The closer we came to the French shore, the more the sheer inadequacy of the books and films hit home.

A mile or so from shore, the ghastly futility of the Dieppe raid sank in. We could see the wide beach, which looked inviting enough for a landing. We could not see that the beach was formed, not of sand, but of large, round stones which, as the men who operated the landing craft and tanks discovered, jammed the wheels and rendered their craft immobile.

There, at each end of the beach, loomed the cliffs with their guns from which there could have been no escape on that wide, inviting stretch of land. No men, no matter how well trained or equipped, could have succeeded against that geography.

As I walked along that beach and through the streets of Dieppe with those who had landed there in 1942, listening to their stories and watching grown men weep, I tried again to imagine the horror of what they knew. When they paraded proudly through the town, while the people cheered and waved their flags, it all seemed slightly unreal, until I remembered that these were the lucky ones—if lucky is indeed the appropriate word—unlike their friends and colleagues who lay in rows on the hill behind the town.

In Vimy, a few years later, the men were much older, of course, survivors of the slaughterhouse that gained a hill in the "war to end all wars." But knowing from the books, as best anyone can, how ghastly Vimy and all the other battles had been, I peered at the creased faces and asked myself what kind of courage I might have mustered in the same circumstances. The easy, comforting answer was that, of course, I would have been as brave. The honest answer was, and is, that I could not be sure.

Beaumont-Hamel: a tiny fragment of the Battle of the Somme, a testament to the military myopia of Douglas Haig, commander-in-chief of the British Expeditionary Force. From the outports of the Dominion of Newfoundland, young men had enlisted to fight for the Empire. The cream of that dominion's youth died in one inferno, hopelessly running across an open plain into the mouth of fire. Would I have run across that plain?

I am, like a majority of Canadians, from generations that have not known war. Remembrance Day for me used to be something quaint. And so it might have remained, but for having seen the rows of graves and the terrain where their occupants fell. It is now, quite literally, a day for remembering, and for asking unanswerable questions of self.

No Government Has Been Immune to the Sweet Seduction of Patronage (November 25, 1994)

The Liberal Party, the once and current government party of Canada, certainly did not invent political patronage. It just practised patronage more frequently, and usually more adroitly, from the accession to office of Sir Wilfrid Laurier in 1896 to this week's flurry of appointments of Liberals to high places.

The latest appointments may at least help mitigate the ahistoricism that has crept into post–Brian Mulroney political writing. Books and articles in recent months have been marked by a forgetfulness, deliberate or otherwise, about what had transpired before the Conservatives' most recent exercise of power.

Mr. Mulroney, of course, brought much justifiable public condemnation on his own performance because it differed so sharply from his 1984 campaign rhetoric. Remember it? "You had an option, sir. You could have done better," he thundered at Prime Minister John Turner in their televised debate. Splendid theatre; splendid hypocrisy.

Mr. Mulroney never intended, not even when he uttered those politically thrilling words, to change the system of political patronage. Imitation being the sincerest form of flattery, he merely intended to turn the system to the Conservatives' advantage. The Liberals, in other words, had taught better than they knew.

Mr. Mulroney departed 24 Sussex Drive with an orgy of appointments, just as Pierre Trudeau had done. He used the Senate, boards, agencies, commissions, the foreign service and, yes, even Rideau Hall, just as the Liberals had done.

The tollgating and pressuring of contractors for contributions and purchase of seats at fundraising dinners, the steering of contracts to friends of the party, the selling of party memberships to those seeking periodic social access to ministers and the prime minister, the use of legal agents in every riding of Canada to reward sympathetic lawyers, the papering of the hall at state dinners with party stalwarts, the massive porkbarrelling of government contracts by ministers in every region of Canada—these were all hallmarks of the Conservative years, just as they had been under Mr. Trudeau and his predecessors.

All that distinguished the Conservatives was the excessive shadiness of certain characters swept in by the Tory tide in Quebec, the desperation for patronage from those who had gone for so long without it and a certain *arriviste* cast of Mr. Mulroney himself and some of those around him.

Nine years removed from office, the Liberal Party has returned and so have its old ways, public rhetoric to the contrary.

Soon after being named Justice Minister, the neophyte Allan Rock expressed the hope that party affiliation would no longer determine the selection of legal agents, lawyers who do federal government work across the country. It did not take long—it never does with neophytes—for the Liberals to educate Mr. Rock so that in every constituency new Liberal lists swept out the old Conservative ones.

When the Queen and foreign leaders are given state dinners, out come the lists of local Liberals. Lobbyists in Ottawa have hired on Liberals, or moved those with Liberal credentials to positions of greater public prominence.

Prime Minister Jean Chrétien has continued in the ways of his Liberal predecessors. Two stalwarts—Jean-Robert Gauthier, a long-time MP from Ottawa–Vanier, and John Bryden, defeated candidate, fundraiser, political organizer and Chrétien kingpin in New Brunswick—have been summoned to the Senate. They follow two former Liberal provincial politicians whom the Prime Minister had named to the Senate—Lise Bacon and Sharon Carstairs.

And, of course, the country is now blessed with a Governor-General–designate, Romeo LeBlanc, whose Liberal loyalty, partisanship and service are scarcely equalled in contemporary politics—press secretary, speech writer, MP, middle-ranking minister, senator and now Governor-General. Happily for those who wish the disappearance of the monarchy, this appointment with its obvious patronage hue has been greeted like such a damp squib outside New Brunswick, the Liberal caucus and the editorial pages of *The Toronto Star* that the whole creaky and increasingly ridiculous edifice of the British monarchy in Canada is further discredited.

Patronage, and especially its misuse, does have its rewards.

Rich Vein Discovered *(September 30, 1988)*

Cholesterol being a national scourge, it's surprising that politicians have not so far addressed themselves to proposing solutions.

Happily, however, an election is on the horizon, and that means we can expect a variety of promises to eradicate cholesterol from our society.

If our politicians are true to form, some will suggest paving all the veins and arteries in those afflicted with cholesterol build-up. Paving would be less cost-effective than plastic arteries, but it would create more jobs in disadvantaged regions. Just as energy projects are no longer justified on energy grounds but on the number of construction jobs created, so the massive paving program will be sold because it will create 32,000 full-time and 23,000 part-time jobs.

It is possible the government will initially deny that cholesterol constitutes a problem. But just as Trade Minister John Crosbie eventually showered $3.4-million on inshore fishermen after denying for weeks they had a problem, so the government will ultimately declare cholesterol a problem and find the money.

Indeed, a mega-effort to eradicate cholesterol could involve a variety of interest-free loans, loan guarantees, grants, tax write-offs and industrial development agreements with asphalt manufacturers across Canada. That paving arteries might be scorned by medical experts will be treated with the political contempt reserved for those bureaucrats who recommended putting the CF-18 maintenance contract in Winnipeg rather than Montreal.

Other politicians will link the fight against cholesterol with the struggle for a clean environment. Clean Air for Clean Pipes might run the government-sponsored jingle. Soon therefore, a party leader will declare a nation-wide campaign against sludge in all its various internal and external manifestations. He will promise a sizeable number of millions of dollars to the effort, but this will immediately be denounced as inadequate by the other party leaders. "The Prime Minister's heart is not in the fight," one leader will exclaim.

Part of this commitment will involve the creation of a task force drawn from every part of Canada to study the cholesterol problem. The medical profession will privately groan, there already being a mountain of evidence on the perils of cholesterol, but so much new research will be commissioned by the task force that the profession will grow silent (and richer).

While this task force grinds along, a federal-provincial conference will address the problem of cholesterol. If the spirit of Meech Lake prevails, the provinces will successfully hold up the federal government for huge wads of cash without being forced to adhere to any particular guidelines. Quickly, thereafter, an opposition party and the National Action Committee on Cholesterol will decry the lack of national cholesterol guidelines.

This will be followed by a constitutional challenge launched by the Canadian Civil Liberties Association asserting that any cholesterol standard abridges the Charter of Rights and Freedoms. "We do not approve of cholesterol," a civil-libertarian will state, "but we will defend to the death a person's right to eat as much cholesterol as he wishes."

Opponents will link cholesterol to free trade, arguing that American fast-food chains will dump more fatty foods into the Canadian market. Supporters of free trade will insist that increased competition and higher productivity will drive down the cholesterol levels of all Canadians. To sort out this dispute, the Economic Council of Canada will be asked for a report.

Finally, the pollsters will proclaim that cholesterol is a bad thing but much liked, and for this insight they will receive many headlines and potfuls of money.

Day of Reckoning *(February 6, 1988)*

And God said unto Jesus as he approached the Pearly Gates: "Have you ever been involved in a conflict of interest?"

"No, Heavenly Father. I put all my worldly goods in a blind trust and registered all my assets with the Deputy Registrar-General."

"But were you not born in a hotel? Did your parents pay for that room?"

"There actually wasn't a room at the inn. We stayed in the stable."

"Yes, but what did it cost? Did your parents receive a benefit in kind?"

"I don't know, Heavenly Father."

"Then you left yourself open to the potential possibility of a perception of a conflict of interest. You disobeyed the first and great commandment: Thou shalt be squeaky clean."

"I tried always to walk in your path, Heavenly Father."

"Were there not some eminent persons who gave you gifts? Did you declare those?"

"I think I told the Deputy Registrar-General about the gold and the frankincense, but I can't honestly remember about the myrrh. They only gave me a couple of grams."

"Did you ever attempt to bribe anyone?"

"I gave people loaves and fishes once during my recruitment campaigns."

"And did you declare these as campaign expenses?"

"Most of them, but apparently I overspent by a little bit, for which I am heartily sorry."

"Did the Chief Recruitment Officer lay charges against you?"

"No, he said my campaign was so successful at attracting converts that I would not be charged. He did charge my baker and fishmonger, though. He sent me a scroll saying he wouldn't charge me, although technically I had offended against the rules."

"What did you do with the scroll?"

"I stuffed it in my mule's feed bag and promptly forgot about it. The Pharisees found it later and made a big stink about it."

"Did you ever compromise yourself by being in places of ill-repute?"

"I once followed Mary Magdalene into a place called Tiffany's where a lot of soldiers used to hang out. She was a nice girl. I tried to put her on the straight and narrow. *The Nazareth Times* ran a big story about it."

"What about the moneychangers' temple?"

"That's true, I went in there once and threw all the bankers out onto the street."

"But the fact that you were seen with them laid you open to another possible perception of a conflict of interest. How was anyone to know that you were not seeking a loan from them?"

"Forgive me, Father, for I knew not what I was doing."

"Did this possible perception of a conflict of interest hurt your recruiting?"

"Somewhat. But I just kept saying the truth would set me free."

"Did anybody believe you?"

"My disciples did, at least all but one of them. Somebody within my ranks kept leaking things to the newspapers."

"I am told that you once gave your disciples a free supper. Did you tell the Chief Recruitment Officer about that expense?"

"Well, it was near the end, you see. So I thought reporting it would have been a bit academic."

"Not good enough. A public man like you must lead the life of an open book."

"But, Heavenly Father, what about those who pressed down upon my head a crown of thorns? They spat upon me every day in the public meeting place in the capital. They mocked and reviled me."

"They, too, will find it easier to pass through the eye of a needle than to pass through these gates. They will be judged, when the time comes, by the same commandments."

The Verdict Confirmed *(July 1, 1987)*

The death penalty died in our time in the small hours of yesterday morning, executed by a twenty-one-vote parliamentary majority.

Like an unwanted visitor, the death penalty seemed never to take no for an answer. The ultimate penalty first expired when Cabinets began routinely commuting death sentences more than two decades ago. It seemed truly buried in 1976, when Parliament wiped the penalty from the statute books.

Yet in the hearts of the true believers, the death penalty never died. And with polls consistently showing a majority in the country in favour of the penalty's resurrection, the true believers found the answer to their dreams in the grasping aspirations of a campaigning party leader, Brian Mulroney.

Or so they reckoned when Mr. Mulroney promised a free vote on the return of the death penalty. What they had not counted on—nor, in truth, had many of us pundits—was the subtle but pervasive decline in the intensity of the public clamour for the death penalty's return. Nor had they understood that the massive Conservative parliamentary majority obscured what ultimately sealed the hangman's fate—the dramatic shift in Quebec opinion.

In 1976, Quebec MPs split almost evenly. Yesterday morning, the vast majority opposed the death penalty, a reflection presumably of conscience and of the now-prevailing attitudes against the death penalty in that province. Not for the first time in Canadian history, French Canadians helped to save us from ourselves.

Criminal lawyer Eddie Greenspan typified, in his decision to campaign for three months against the death penalty, how much better organized the abolitionists were than their opponents had suspected. ("Abolitionists" is used here, as in 1976, to refer to those opposed to capital punishment.) Mr. Greenspan, seated for the vote in the Prime Minister's gallery, smiled and flashed the victory sign to his fellow abolitionists in the chamber below when the jubilation of the moment drove erstwhile enemies into the centre aisle for precious scenes of mutual congratulations.

There stood the three party leaders, abolitionists all, each shaking hands with MPs from other formations. On the Tory benches, ministers Barbara McDougall and Monique Vezina, seatmates in the second row, embraced like dear friends suddenly reunited after a painful absence. On the Liberal side, whip Jean-Robert Gauthier stood with outstretched arms and a broad grin, like a kid who'd just scored his first touchdown. And in the galleries, packed with abolitionists despite the ungodly hour, the protocol of silence yielded to the exultation of unexpected triumph.

For indeed no one had predicted, even in the minutes preceding the vote, that the majority could rise to twenty-one. The drift against the death penalty, which gathered momentum on the day of the vote, had been evident from the beginning of the debate. Indeed, Forestry Minister Gerald Merrithew did not make up his mind until just before entering the chamber, an abolitionist gain that sent Conservative MP James Jepson, a proponent of the death penalty, scurrying to Mr. Merrithew's side hoping for literally a last-minute change of heart.

Not a single MP previously opposed to the death penalty switched sides, whereas important conversions marked some who had once voted for capital punishment. The sincerity of MPs who searched their consciences, such as Conservatives Jack Murta and George Hees, or Liberals such as Doug Frith, Len Hopkins and Carlo Rossi, testified to the seriousness with which parliamentarians took their responsibilities. So, too, did the turnout—only three absentees.

If those who would restore capital punishment, blessed with such a lopsided Conservative majority, could not muster a parliamentary majority, the death penalty has breathed its last in Canada.

Why Hugh MacLennan Was a Rarity Among Canadian Novelists and Poets

(November 9, 1990)

"Love consists in this, that two solitudes protect and touch and greet each other."—Rainer Maria Rilke

With those words for a frontispiece, Hugh MacLennan began his 1945 novel *Two Solitudes*. The title passed into both the English and French languages, but not perhaps as Mr. MacLennan had hoped.

Two solitudes, in conventional parlance, came to mean division: two groups that could never understand or appreciate each other. His own novel suggested the contrary: that hope did exist for understanding and tolerance between French-speaking and English-speaking Canadians.

The few times I ever heard Mr. MacLennan's novel and other works discussed by French-Canadian journalists or literary figures, he was lightly dismissed as quaint at best, naive at worst. He tried to learn French, but failed owing to a hearing impediment, and his depiction of French-speaking Quebeckers seemed stilted and stereotypical.

But whatever Mr. MacLennan's reputation, he was at least trying to grapple with what has been, for better or worse, part of the enduring Canadian story: the relations between the two large linguistic groups.

That alone makes him, if not an exception, then a rarity among English-language writers in Canada. And it begs ruminating upon why so few novelists and poets in Canada—people who ought to be wrestling with a country's central myths—have tackled the subject Mr. MacLennan wrote about in *Two Solitudes*, *Return of the Sphinx* and other works.

Historians and journalists, writers of non-fiction, have not shied from the subject of Quebec in particular and English-French relations in general. Indeed, it is a paradox that a vast majority of biographies written about major French-Canadian political figures have been by English-speaking writers. That fascination continues today. Witness the new book by Stephen Clarkson and Christina McCall on former prime minister Pierre Trudeau.

But the novelists and poets have largely given the subject a pass. Rick Salutin, the playwright, novelist and essayist, is one who has tried, especially in his plays *Les Canadiens* and *1837*. Leonard Cohen, like Mr. MacLennan an English-speaking Montrealer, touched the issue in *Beautiful Losers*. Scott Symons, the Toronto writer, is another who tackled the subject.

Mr. Salutin, who has supported Quebec independence for years, thinks part of the answer lies in the fact that French-speaking and English-speaking Canadians have lived different historical and cultural realities. Therefore, it becomes difficult, and perhaps fruitless, for writers of fiction to try to capture the other reality. He notes that the Riel Rebellion did produce some writing and an opera, and that this political event, given the characters involved, certainly touched the French-English dynamic of Canada.

Elspeth Cameron, Mr. MacLennan's biographer and an expert on Canadian literature, put the same point another way. Relations between French-speaking and English-speaking Canadians have usually been at the level of laws, not cultures.

Non-fiction writers can grapple with laws and institutions, and through them with the English-French dynamic. But fiction writers are rooted in place. They absorb their surroundings "through their pores," to use Ms. Cameron's phrase, and therefore have difficulty adequately feeling a reality that has not been their own.

Ms. Cameron also observed that the Canadian tradition of the "political novel" is weak. It would be through that kind of novel that the French–English dynamic would be most easily explored. Perhaps because Canada was an evolutionary society, rather than one forged in war or revolution, the country never produced the great political-historical novels that characterize American and French literature.

So, too, she observed that many Canadian fictional characters are rather ordinary people, caught up not in momentous clashes, but with moral and ethical conflicts full of shadings. Survival, as Margaret Atwood wrote, has been the enduring Canadian experience.

In any event, Mr. MacLennan was one of a very small band of fiction writers who dealt with what at the level of laws and government and politics has been central to the Canadian experience—indeed, too central for many English-speaking Canadians. That more writers did not follow his path says something not just about the state of literature, but perhaps about Canada, too.

PART 9 *United States*

A Visitor's Guide to the American Century (Reprinted from Queen's Quarterly 102/3 [Fall 1995])

Sir Wilfrid Laurier predicted in a fit of hope over prescience that the twentieth century would belong to Canada. Walter Lippman, the American columnist and author, was right. The twentieth century, he wrote, was The American Century.

As the millennium approaches, we all live in The American Century. It did not begin that way. Isolationist in foreign policy and possessed of a vast internal market, the century dawned with the United States preoccupied with self. It entered the First World War belatedly, and shortly after that war's end, it became conventional wisdom in the United States that participation had been a mistake.

It was against that backdrop that Americans witnessed the beginning of the Second World War. Constrained by public opinion, President Franklin D. Roosevelt could not convince his country to enter the war until bombs dropped on Pearl Harbor.

Some half a century later, the United States is incontestably the world's only superpower, its attention sought in every corner of the world, its decisions, or lack thereof, consequential far beyond its borders. Its cultural products, usually of the mass variety, penetrate homes everywhere; its economic might, although battered by a chronic trade imbalance, extends to every continent; its diplomatic ear is sought by friend and potential foe.

Militarily, the demise of the Soviet Union has rendered the United States the only power capable of exerting its force where and when it chooses. Think of areas or countries roiled by conflict: the Persian Gulf, Haiti, the Middle East, ex-Yugoslavia, Northern Ireland. In each instance, the power of influence of the United States was critical—and in every case in the direction of stability and peace. For all the criticism sometimes heaped from abroad upon the United States, and for all the frustration and wonder with which foreigners observe the complicated political structures of that country, rarely has an undisputed superpower projected its power so benignly.

Whatever one's view of America and its history, in this American Century the satisfactions of ignorance about the United States are as comforting as they are dangerous. Nowhere is that comfort higher than in Canada. It is an everyday assumption in Canada that Canadians know more about the United States than vice versa, an assumption easy to verify, and that therefore Canadians need know nothing more. Indeed, it is sometimes argued that since Canadians need to understand their own country better, any focus on the United States diverts attention from the more pressing priority.

That Canadians should understand their own country better goes without saying. That this quest would somehow be diverted by a better grasp of things American is fallacious. The United States is far more consequential to Canada than vice versa. American ignorance may be irritating; it should not give Canadians comfort with their own level of knowledge. In this age of globalization, free trade and instant communications, it will help rather than hinder Canadians' search for their own special identity if they understand better the political system, economic structure, history and culture of their southern neighbours.

It is an observable irony of American life that so many of its historical heroes—men and women after whom cities have been named and monuments erected—contributed in the sphere of government, and yet Americans have always been decidedly ambivalent about the appropriate role of government in their national life. The constitution of the United States, which was argued over from the Continental Congress of 1776 to the Bill of Rights of 1792, and thereafter in an important sense until the Northern victory in the Civil War, established divided government. It did so because a large number of eighteenth-century Americans worried about the concentration of political power which they felt had corrupted the politics of the Mother Country. Strong government, in their eyes, was the enemy of "life, liberty and the pursuit of happiness."

Of course, there were Founding Fathers such as Alexander Hamilton and James Madison who despaired of the untidiness, indeed the unruliness, of the early American governments. They distrusted so-called states' rights and believed that only a strong central government could turn the United States into a powerful country. Madison even preferred that the national government possess an unlimited veto over all state laws.

These were the so-called Federalists, and they were bitterly opposed at the founding conventions and for decades thereafter by the so-called Anti-Federalists who perceived the United States as a confederation of powerful states which would delegate certain restricted powers to the central government. The Anti-Federalists, at the risk of an excessive generation, represented a combination of those who distrusted government power *per se*, and those who distrusted centralized power in Washington.

The Civil War decided the issue of secession. It did not quell the debate about the appropriate powers exercised by Washington and the states. Indeed, after the post–Civil War Reconstruction period, "states rights" became a dogma in the South which, among other consequences, allowed southern states to pass laws and enforce segregation by other means of segregation.

The role of the central government expanded at first slowly under the New Deal, then quite dramatically with America's entry into the Second World War. Washington reached the apogee of its power in the 1960s with the civil-rights movements, the Vietnam War and continuing strong economic growth.

Now, of course, a strong movement is afoot to curb Washington's power *vis-à-vis* the states. This movement is being driven by the old American suspicions both of centralized government and of government power *per se*. It is being accelerated by economic forces that include the massive federal government debt and deficit, and by a visceral antipathy to taxation that is everywhere apparent in the United States. There is no observable constituency, or set of constituencies, that could be shaped into a political coalition in favour of higher taxes, the revenues from which in turn might be used by government to lead a collective effort to grapple with America's growing social problems.

The Republican Party's "Contract With America," acted upon by the Republican-dominated House of Representatives under the leadership of Speaker Newt Gingrich of Georgia, reflects this antipathy to taxes, and more profoundly, to government itself. Indeed, so powerful is the anti-government message in the Contract that many Democrats entered a political bidding war with the Republicans to offer tax cuts and spending reductions. The partisan debates were therefore about the modalities of reducing the size of government in Washington. The 1996 presidential campaign, coupled with the House and Senate races, will undoubtedly feature fierce debates about the means for reducing the size of government.

It is worth asking, given the centrality of antipathy to government, what has brought about this widespread attitude. Some of the antipathy merely reflects the old and ongoing discussion about American federalism and the enduring American suspicion about government *per se*. But more recent factors have highlighted these suspicions.

As had been widely noted by both political parties and commentators, the American middle class has struggled to keep family incomes rising in real terms. Huge swaths of the American economy have been decimated by foreign competition and recession, eliminating hundreds of thousands of blue-collar jobs. As Kevin Phillips argued in his book *Boiling Point*, "Despite unprecedented prosperity at the top, the proportion of people whose purchasing power of defined incomes made them 'middle class' was certainly 5 to 10 percentage points smaller than it had been ten or twenty years earlier."

While families struggled to maintain their real incomes, even after the massive entry of women into the workforce, they asked themselves why they did not seem to be making the kind of economic progress commensurate with their hard work. The answer struck many as taxes, although many Americans did not realize that the 1980s under President Ronald Reagan featured a shifting of the overall tax burden from the wealthy to the middle class. Not only did many white Americans resent government taxation at a time of declining real incomes, they did not see either an improvement in government services or new services of benefit to themselves. Instead, many white Americans believed tax dollars were being disproportionately spent on minority groups and special interests whose members did not deserve the help governments provided. Nor did they feel that such programs as welfare and the public education system were delivering value for money. This resentment was then fuelled by demographic shifts in American society.

Americans have always been a mobile people, and they remain so today. Recent decades have featured four mass migrations with profound consequences for American life. There was what the author Nicholas Lehman in his brilliant book, *The Promised Land*, called "The Great Migration" of blacks from the south to the cities of the north, and from the agricultural south to the urban south. This migration fundamentally altered the demography and subsequently the politics of America's large cities.

There was the equally huge, and in many cases related, movement of whites (and more recently middle-class blacks) from the inner cities to the suburbs. The last U.S. census recorded that for the first time the largest number of Americans—46.2 per cent of them—lived in census districts described as suburban. In 1989 and 1990, central cities lost 2 million residents, while suburbs gained 3.5 million. During the 1980s, fifteen states recorded a decline in the population of their central cities. Only four of thirty-nine cities with a population of more than 1 million gained residents: New York because of immigration; Portland, Charlotte and Columbus because they annexed adjacent suburbs. This population shift has kept right on going, past the suburbs into what is called "ex-urbia," sprawling suburban areas of largely single-family homes and shopping centres with clusters of commercial offices and light-industrial factories beyond the postwar suburbs.

There has also been the widely noted migration toward the west and south. If you think of America as a plate, the central point from a population point of view is now ninety-five miles southwest of St. Louis. The fastest growing states from 1980 to 1989 in order were: Nevada, Florida, Arizona, New Hampshire (an exception caused presumably by low taxes), California, Georgia, Alaska, Texas, Virginia and Washington. Put matters another way.

The cities with the fastest-growing rates of population from 1980 to 1990 were: Fresno, Sacramento, Austin, San Diego, San Jose, Phoenix, Tucson, Los Angeles, El Paso, San Antonio, Jacksonville, Fort Worth.

There are two other demographic migrations worth noting. The lesser of these relates to the more important, and can best be seen by the demography of California, America's most populous state. For more than a decade, a sizeable number of whites have been migrating from California. They began heading north to Washington and Oregon; in recent years they have migrated to all the other western states in search of new opportunities, but also to flee from increasingly violent and difficult California cities.

And yet California's population, despite this exodus, continues to increase. Why? Largely because of immigration. White non-Hispanics now account for about 17 million of California's nearly 30 million people. If anything like current trends continue, California in the first decade of the next century will become America's first state outside the Deep South in the last century with a white, non-Hispanic minority.

More than 800,000 people arrive as legal immigrants to the U.S. every year. The number of illegal immigrants can only be estimated, but some credible observers suggest 700,000-800,000. Not since the first two decades of this century has America seen these levels of immigration. Demographic change is everywhere apparent in urban America, most obviously in the cities along the Mexican border and the big cities of the coastal northeast and Pacific, but ethnic change is apparent in almost every corner of urban America.

For example, Hispanic gangs, apparently from southern California, appeared in the summer of 1993 in Salt Lake City, shocking the Mormons. The number of Asians tripled in Minneapolis in the 1980s to 77,000. Thousands of Vietnamese arrived in Quincy and Lowell, old Massachusetts mill cities. In Fresno, in California's central valley, the phone book now lists as many Vangs—Hmong refugees from Laos—as Joneses. Streetcars in San Jose carry signs in both English and Vietnamese.

In the 1980s, the white population across America grew by 6 per cent, the black population by 13 per cent, Hispanics by 53 per cent and Asians by 108 per cent. In California, blacks are now outnumbered slightly by Asians and hugely by Hispanics. Hispanics are more numerous than blacks in Texas, Massachusetts and most of the states of the southwest. Hispanics will soon be more numerous than blacks in Florida, New York and New Jersey. And, by the turn of the century, blacks will be outnumbered by Hispanics in the U.S. as a whole.

Hispanics, of course, vary enormously. Of the 13.5 million Americans of Mexican ancestry, 4.5 million were born in Mexico or slightly more than one-third. Of the more than 1 million Cubans, almost three-quarters were born in Cuba. There are 2.7 million people from Puerto Rico, and 5 million other Hispanics from various Spanish-speaking countries. Cubans, Puerto Ricans, Dominicans, Mexicans—they may all have spoken, or still speak, Spanish as their native language, but their political outlooks differ, as do the customs of their native countries. To speak, then, of Hispanics is misleading, since they do not form a homogeneous block. The same can certainly be said of so-called Asian Americans, who come from dozens of countries. Neither Hispanics nor Asian Americans have yet achieved political power commensurate with their growing numbers. But it is inevitable that they will achieve greater prominence in public life, heightening the competition for public positions, just as they now jostle for positions in the private sector and universities. Although some people on the political left, or what is left of the American Left, speak of a "rainbow coalition" of oppressed minorities, my own sense is that an uneasy truce at best exists among these groups. Relations among these groups, in reality as opposed to political rhetoric, is more conflictual than collaborative.

These fresh waves of immigrants, largely from non-European and Canadian sources, arrived during and after the blacks' civil-rights movement that changed the laws and challenged the political culture of the United States. That movement's aims slowly shifted from the elimination of barriers, racial integration and emphasis on individual rights to include affirmative action, racial separation and emphasis on group rights. That shift, which divides the black community today, now divides the new ethnic communities.

Blacks had two claims on the American conscience—a moral one based on slavery, the failure of Reconstruction, Jim Crow, segregation and systemic discrimination; and a demographic one based on numbers. Previous immigrants may have arrived by the millions, but no single group was sufficiently numerous to eclipse the black's demographic claim.

Now, however, blacks find both moral and demographic claims contested by new immigrants, not by direct refutation so much as by the flattering means of imitation. Some of the new immigrants are seizing upon the very tools crafted in the later days of the civil-rights movement to advance their own purposes. Affirmative action must now apply to Asian Americans, Hispanics, Chicanos (not to be confused with Hispanics), American Indians, gays—and, of course, women.

Political representation, university curricula, civil services, apportionment of public monies, practices of private corporations—these elements of American life are now scrutinized from a variety of sources for their "representativeness," not just by the first civil-rights crusaders, the blacks, but by a plethora of groups.

A staple of American public discourse is much less the classic debate between those who favour redistribution of society's rewards on an income basis—that is, the traditional left–right distinction—but on what Canadian philosopher Charles Taylor has called the "politics of recognition" among competing minority groups. At the lower end of the income scale, it is noticeable that tensions between blacks and Asians erupted in Los Angeles during the riots, in New York City, Miami and in several other hot spots of urban America. Certain Asian-American parents whose children have done so well in educational testing have been among the most vocal opponents of mandated affirmative action by universities and other public bodies to assist blacks and Hispanics. The backlash against affirmative action, which began in a political sense in California, has now swept across the entire nation.

The blacks' moral claim is weakening as time passes from slavery, Jim Crow and the civil-rights movement. There is a widespread feeling outside the black community that the debt of past discrimination has been paid so that the moral claim so powerfully advanced by the civil-rights movement, and subsequently enshrined in various preferential policies, has now worn thin.

The age-old "American Dilemma," then, still plagues American society; indeed, it remains one of the pivots around which American society and politics moves. Since the civil-rights movements, blacks have both done better, but also in a distressingly large number of cases done seriously worse than before, at least in terms of income and social breakdown. Everywhere in America, stunning examples testify to the progress that blacks have made in the short space of one generation, and not just in sports and entertainment. A black middle-class exists; universities compete with each other to recruit academically talented blacks; public services often mirror, when they do not actually exceed, the portion of blacks in the tax-paying population.

And yet, while many blacks have moved up the income ladder—often moving away from the inner cities in quest of better neighbourhoods—many others are trapped in vicious cycles of poverty, violence and family breakdown. Blacks have suffered terribly from the economic hollowing out of blue-collar employment, as the sociologist William Julius Wilson has convincingly demonstrated. For example, the black unemployment rate was a multiple of 2.09 higher than that for whites during the 1960s; 2.02 higher during the 1970s, but 2.37 higher in the 1980s. In 1993, black unemployment was 12.9 per cent compared to 6 per cent for whites. (Two caveats here. First, American unemployment numbers would be higher if they used Canadian methods of calculation. Second, more blacks are missed in official statistics.) Blacks are now likely to suffer again as public services are reduced, both because blacks depend more upon those services than whites and because blacks are more dependent on public-sector employment than whites are. Blacks are three times more likely to live below the poverty line than whites across America, except in the west, where they are twice as likely.

The breakdown of black families has been widely noted, much analyzed, frequently argued over, endlessly rationalized, incessantly moralized and sermonized about, but increasingly accepted, by black leaders themselves, as a contributing factor to the black community's difficulties. More black women than men are in the labour force; two-thirds of black children are living in single-parent homes; the gap between black and white family income would be 22 per cent instead of 44 per cent if the percentage of two-adult families was the same for blacks and whites; two-thirds of black children live in one-parent families, compared to a national average of one in four. Sixty-eight per cent of black births are out of wedlock, compared to 36.6 per cent for Mexicans and 18.5 per cent for whites. That compares to 37.6 per cent of black births out of wedlock in 1970, and 5.7 per cent for whites. Here are pregnancy rates for every thousand teenagers: Sweden 35, France 43, Canada 44, England and Wales 45, white Americans 93, black Americans 186. Fifty-five per cent of black households are headed by women who have never married, up from only 11 per cent in 1960 and compared to 16.5 per cent of white women today.

Crime is now rampant in inner-city America, although crime rates have marginally declined for certain serious crimes. The fastest growing category of housing in the U.S. during the 1980s was prisons, where more than 1 in 250 Americans reside—and the political momentum to build more prisons is relentless. There are 1.5 million inmates in federal and state prisons and local jails, and another 3.5 million criminals on probation or parole, according to the Justice Department. Very soon, if current trends continue, there will be more Americans behind bars or on probation or parole than there are people enrolled in four-year colleges and universities.

Blacks account for about 12 per cent of America's population, but 45 per cent of the prison population. Almost half of America's murders are blacks against blacks. Seventy-one per cent of assailants in robbery cases are blacks. Whole swaths of American cities are now plagued by drugs, gangs and violence, not all involving blacks to be sure, but preying upon black communities nonetheless with a special vengeance.

I mentioned before some of the mass migrations that have occurred in the United States, and in particular the flight of white Americans—but of middle-class blacks too—away from the inner cities. I mean flight in two senses: physical and psychological. I also mentioned the aversion to tax and the stagnation of family income. These can be tied together in this way: millions of white Americans have given up on the inner cities and on the people who remain there. They do not go to the inner cities often; they resent their tax money being drained toward the inner cities; they do not want their children educated there; they do not want their place of employment to be located there. There is nothing new or startling in these observations; they have been made and chronicled countless times. I mean only to suggest that the flight—physical and psychological—has intensified. Attitudes have hardened; political reaction has deepened; and frustration has intensified because no matter how hard many Americans try to flee, the problems from which they have fled do not seem to remain far away.

There are now older suburban areas where some of the social pathologies and problems of the inner cities are manifest—the so-called bedroom communities around New York and Los Angeles, for example. Cities such as Salt Lake City, Denver, Minneapolis, the cities of California's central valley (Fresno, Bakersfield, Modesto, Sacramento) are experiencing for the first time some of these pathologies. So even are smaller cities. And whether Americans are right in objective terms to feel less physically safe, every evening newscast in the United States in urban areas nightly reinforces the message of crime and violence and sensationalism. This flight, and the frustration that it is apparently impossible to flee fully from the problems have fused popular resentments around the themes of race, taxes and rights.

Thomas Byrne and Mary D. Edsell in their book, *Chain Reaction*, come very close to the mark when they write about taxes: "No longer the resource with which to create a beneficent federal government, taxes had come for many voters to signify the forcible transfer of hard-earned money away from those who worked, to those who did not. Taxes had come to be seen as the resource funding a liberal federal judiciary, granting expanded rights to criminal defendants, to convicted felons, and, in education and employment, to 'less qualified' minorities. Federal taxation had become, in the new coded language of politics, a forced levy underwriting liberal policies that granted enlarged rights to members of society who excited the most negative feelings in the minds of other, often angry voters." They write elsewhere, "Fairness . . . no longer symbolized Democratic struggle to achieve tax equity for 'average' working men and women, to provide access to middle-class homes and incomes, or to insure the rights to bargain with management for just compensation; 'fairness' now meant, to many voters, federal action to tilt the playing field in favour of minorities, government unions, feminists, criminal defendants, the long-term jobless, never-wed mothers, drug addicts and gays."

The country's newspapers, properly read, provide weekly evidence of the phenomenon described by the Edsells. *The New York Times* reported earlier this year that a federal judge, citing what he called a "crisis," took the extraordinary action of placing the entire 70,000-student Cleveland school system under the direct control of the superintendent of schools. The system which had exhausted its $500-million budget halfway through the school year, was more than $125-million in debt. The fiscal crisis reflected, in large part, the fact that Cleveland voters have not approved an increase in school spending in more than a decade. They rejected two ballot proposals last year that would have increased taxes for schools. The reasons for this rejection lie in demography. The total population of Cleveland proper declined from 800,000 in the 1950s to about 500,000 today. More than twice as many whites left the city as blacks. The schools are 70 per cent black. When the ballot measured where voted upon, black turnout was low; that of whites who send their children to Catholic schools was large, and the tax increases were defeated.

In San Jose, near where I lived last year, about half the students are out of school at 1:30 p.m. because there is insufficient money to provide more than five periods of daily education. There, too, voters reject tax increases, because those with money have taken their children out of the public system, or placed them in "charter" or "magnet" schools.

Another example of this reaction is the revolt against welfare. A campaigning Bill Clinton promises to end "welfare as we know it." Nothing has yet been done about the promise, but Congress has been awash with proposals to curtail programs for welfare, or to turn federal programs over to the states in exchange for block grants. Middle-class entitlements such as social security and mortgage and property-tax deductibility are sacrosanct, but welfare is politically vulnerable, since it seems to be expensive, counterproductive in getting people back to work, and, of course, disproportionately used by blacks.

The political reaction analyzed by the Edsells began in the 1970s following the turbulence of the 1960s. Under Presidents Richard Nixon, Gerald Ford, Ronald Reagan and George Bush, and now under Speaker Gingrich and his Republican's congressional majority, this reaction has dominated presidential politics and heavily influenced policies in Washington and increasingly in the states. It has been heavily overlaid with a kind of *Kulterkampf*, or cultural war, led by conservatives who see so-called traditional American values of patriotism, family unity, hard work and individual rights threatened or eroded by a variety of forces ranging from minority groups, guilt-edged liberals, craven politicians, complaint courts, insensitive and swollen bureaucracies and a hedonistic media. It is among the supreme ironies of contemporary America that the young and self-confident conservative "intellectuals," many of whom reside in New York and Washington and have been educated at Ivy League and other establishment institutions, cottoned on to this heartland dissatisfaction and made it their own, although they themselves would never be caught dead in the heartland, unless to give a paid speech on a university campus in Des Moines on a Thursday night.

It is curious, the virulence of this *Kulterkampf*, since the end of the Cold War meant that democracy emerged triumphant and left America militarily unchallenged. The Cold War's conclusion did not mean the "end of history," but it left democratic values and institutions dominant as a role model for a majority of countries around the world. Such a *Kulterkampf* elsewhere has often occurred in the aftermath of military defeat or domestic upheaval, neither of which have taken place in the United States. What the Cold War did produce was an increasing introspection in the United States, which seems to me entirely appropriate, since it would allow the United States to focus on urgent domestic priorities. Although it is fashionable in certain quarters abroad to deride the American contribution to maintaining a balance of power and enforcing a kind of containment against the Soviet Union, that effort was valuable for America's allies but it inevitably influenced American spending priorities.

It is difficult for those who have not lived in the United States to appreciate the degree to which the Cold War, the first sustained international peacetime engagement of the United States in its entire history, commanded commitment in that country. It was the axis around which the country's foreign policy turned; it was the prism, sometimes distorted with tragic results to be sure, through which Americans viewed the world; it was the priority which enabled presidents to mobilize public resources. Harry Truman used the Communist threat to gather congressional support for the Marshall Plan and the Truman Doctrine; Dwight Eisenhower used it to secure congressional funding for the inter-state highway system; John Kennedy launched the American space effort to compete with the Soviet challenge; Lyndon Johnson pushed America into Vietnam but also urged an end to segregation because of the adverse publicity it gave the U.S. abroad, and so on. Large swaths of the American economy, its research effort, its technological advances were bent to the needs of military preparedness. And now, with the threat gone, the considerable constriction of the military infrastructure is putting tremendous pressure on many communities and states across the country. In California, the closing of military bases, the ending of lucrative defence contracts and the consequent unemployment have disrupted thousands of lives. The same constrictions have sorely affected states from Connecticut to Texas. The constriction has occurred while the economy was already in profound restructuring, increasing uncertainty in literally millions of American families about their economic future and that of their children.

The Cold War effort did allow presidents from time to time to mobilize a national constituency to override isolationism or at least skepticism about international commitments. It also enabled them periodically to mobilize domestic constituencies to cut through the labyrinth of domestic political process, although the Vietnam morass led to many charges about the "imperial presidency." At the heart of the American system is the division of powers, but increasingly this system should be described as the "division of power with divisions of power within divisions of power." When George Bush, mouthing his speechwriter Peggy Noonan's words, called for a "thousand points of light" to encourage Americans' philanthropic spirit, he might have been referring to the political system.

With so many points of influence in the U.S. system, a president must forge a fresh coalition on every issue, and of course this coalition-building is exceptionally difficult when different parties control the presidency and Congress. Since party discipline is weak—although the House Republicans are showing considerable unity this far—a president must cajole, threaten and politically bribe even members of his own party as he attempts to assemble majorities. For example, Mr. Clinton's first budget after the 1992 election was passed by only one vote, although the Democrats then controlled the House, only after a full-court press (American politics revels in sports metaphors) by him and Vice-President Al Gore.

One of the enduring ironies of U.S. politics—or perhaps it is not ironic, given American suspicions of government—is that presidents, who sit atop the national government, are frequently driven to campaign against the very government they wish to run. Even in office, they seem to complain endlessly about the "system." No one mastered this art better than Ronald Reagan. As an outsider he spent decades lambasting government; when in the White House, he continued to portray himself as a constant battler for the people against government, especially the "big spenders" in Congress.

For all the critic's complaints, Americans overwhelmingly admire their political institutions. What messes up these institutions, according to the common refrain, is not their inherent nature or structural flaws, but those who operate them. The reforms much debated these days are not about fundamental reform of the institutions, but rather about ways of preventing politicians from allegedly abusing them by overspending or staying too long in office. Hence the movement for term limits. Fifteen states have now adopted laws capping terms; action in other states is pending. Hence the ongoing debate, not about publicly financed elections, but about how to trim the excesses of the system that makes politicians so dependent upon private fundraising.

There has been no measurable reform, therefore, to the tremendous costs of politics. There are spending limits for presidential candidates who want to be reimbursed partially from the public treasury. Those who eschew reimbursement can spend what they wish, as Americans witnessed with billionaire Ross Perot in the 1992 campaign. There are no limits for Senate and House races, and senators and congressmen must literally spend time each week raising money. With the costs of political entry and survival so high, it's little wonder that politicians are dependent upon Political Action Committees that were set up by lobby and special interest groups to get around limits on individual contributions. Lobbyists' influence is also related to their ability to mobilize constituencies. Direct mail, media outlets, satellite communications—the entire technology revolution in communications—has enabled lobbyists to direct their message to specific groups more adroitly than ever. The latest development in political communication is the explosion of talk radio, which is disproportionately controlled by conservative voices. Hot-line shows, usually staffed by right-wing zealots such as Rush Limbaugh, former Watergate felon Gordon Liddy and most recently Oliver North, crackle with venom against liberals of all kinds. All these developments have made divided and complex government even more difficult to work than ever.

Conservatives, and white Americans of many stripes, are now mobilizing to contest the affirmative action policies that have been developed in the last quarter-century. This debate has the potential to be among the nastiest in recent memory, pitting racial and ethnic groups against each other in an increasingly diverse society. As so often happens, this movement against affirmative action is beginning in a formal way in California. What's bubbling in California is being eagerly watched across the United States by opponents of policies such as affirmative action.

At issue is a proposed plebiscite—to be held either next March with the California presidential primary or in November with the 1996 presidential election—that would ban state-sponsored affirmative action. The plebiscite, the brainchild of two university professors, reads that the state shall not "use race, color, ethnicity or national origin as a criterion for either discriminating against or granting preferential treatment to any individual or group in the operation of the state system of public employment, public education or public contracting." Polls of California opinion suggest the measure will win easily. Republican Governor Pete Wilson, a candidate for the Republican presidential nomination, has endorsed the plebiscite. So have all the other Republican presidential contenders. President Clinton, while not abandoning affirmative action, has stepped up his disclaimers about quotas and has ordered a review of federal policies to ensure their "fairness." Republicans are correct in believing that attacking affirmative action will drive wedges into the Democratic Party.

Public agencies in California and elsewhere have been roiled for years over affirmative action. Universities, police forces, civil services have been riven by particularistic disputes. This latest plebiscite, which comes at a time of economic uncertainty for millions of Americans despite a booming economy, reflects anger among whites at what they feel is preferential treatment for those they consider less qualified. It offends their sense of individual rights and merit, and of course it threatens their sense of self-interest. They reject arguments that preferential policies are needed to reverse past injustices. The great unknown in this debate is how women will react, since they have benefited from many of the policies now under attack. While American males may believe preferential policies are unfair, it remains to be seen how white women, especially in the professional middle classes, will react. But since this issue does not just go to the heart of racial and ethnic issues, but speaks to conflicting definitions and perceptions of past history and defence of rights, it has a potential for political explosiveness that we have not seen since the issue of court-ordered busing of schoolchildren in the 1970s.

These scattered reflections about some of the divisions in American society, and some of the forces that are at work changing American society, should not be read as a cry of despair for the United States, for there is a sturdy and impressive overall unity about the United States, and extremely vigorous public debate. Voter turnout in elections is far lower than in any Western democracy, but the vibrancy of American democracy remains something to behold, whatever its excesses, twists, turns and decisions that sometimes produce despair. Americans may not respect their politicians, but they admire their political institutions, which have stood the test of time in the world's oldest federation. The American model of government, American culture, American ideas, American universities, American industries continue to impress others around the world. America remains, for all its faults, a magnet for millions who wish to move there, a country which provides a high standard of living for the majority of its people, a country with an abiding sense of individual rights, a country whose participation in world affairs is eagerly sought by dozens of other countries. Foreigners in Asia, Latin America, Europe or the Middle East may sometimes complain about America; until they face the prospect of America withdrawing from their part of the world, at which point they start to worry. It is a testament to the international commitment of America that, despite the end of the Cold War and pressing domestic problems, it has remained engaged in the world, resisting the siren songs of isolation sung by certain American politicians. As for Canadians, on whose birth certificates seem to be written the liberty to complain about and admire the Americans, perhaps Prime Minister Lester Pearson said it best when he quipped: "Americans are our best friends, whether we like it or not." Their problems are not always ours; but their ideas and their society cannot leave us indifferent, nor should our predisposition to believe that we know more about America than vice versa blind us to the need to understand more deeply still the country whose influence upon us overshadows that of all other countries combined.

Reinventing Canada *(November 9, 1994)*

This piece is excerpted from a speech given as The Charles R. Bronfman Lecture in Canadian Studies.

To those who prefer the long view, there is nothing inherent in Canadian history about fiscal profligacy. If you examine the national accounts dating back to 1867, you will see that Canadian federal government budgets in peacetime that carried large deficits were not the rule. In the twenty-four years, from 1947 to the last budget in surplus, 1974, for example, fifteen federal budgets were in the red (but none of them seriously), eleven in the black and one was balanced. The large deficits the country assumed to fight the Second World War were followed by nine budgets in eleven years in surplus, as governments paid down the wartime debt. By the late 1960s, the national debt stood at a paltry $19-billion.

I remind you now of some doleful facts:

- Federal governments have run deficits, of gradually rising absolute size, in every year without exception since 1975.
- The federal government's debt is fast approaching $600-billion; the provincial debts, $200-billion.
- In 1971, the per capita share of the national debt for each family of four was $3,500. Today, it is $76,300. If current trends continue, the family-of-four debt will rise to $115,000 by 2001.
- The ratio of federal and provincial debt to gross domestic product, one of the important ways economists measure a country's ability to pay, is now 95 per cent, and will soon exceed 100 per cent.
- In every year of the past fifteen—that is about five years after the string of deficits began—the federal debt has grown faster than the Canadian economy.
- Interest payments on the federal debt are now the largest single item in the federal budget. Interest payments account for 35 per cent of all federal revenues, compared to 11 per cent in 1974, when the string of deficits began.

- Governments are now caught in the so-called deficit/debt trap whereby their "savings" from a reduced rate of increase in operating costs, or an actual decrease, are wiped out by higher debt-servicing payments. For example, program spending in Ottawa in 1994-95 will rise only 0.6 per cent; debt-servicing payments by 6.5 per cent. In Alberta, program spending (courtesy of cuts made by Premier Ralph Klein's government) will drop 9.2 per cent in 1994-95; interest payments on the provincial debt will rise 8.0 per cent. In Ontario, the NDP government cut program spending by 1.6 per cent last year (thanks, in large part, to the social contract) but interest payment on the provincial debt rose 13.7 per cent.
- The federal government this year will spend $1.32 for every dollar it raises in taxes.
- Thirty-three cents of every dollar we send to Ottawa goes to pay interest on the public debt.
- The total deficits for all governments—federal and provincial—this year will total $57-billion.
- Every day, the federal government takes in $340-million in revenues and spends $448-million. The deficit therefore grows every day $108-million, or $4.5-million per hour, or $75,000 a minute.
- The operating budget of the federal government enjoys a $5-billion surplus, but debt-servicing charges cost $44-billion. Since 1988-89, the federal government has amassed a cumulative operating surplus of $21-billion, but compound interest on the debt has totalled $199-billion.
- The percentage of our national debt held by foreigners has increased to $313-billion, a percentage three times higher than Italy, which used to be considered the country with the least fiscal discipline in the G7.

The severity of this situation has been brought home to every government in Canada. That severity, coupled with the length of time it took the country to arrive at this situation, means that we face many years—I will not predict just how many—of wrenching change to restore some semblance of balance to our national fiscal accounts. More ominous still is the prospect that if important remedial steps are not taken we will be even more strapped when the next recession comes than we were in 1990-91, just as we were much more vulnerable then than in the recession of 1981-82. Of course, political upheaval that would undoubtedly follow the secession of Quebec would severely compound problems. Both Canada and Quebec would suffer economically from separation; Quebec would have an especially difficult time financing its share of the national debt on top of a provincial debt which is among the highest per capita in Canada. But it is worth noting, as a sign of the times if nothing else, that whereas federalists during the 1980 referendum could argue that in separating from Canada, Quebec would be leaving an economic powerhouse, the arguments federalists now advance are in the form of warnings about Quebec's ability to finance its share of the national debt.

How did we arrive at this state of affairs, since there is nothing in the long history of Canada—and this is the world's second-oldest federation—that suggests fiscal profligacy in peacetime?

Back in the 1960s, economic growth averaged about 4 per cent over the decade. There were dips in yearly growth, to be sure, but the economy was producing jobs, growth and revenues. In the 1960s, when all seemed possible, government embarked upon or enlarged a series of programs which became hallmarks of the modern-day Canadian identity. I refer to the Canada and Quebec pension plans; Medicare, publicly financed health and hospital insurance; federal assistance for post-secondary education; the Canadian welfare programs.

Then, in 1971, amid a mild recession, the Liberal government of the day drastically overhauled and expanded the unemployment insurance program, widening eligibility for benefits and introducing payments for seasonal work. The scheme thereby changed fundamentally from one of providing insurance to an income supplement. During the same years, the government launched formally and expensively what had been done haphazardly and largely through political influence in previous generations—regional development.

All these programs were designed with the best of intentions, and some of them have worked exceedingly well. As a wag once said in another context, the founders built better than they knew. But those who built the programs did so on the basis of one flawed assumption: that economic growth would continue at the rates of the 1960s, and that the federal government would continue to experience sufficient revenue growth to finance its enlarged responsibilities. So, too, provinces expanded their spheres of activity enormously—schools, hospitals, community colleges, universities, municipal transportation systems. Provincial expenditures, fuelled in part by generous federal transfers, were rising even faster than those of the federal government.

Then came the OPEC crisis of 1973. Suddenly the Western economies were thrown into neutral, even reverse. Economic growth rates dropped; joblessness grew; the increase in government revenues declined. Soon, the word stagflation entered the economists' lexicon: the cruel and simultaneous appearance of both high unemployment and inflation.

The effects on federal finances were immediate. The federal budget was in deficit in 1973, in surplus in 1974, and in deficit again in 1975, never since to return to the black. The jobless rate, which had averaged 5.1 per cent in the

1960s (or about 2 per cent in real terms) jumped to 6.7 per cent in the 1970s, with much higher inflation as well. The emergence of oil as a commodity for which the price was escalating rapidly in real terms set off a decade-long struggle between consuming and producing provinces, and between the federal government and Alberta. Programs which had been designed in the higher-growth 1960s began to see costs rising rapidly as higher joblessness pushed more people onto unemployment insurance and welfare. Economic growth averaged 3 per cent over the decade, governments changed tax policies to boost economic activity. Ottawa subsidized the price of imported oil, at considerable cost to the treasury. It was the era of de-indexing of personal income tax rates, new credits for research and development, investment incentive programs with acronyms such as MURBS, and registered retirement savings programs.

A quite deliberate decision was made by Liberal governments—decisions that were defended in a series of budgets in the mid-1970s—to cushion Canadians to the greatest extent possible, from the post-OPEC period of slow growth. The result was a remorseless increase in government spending. It rose 22.6 per cent in 1973-74, 28.3 per cent in 1974-75, 18.5 per cent in 1975-76, 7.1 per cent in 1976-77, and by 1979-80 it was still rising at 10.4 per cent per year. In his politically fatal budget of December 1979—the one that promised "short-term pain for long-term gain" and brought down the Joe Clark government—Finance Minister John Crosbie boasted of reducing spending increases to only 10 per cent. He was considered tight-fisted and worthy of being ejected from office!

Paradoxically, each budget in these years featured ministers of finance professing to be worried about excessive government spending and promising to reduce at least the administrative costs of government. In 1976, the federal budget promised "close control over government spending." In 1977, the budget said, "as the slack in the economy is taken up, the deficit will be reduced." Allan MacEachen promised in 1980 a "steady reduction in the government deficit and financial requirements." In his second budget, with recession driving the deficit skyward, he intoned, "we must reduce our deficit and borrowing requirements substantially." The same mantra continued under successive Liberal, Conservative and now Liberal ministers. But ministers also believed—as they do today—what Jean Chrétien, then president of the Treasury Board, said on Dec. 18, 1975: "When you carry out . . . a review, you come to a conclusion [that] cannot be described too often—particularly to those who talk glibly about cutting expenditures, as if it were an easy thing to do. That conclusion is that there is very little, almost nothing, that can be cut without hurting someone."

Once again, I repeat that these programs were designed with the best of intentions. Each was—and can still be—easily defended as contributing to a sense of national community, inter-regional and interpersonal sharing and caring, and even economic efficiency, since I have always argued—in contrast to some of my colleagues—that social justice and economic efficiency are not polar opposites; that, in fact, countries with fairer income distributions than those in Canada are also more efficient because more of the population is equipped to participate fruitfully in the economy.

The deficit in the late 1970s, although rising slowly, was still a fraction of today's and there was an assumption, or at least the hope, that economic growth would resume to such an extent that the deficit would take care of itself.

In 1978, Prime Minister Pierre Trudeau returned from the Bonn economic summit having been chastened by a lecture from German Chancellor Helmut Schmidt about Canada's worsening fiscal situation. Without informing his minister of finance, Jean Chrétien, Mr. Trudeau abruptly ordered $2-billion in spending cuts. It would be amusing, were it not otherwise tragic, to recall Mr. Trudeau's words warning about the perils of a $7-billion budgetary deficit: "We must have a major re-ordering of government priorities. We must reduce the size of government . . . *Canadians within several years would almost certainly be faced with a fiscal crisis* [italics mine]."

When the Tories arrived in office in 1979, they looked at the widening trend lines between expenditures and revenues. They decided to try to reverse the trends and proposed a deficit-tightening budget, hinged in part on an excise tax on gasoline. The rest, as we know, is history.

The 1980s began with the sharpest recession since the 1930s: interest rates reached 22 per cent, unemployment skyrocketed, government revenues declined, the multiplier effect of government programs increased government spending. From $14-billion on the eve of the recession, the deficit rapidly jumped above $30-billion. When the Conservatives took power in 1984, the forecast deficit was $38-billion.

The 1980s were curious from the point of view of economic growth: the early years, which were catastrophic, were followed by strong growth in the middle of the decade, and starting in 1989 by much slower growth. Economic growth, which had been 4 per cent in the 1960s, averaged 3 per cent in the 1970s, but was only slightly more than 2 per cent in the 1980s, with an unemployment rate averaging 9.3 per cent.

As various reports in the early 1980s from the Economic Council of Canada showed, the revenue-raising policies of the federal government could no longer keep pace with spending increases. All the attempts to stimulate the economy with tax expenditures had put holes in the government's ability to raise revenues. So, any government coming to power after the recession at the beginning of the 1980s would have had to attack the huge problem of the deficit, and it would have been tempted to raise taxes. That's what the Conservatives did. According to the OECD, taxes as a portion of gross national product rose faster in Canada in the 1980s than in any other member country. It's not surprising, in the light of this fact, that politicians of every stripe have encountered tax fatigue. The Conservatives, to give them their due, reduced the deficit as a percentage of GNP. They reduced considerably the operating costs of government, but the situation was so serious that even though the operating budget of the government was in considerable surplus when the Conservatives left office, the deficit still remained at $36-billion.

The Tory record was decidedly mixed. Under the Conservatives from 1984 to 1991, total budgetary expenditures rose an average of 5.1 per cent per year. It is worth breaking down this figure to illustrate an aspect of our remorseless arithmetic. The Conservatives in those years kept the operating costs of government—salaries, goods and services—to average annual increases of only 2.2 per cent. Debt charges, however, rose yearly by an average of 9.1 per cent. The deficit/debt trap was at work. But the Conservatives were actually less robust than their sometimes messianic rhetoric about the dangers of deficits and debt suggested. Non-operating program spending rose 3.9 per cent.

For example, payments to the elderly rose 7.1 per cent a year; cash to science and technology by 7.1 per cent; budgets for Indian and Inuit programs by 10.8 per cent; agricultural subsidies rose 9.5 per cent.

The Cabinet was variously structured to focus attention better on spending priorities. The Trudeau government instituted an elaborate series of Cabinet committees, ostensibly to improve co-ordination. Then it developed, and subsequent governments accepted, a so-called envelope system for expenditures whereby the budget was subdivided and ministers were told that any new money must come only from funds within their subdivision. That system broke down. Then something called the "expenditure review committee" was established in the second half of the Mulroney years. It had some modest success, but it could not keep federal program spending below the inflation rate in the early 1990s.

Nor did outside actors have any more success. The most dramatic of these was the so-called Nielsen task force, established in the early days of the Mulroney government. This exercise brought to Ottawa people from outside government to take a hard look at government spending under the direction of Deputy Prime Minister Erik Nielsen. The groups produced nineteen reports and recommended one-time reductions in spending and tax expenditures totalling $7-8-billion. Subsequent studies estimated, however, that the government had acted on enough recommendations to reduce spending by only $280-million and tax expenditures by $215-million.

So, a variety of mechanisms, or systemic responses if you like, were adopted in the last quarter-century in Ottawa to rationalize decision making, establish priorities and contain spending. They all failed, in whole or in part, because a crucial ingredient was missing: political will.

The question, of course, is why that will was lacking with any kind of consistency? After all, Canadian governments before those which presided over this string of deficits had operated on the assumption that continuous deficits could not be sustained, at least in peacetime. So what changed?

I would offer the following list of reasons, in no particular order, fully aware that the list is incomplete and that each item could take a volume to explore.

- Once the expansion of the federal government began in earnest in the 1960s, the number of citizens with a direct financial stake in government spending or tax expenditures rose dramatically. This, in turn, produced a deepened and widened sense of entitlement among beneficiaries of government decisions who viewed those entitlements not as discretionary decisions of temporary political leaders but as rights of citizenship.
- The Liberal Party underwent a sea change in fiscal approach under Prime Minister Pierre Trudeau. Under his three predecessors, the role of the state in Canadian society was considered vital, but that role had to be measured against ability to pay.

Ironically—and historians often forget this about Mr. Trudeau—he did not enter 24 Sussex Drive urging government to do more, but rather to do less. A close reading of his speeches in the Liberal leadership race of 1968 and the "Trudeaumania" campaign of that year reveals a leader worried about citizens expecting too much from the state. Lowering expectations— in constitutional reform as in fiscal matters—was a persistent theme in his standard speeches from those years.

After his near-deficit in 1972, and with the onset of the OPEC crisis in the next year, Mr. Trudeau was willing to countenance a considerable and costly expansion of government activities with less regard for ability to pay. Part of this shift undoubtedly reflected changes in the composition of Liberal Cabinets and voting support. As time went by, the more fiscally prudent elements in the Liberal Cabinets which had always been present under Prime Ministers King, St. Laurent and Pearson gave way to more activist-minded ministers, so that toward the end of the Trudeau period there were almost no ministers with solid ties to the nation's business leaders, and those who were fiscally prudent had been marginalized in Cabinet.

The last two decades have featured governments largely flummoxed by how to return to steady and sustained economic growth based on rising productivity. Instead, productivity has been flat in Canada, and rising productivity is the key to more jobs. The consequence of this state of affairs has been a weakening of the social contract that prevailed for almost three decades following the Second World War whereby governments committed themselves, and delivered, low unemployment and a welfare state for those temporarily in need, and, in exchange, were accorded a legitimacy to cut whatever deals and make whatever arrangements political leaders considered best.

In an era of low unemployment, steady growth and burgeoning public revenues, it was far easier to make inter-regional trade-offs that lay at the heart of the traditional Canadian political culture than in periods of high unemployment, erratic growth and burgeoning deficits and debt. The political challenge of negotiating win-win solutions was replaced by the much tougher ones of win-lose or lose-lose. Put another way, the politics of joy has been replaced by the politics of pain, courtesy of the remorseless arithmetic of the last two decades. The politics of pain has undoubtedly contributed to the anti-political mood of the recent years and to the deep, if misguided, notion that the solution to our fiscal woes lies in curbing the excesses of political remuneration and that old standby of eliminating "waste and duplication" in the federal government. Finally, the politics of pain is made more acute by the long delay in Ottawa in addressing the mounting fiscal crisis. Decisions today are made more painful by the refusal to have made them yesterday.

Canada's job-creation record, in the last twenty years, has actually been good, but it did not come from higher productivity. The country has experienced two demographic surges that soaked up the jobs—and contributed in some measure to economic growth. Female participation rates in the labour force soared, such that 80 per cent of all employment growth from 1975-89 was among women aged 25-54. Immigration, too, has soared in recent years. From 1977 to 1986, immigration averaged 106,000 people per year; from 1987 to 1993, the yearly average was 179,000. If the 1977-86 immigration levels had been maintained through 1987-93, there would have been 511,000 fewer people in the country, not all of whom of course would have been in the job market.

Every government has feared the political reaction to spending reductions, which partly explains why until recently governments often preferred tax increases when struggling with the deficit. Considerable polling data showed that deficit reduction ranked far below other concerns, as it may still today, and every suggested cut was bound to outrage certain interest groups which would try, in turn, to make life politically miserable for the government. Similarly, there were strong regional pressures in every Cabinet to continue expenditure programs, and to add new ones. Prairies ministers went to bat for higher agricultural subsidies; Quebec ministers warned throughout the period of the menace of separatism; Atlantic ministers pointed to the depressed state of the region's economy and to its dependence on government.

What former Quebec Cabinet minister Richard French once called Canada's "malignant form of regional envy" influenced every federal government. Programs designed to benefit particular regions, especially Quebec, were frequently extended to other regions, or offset by spending elsewhere to placate anticipated cries of favouritism. Curiously, it is my experience that this kind of spending seldom sealed political support, but it was undertaken because politicians feared political retribution rather than anticipated political gain.

The dynamics of parliamentary life, and the way the media often portray them, contributes to opposition parties outbidding governments for political support. Because no premium is placed on thoughtful policy development by opposition parties, and no penalty is imposed upon them by the media, which favour opposition parties only for their shrieking, opposition MPs seldom do more than oppose, which ill prepares them to govern. They are thereby hung on promises whose fiscal implications, among others, have not been clearly thought out.

I have no crystal ball into which I can peer to predict with any degree of precision what the consequences of this deficit/debt crisis will bring. I am painfully aware as a journalist that those who gaze into crystal balls often must wind up eating broken glass. I therefore often only speculate about what lies ahead.

I do believe in general terms that this crisis will change the relationship between citizens and the state, and that it will change the structure of the Canadian federation.

Governments of every stripe will be forced in a variety of ways to trim their expenditures, at the very least by reducing the increase, and probably to reduce them in absolute terms. This will be a politically difficult job, since Canadians have come to expect a wide range of services from their governments.

Among the strategies governments will use are those we are already witnessing. In some cases, governments have simply stopped providing services. For example, there are certain medical services no longer covered by publicly financed medicine. I suspect the list of these services will grow, especially as the population ages.

In other instances, governments will commercialize or privatize services they have previously provided. Major government construction projects will be contracted out to the private sector, which will, in turn, receive payments from users of the projects. This has already been done for the bridge to Prince Edward Island, a new toll road near Toronto, and airports.

Governments will also increasingly require taxpayers to pay for specific services that used to be underwritten in whole or in large part by general tax revenues. University fees, which have been rising in Ontario at 7-10 per cent per year, will continue to increase. Fees for all manner of government services will rise.

Governments will attempt to provide services with fewer employees. Public-sector unions will find both their numbers reduced and their remuneration rising more slowly than inflation.

Governments will reshape major existing programs to try to target them toward those most obviously in need. The government's social-policy discussion paper provides a very general sense of direction of where the present Liberal government wishes to move.

Governments will also raise taxes, although not immediately. The existing tax fatigue will eventually yield to a recognition by governments that some mixture of spending reductions and tax increases will be required, since I cannot believe that on a national basis a constituency can be built to tackle the problem entirely by spending reductions. As sure as we are here today, higher taxes follow large deficits. That was the lesson of the 1980s, and after this current pause in tax increases, it will be a lesson to be revisited later in the 1990s.

Where those taxes will fall I cannot predict, but I would guess that it is not unreasonable to expect governments to look at the savings and borrowings of our generation.

There are, of course, enormous political, ideological and bureaucratic obstacles to these changes, and there will continue to be fierce regional pressures brought to bear on ministers not to make changes that adversely affect particular regions and specific sectors of the economy.

I think, too, these fiscal pressures will restructure Canadian federalism. What we are witnessing in Ottawa is overstretch: the federal government simply cannot maintain itself at existing levels of personnel and spending within existing rates of taxation.

The fiscal crisis will, I believe, reduce Ottawa's role *vis-à-vis* that of the provinces, leaving Canada, which is already the world's second most decentralized federation after Switzerland, even more decentralized than it is today. Of course, if Quebec decides to secede from Canada, all bets are off, since the nature of the Canadian federation as we have known it would be

drastically altered, and what form the remainder of Canada would take—
and for how long it could survive as a geographically divided, Ontario-
dominated country is anyone's guess and quite beyond the scope of my
remarks today. If I am correct, however, about decentralization brought on
by the fiscal crisis, it will be incumbent upon provinces to improve their
own interprovincial co-ordination to assure national standards and porta-
bility of benefits. Alas, the track record in this area is spotty indeed.

Our fiscal situation, now building for two decades, is incapable of being
sustained. We can make progress against this situation ourselves, or we can
be forced into progress by external forces. That is the underlying, stark
choice we face.

It is an unsettling, back-to-the-wall kind of choice that most of us make
with the greatest of reluctance. Some of the neo-conservatives whose voices
are so prominent today positively relish what lies ahead, because this crisis
they believe will produce the Canada of their ideological dreams: with the
largest possible scope for the free market, whatever the consequences for
social justice, and a government in full—and they hope—permanent
retreat. I do not relish that prospect, because I continue to believe that government, with all its faults and broken promises, remains a major vehicle for
extending the "life chances" of citizens. It cannot, however, play this role
constructively if it remains encumbered by deficits and debt of the current
size. And therefore, the stark challenge remains: either we tackle this problem ourselves, with our own priorities and real urgency, or we will be forced
into tackling it by others.

This long period of readjustment and redefinition brought on by this
unsustainable fiscal situation is now upon us, and will remain with us into
the next century. It took almost a quarter of a century for Canada to get
into this situation; it will take to the year 2001 and beyond to recover from
the legacy of the last twenty years.

Index